新东方 NEW ORIENTAL

新东方雅思(IELTS)考试指定辅导教材·基础培训

IELTS Speaking
雅思口语胜经

新东方教育科技集团
雅思研发团队 编著

群言出版社
Qunyan Press

图书在版编目(CIP)数据

雅思口语胜经 / 新东方教育科技集团雅思研发团队编著. —北京：群言出版社，2006（2009.3 重印）

ISBN 978-7-80080-579-0

Ⅰ. 雅…　Ⅱ. 新…　Ⅲ. 英语—口语—高等学校—入学考试，国外—自学参考资料　Ⅳ. H319.9

中国版本图书馆 CIP 数据核字(2006)第 052979 号

雅思口语胜经

出 版 人　范　芳
责任编辑　王　超
封面设计　王　琳
出版发行　群言出版社(Qunyan Press)
地　　址　北京东城区东厂胡同北巷 1 号
邮政编码　100006
网　　站　www. qypublish. com
电子信箱　qunyancbs@126. com
总 编 办　010—65265404　65138815
编 辑 部　010—65276609　65262436
发 行 部　010—65263345　65220236

经　　销　新华书店
读者服务　010—65220236　65265404　65263345
法律顾问　中济律师事务所
印　　刷　北京画中画印刷有限公司

版　　次　2006 年 6 月第 1 版　2009 年 3 月第 12 次印刷
开　　本　787×1092　1/16
印　　张　13.75
字　　数　280 千字
书　　号　ISBN 978-7-80080-579-0
定　　价　35.00 元

心中的罗马(代序)

在人生发展的道路上，人们总希望有更多的选择，有更多的改变命运的机会，从而使自己的生活变得更加丰富多彩。

上世纪80年代的中国学生还没有太多的选择，他们毕业后通常都是由国家分配工作。大多数学生都是“本分”孩子，高高兴兴地走上了他们被分配的工作岗位，继而在祖国最需要的地方认认真真干一辈子。

90年代的学生开始有了选择。随着中国的改革开放，国家鼓励出国留学，学生们开始把眼光投向了国外。或为了知识或为了生活，留学成了中国学生的重要追求之一。90年代的留学，大家的眼光多关注于美国，因为只有美国能够给中国学生奖学金，使一些贫困的中国学生在不需要自己花费的情况下就能够得到很好的教育。为了能够争取到美国读书，中国学生使尽浑身解数，把两门到美国去的必经考试TOEFL、GRE考到了奇迹般的水平，出现了很多的满分，中国学生的互相竞争到了白热化的程度。

2000年以后，中国学生有了更多的选择。随着中国的发展，有一些家庭变得富有起来，已经能够自费出国留学。在美国固执地认为中国人太穷付不起学费时，他的兄弟国家如英国、澳大利亚等却像猎狗一样，敏锐地嗅到了中国学生出国留学的热情和其中的商机，开始大量地录取中国学生到他们的国家去读书。中国学生面对突然出现的众多选择，一时眼花缭乱，蜂拥而出。和TOEFL相对应的英联邦国家的语言水平考试IELTS便成了中国学生选择的另一门重要的留学必经考试。

当美国人满足于他们自己的既定标准，并且坚持认为TOEFL是全世界最好的语言测试系统时，IELTS却向更实用的方向发展，强调学生的听、说、读、写四大能力在语言测试中的重要性。这一方向赢得了英联邦国家大学的认可，甚至越来越多的美国大学也开始认可雅思考试。于是，在短短的几年内，雅思考试成为中国学生出国的首选考试，考试人数在一段时间内超过了TOEFL考试人数。

当美国人意识到自己所犯的错误，开始对TOEFL考试进行改革时，已经有成千上万的中国学生到英联邦国家去读书了。由于相对宽松的录取政策，还有更多的学生正在准备到这些国家去读书，很多学生甚至到了牛津、剑桥这样的名牌大学。到英联邦国家去留学这一选择，已经成为越来越多的中国学生的日常思维。美国大学不再是中国学生的惟一选择。这一情况的出现，给中国学生至少带来了两大好处：一是IELTS和TOEFL这两门考试的不断改革，使其更加切合实际，中国学生通过对于这两门考试的准备，能够真正提高英语水平，不再存在高分低能的现象；二是美国的骄傲心态开始改变，开始愿意给中国学生更宽松的政策和更多的学习机会。

这无疑是一件好事，中国学生有了更多的选择，也许会出现更多的惊喜，生命也许会更加灿烂。而 IELTS 和 TOEFL 这两门考试的竞争将会给中国学生带来更多的方便，比如考试形式更加灵活、服务更加周到等。总之，选择带来希望，竞争造就优质。也许，中国学生的未来还有更多的选择，现在很多学生已经开始到法国、德国和其他非英语国家去留学。从大趋向上来说，无论是对于个人还是对于国家，这肯定是一件好事。

只是希望中国学生不要在选择中迷失了自己，不要为了选择而选择。生命的道路有很多，最好一开始就选对道路，否则回头重走会倍加艰难。也许你会问：选择哪一条道路好呢？条条大路通罗马，关键是你要知道罗马在什么地方。罗马，就是你心中最割舍不下的理想。

新东方也在为心中割舍不下的理想而努力，那就是在中国学生前进的道路上出一把力，成为中国学生越过人生障碍的垫脚石或者加速前进的助推器。这套雅思书籍的出版，就是我们所做努力的一点小小的证明。也许这不一定是最好的雅思书，但是它们倾注了新东方雅思老师的全部心血，融入了老师们近十年的教学经验。这些心血和经验，在全书的字里行间都能够读出来。

生命的梦想需要很多努力才能实现，雅思考试本身尽管无聊，但背后包含的意义是丰富的，它是你为自己的梦想努力过的证明。也许因为这一努力，你的生命将会从此与众不同。

P63、 P61. P139.

P43.10.

新东方教育科技集团董事长兼总裁

目 录

CD 曲目列表

第三章　雅思口语考试常考问题和卡片话题

雅思考试总论

1. 什么是雅思（IELTS）考试

雅思（IELTS：International English Language Testing System）是专门为准备进入以英文教学的学院或大学深造的学生而设的英文水平测试。雅思注重学生在专业范畴内需具备的英语能力，所以许多英语国家的学校都鼓励学生参加雅思测试。雅思测试由澳洲大学联盟（IDP Education Australia）、英国文化协会（British Council）以及剑桥大学测试中心（UCLES）共同举办，由剑桥大学测试中心统筹管理。

2. 雅思的测试对象

凡计划前往英语国家就读本科、研究生、专科技术学院或预科等课程的考生，以及想要申请赴澳洲、新西兰、加拿大等地移民的移民者都可参加雅思考试。目前，全世界共有40多个国家或地区认可雅思成绩，主要包括英、美、加、澳、新西兰、爱尔兰和南非等英语国家，此外还有很多欧洲及亚洲国家，如瑞士、挪威和新加坡等都认可雅思；而且，它是赴澳大利亚、荷兰留学受认可的惟一的语言测试；所有的加拿大教育机构都认可雅思成绩；根据雅思考试官方网站透露，在美国，现在已经有380余所大学和研究生院正式认可雅思成绩。目前，在全球120个国家的超过400个测试中心定期举办雅思考试。

3. 雅思的计分方式及考题类别

（1）**计分方式**：雅思分Listening、Reading、Writing、Speaking四大项目，各项目独立计分，最后所得成绩取四项成绩的平均值。IELTS满分为9分，成绩能达至9分者，代表其英语能力与母语为英语的人能力相当，反之若只考1分者则表明其不具有英语能力。

（2）**考试组别分类**：Reading与Writing部分采取分组方式，共分为Academic和General Training两组；Listening和Speaking两项则不分组。

（A）**Academic**：适用于申请正式课程者，例如研究所、大学、专科学校或要求此组别者。

（B）**General Training**：适用于申请移民者及欲申请学校要求此组别者。

4. 雅思的测试方式及时间

测试时间：约2小时45分

测试顺序如下：

笔记区

雅思测试顺序	
(1)Listening 听力	测试时间：约30分钟，另有10分钟誊写答案 测试方式：分4段进行，每大题前会有30秒时间阅读题目及答案选项，每段测试之后，还会有30秒时间检查答案。 测试题数：4道大题，共40个问题
(2)Reading 阅读	测试时间：60分钟 测试方式：填空/选择/问答/匹配
(3)Writing 写作	测试时间：60分钟 测试方式：第一篇作文至少需写150字，主要是对所提供的数据、图表加以描述；第二篇作文至少需写250字，主要是就某个主题发表自己的想法及意见。 测试题数：2篇
(4)Speaking 口试	测试时间：10~15分钟 测试方式：口试官和考生进行一对一的口试。

5. 考试流程

考生(candidate)在考试当天必须携带身份证原件和准考证，在8:30之前到考场门外等候，然后逐个验证入场。入场后考生可依次找到自己的座位。考场大多是语言实验室，使用耳机。桌上有一张印有考生姓名(拼音)、考号、生日和类别(Academic类还是General Training类)的纸条、一支HB铅笔和一块橡皮。待全体考生就座，主考官介绍考试规则后分发答题卡和听力考试的试题本(booklet for the listening test)。

在答题卡的正面答听力题，背面答阅读题。考生应在答题卡的正面填写自己的姓名(拼音)和考号(candidate number)，并用铅笔将相应的长方形小框涂黑。之后，听力考试开始。

听力考试结束后由监考人员收走听力试题本，然后分发阅读试题本。考生应在答题卡背面标明考试类别（Academic类还是 General Training类），然后开始阅读考题。

需特别指出的是，听力磁带约为30分钟，考生答题时，需先将答案写在试题本上，待磁带上的试题内容放完后，有10分钟的时间将答案誊写到答题卡上。

阅读考试的答题则应直接写在答题卡上。阅读考试的时间为60分钟，考生不再有额外的时间誊写答案。在做阅读题时，可以用笔在试题本上划线或做标记。考官会在阅读考试进行到30分钟和55分钟时提醒考生考试时间。阅读考试结束后监考人员将试题和答题卡收走。考生要注意的是，从2003年9月开始，阅读与写作之间没有休息时间，考生不得以任何理由离开考场。监考人员会分发作文题和作文纸。同样，考生需填写candidate name，candidate number，date，centre name，module。作文考试的时间也是60分钟，考官会在考试进行到20分钟、55分钟时提醒考生时间。作文考试结束后，笔试部分全部结束。

考生考完笔试后，监考人员会提醒考生有关口试的注意事项。口试的时间

笔记区

写在考生桌子上的一张小纸条上。考生应记住自己口试的日期（是当天或是第二天）、时间(几点几分)和地点(口试考场房间号)。口试顺序的安排一般是先外地考生,再本地考生。但这只是一般原则,具体安排会因两部分考生的比例不同而有所不同。一般而言,考生尽量不要在笔试的第二天(一般是星期日)安排其他活动,以免与口试发生冲突。

口试时应提前一个半小时左右到达考场附近,因为前面的考生可能会迟到,或者因笔试考得不理想而放弃口试。出现这种情况时,后面的考生应能够及时补上,以避免考场出现空档。

6. 考试成绩

考试结束的第十个工作日之后考生可以登录http://ielts.etest.net.cn查询成绩。雅思考试成绩有效期为两年。

（1）每名考生只有一份考试成绩单原件,需妥善保存。成绩单的真实性可以通过网络进行核查。详情请登录www.ielts.org查阅。

（2）考试结束两周后,英国使馆文化教育处考试部会将考生的成绩单寄往考生报名时提交的邮寄地址。

（3）考生如需额外成绩单,需向英国使馆文化教育考试部提交申请。

7. 2006年雅思考试新变化

2006年,雅思考试在考务方面进行了一系列的改进,包括通过电子邮件寄送成绩单、成绩复议费下调和取消90天内不得重考的规定。

从2006年4月1日起,雅思成绩单的寄送效率有了显著提高,不仅寄送时间大为缩短,而且考生还可以向英国文化协会中国办公室考试部提交寄送考试成绩单申请。考生提交的寄送成绩单申请经受理后,成绩单就可以立刻以Email的形式送至考生指定的成绩单接收机构。这种快速操作过程给考生和接收机构都带来了便利。考生除在考后提出申请外,还可以选择在报名考试时填写指定成绩接收人地址。此外,考生也无须再承担寄发成绩单的邮资。如果需要以国际航空平信形式寄送,相应邮资也无须考生承担。雅思的免费"额外成绩单"代寄最多可达5份。

另外,雅思成绩复议价格也有所降低。根据雅思考试规则,对分数有疑义的考生可以在成绩公布28天内提出复议,从4月1日起,复议的费用由过去的950元降为860元。复议后如成绩确实存在误差,该费用将退还给考生。

雅思考试还取消了考生在考试90天以后才能够重新报考的限制。考生可以根据自己的情况随时报名重考。据悉,目前世界各地有大量机构采用雅思成绩、他们不仅对考生的总分有要求,对单项成绩也有要求,考生有可能总分达到了要求,但是单项成绩不合格,而"90天不得重考"这个规定的取消,无疑给考生带来了方便。

笔 记 区

8. 雅思考试评分标准细则

成绩评分标准

BAND9 Expert User：能自如地运用英语，表达恰当、准确、流畅并且理解透彻。

BAND8 Very Good User：能自如地运用英语，只是偶尔会有语言不够连贯、不够准确的问题。偶尔会无法理解不够熟悉的情景。能较好地掌握复杂的说理论辩。

BAND7 Good User：在某些情景中偶尔会有语言不准确、不恰当以及不理解的情况，但具备语言实际运用能力。基本上可以较好地理解较复杂的英语和详细的论证，尤其在熟悉的场景中。

BAND6 Competent User：大体上能比较有效地运用英语。虽然有时出现表达不准确、不恰当和不理解的情况，但能够理解和运用较复杂的英语，尤其是在熟悉的场景中。

BAND5 Modest User：具有部分运用英语的能力，在大多数情况下可大致了解大意。虽然出现不少错误，但是基本可以在自己所熟悉的领域内沟通。

BAND4 Limited User：只限于在熟悉的情景中具有基本交际能力，理解和表达方面经常会出现错误，无法使用复杂的英语。

BAND3 Extremely Limited User：只能在简单的情况下表达和理解大概含义。频繁出现交流障碍。

BAND2 Intermittent User：无法进行真正的交流。只能在极熟悉的场景中用只字片语来满足紧急需求。理解书面语和口语方面有重大障碍。

BAND1 Non User：仅能说几个不关联的单词，根本无法沟通。

成绩评分标准细则

按照《IELTS评分标准、分数报告和解释》，考生成绩从1~9共分为九个等级。成绩报告单上有听、说、读、写四个单项的得分和总分（四个部分所得分数的平均分四舍五入之后就是考生的总分）。

总分、听力以及阅读部分的分数是整级或半级。例如，如果四项平均分等于或大于6.25分，则取6.5分；如果平均分等于或大于6.75分，则取7分。写作和口语部分的分数只按整级计算。

听力和阅读部分各包含40道题，每答对一道得一分。考生这两部分满分的原始分均为40分，考生依据其原始分获取1~9的等级分。

等级分/原始分如何换算

部分等级分及原始分换算表（听力/阅读）

听力		学术类阅读		普通培训类阅读	
等级分	原始分	等级分	原始分	等级分	原始分
5	16	5	15	4	15
6	23	6	23	5	23
7	30	7	30	6	30
8	35	8	35	7	34

笔记区

写作评分细则示例

雅思写作通常有Task1和Task2两个部分，考官给以下四项分别评等级分：任务完成（Task 1）/任务反应（Task 2）、连贯与衔接、词汇以及句式多样性和语法准确性。

以Task1为例，一名在雅思学术类考试中写作部分获得6分的考生，其这一分数所对应的写作水准应是：

（A） 任务完成方面：达到写作任务各项要求、能确切选择有用信息进行全面评述、呈现并强调主要特点或要点，但细节可能与要点无关、不恰当或不准确。

（B） 连贯及衔接方面：信息和分论点安排连贯，论证过程清楚，有效使用衔接手段，但句内或句间衔接有错误或显机械呆板，有时指代不清晰或不恰当。

（C） 词汇量方面：相对写作任务而言，所运用的词汇量充足，尝试运用非常见词汇但有时出现错误，拼写和构词出现一些错误，但不影响交流。

（D） 句式多样性和语法准确性方面：混合使用简单和复合句，语法和标点出现一些错误但基本不影响交流。

口语评分细则示例

同样，在雅思考试的口语部分，考官也是按四项标准分别评等级分：流利度和连贯性、词汇、句式丰富性和语法准确性以及语音。以一名口语获得6分的考生为例，这一分数所对应的口语水准应是：

（A） 流利度及连贯性方面：愿意进行详细描述，但有时因重复、自我更正或停顿而造成不连贯，运用不同的连接词和语篇标记，但有时不恰当。

（B） 词汇方面：尽管有时词汇运用不恰当，但词汇量足以详细表述主题，表意清楚，总体上能成功地变换措辞进行复述。

（C） 句式多样性及语法准确性方面：混合使用简单句式和复合句式，但不够灵活；使用复合句式时经常出错，但并不因此影响理解。

（D） 语音方面：总体能听懂，偶尔因发音错误对听者的理解造成负担。

评分受质量监控

据《IELTS评分标准、分数报告和解释》，所有雅思评分都由评卷官和考官在考试中心完成。所有评卷官必须事先接受培训，以确保其理解评分规定，并且证明其能够根据评分标准进行评分。评卷官每两年要重新接受测试，以确保其评分符合标准。每次考试都有系统监测，并对部分答卷进行二次评分。

笔 记 区

相关原文（摘自www.ielts.org）

Score processing, reporting and interpretation

All IELTS marking takes place at the test centre by trained markers and examiners. Markers are trained to understand the IELTS marking policy and are required to demonstrate that they are marking to standard before they are allowed to mark Listening and Reading papers. Markers are re-tested every two years to ensure that their marking remains up to standard. Systematic monitoring and double marking of a proportion of answer sheets are carried out at each administration.

Examiners for the Writing and Speaking modules are recruited and trained in line with agreed standards. They are required to demonstrate that they are marking to standard every two years in addition to on-going monitoring of their performance.

Candidates receive scores on a Band Scale from 1 to 9. A score is reported for each skill module of the test. The four individual module scores are averaged and rounded to produce an Overall Band Score. Overall Band Scores and Listening and Reading scores are presented as whole or half bands; Writing and Speaking band scores are reported in whole bands only.

Overall Band Score

Candidates receive a Test Report Form setting out their Overall Band Score and their scores on each of the four modules, Listening, Reading, Writing and Speaking. Each of the module scores is equally weighted. The Overall Band Score is calculated by taking the mean of the total of the four individual module scores.

Overall Band Scores are reported to the nearest whole or half band. For the avoidance of doubt, the following rounding convention applies; if the average across the four skills ends in .25, it is rounded up to the next half band, and if it ends in .75, it is rounded up to the next whole band.

Thus a candidate achieving 6.5 for Listening, 6.5 for Reading, 5.0 for Writing and 7.0 for Speaking would be awarded an Overall Band Score of 6.5 （25 ÷ 4 = 6.25 = Band 6.5）.

Likewise a candidate achieving 4.0 for Listening, 3.5 for Reading, 4.0 for Writing and 4.0 for Speaking would be awarded an Overall Band Score of 4.0 （15.5 ÷ 4 = 3.875 = Band 4.0）.

笔 记 区

On the other hand, a candidate achieving 6.5 for Listening, 6.0 for Reading, 6.0 for Writing and 6.0 for Speaking would be awarded Band 6 (24.5 ÷ 4 = 6.125 = Band 6).

Listening and Reading

IELTS Listening and Reading papers contain 40 items and each correct item is awarded one mark; the maximum raw score a candidate can achieve on a paper is 40. Band scores ranging from Band 1 to Band 9 are awarded to candidates on the basis of their raw scores.

Although all IELTS test materials are pretested and trialled before being released as live tests, there are inevitably minor differences in the difficulty level across tests. In order to equate different test versions, the band score boundaries are set so that all candidates' results relate to the same scale of achievement. This means, for example, that the Band 6 boundary may be set at a slightly different raw score across versions.

The tables below indicate the mean raw scores achieved by candidates at various levels in each of the Listening, Academic Reading and General Training Reading modules during 2004 and they provide an indication of the number of marks required to achieve a particular band score.

Listening		Academic Reading		General Training Reading	
Band Score	Raw Score out of 40	Band Score	Raw Score out of 40	Band Score	Raw Score out of 40
5	16	5	15	4	15
6	23	6	23	5	23
7	30	7	30	6	30
8	35	8	35	7	34

The Academic and General Training papers are graded to the same scale. The distinction between the two modules is one of genre or discourse type. Academic papers may contain source texts featuring more difficult vocabulary or greater complexity of style. It is usual that, to secure a given band score, a greater number of questions must be answered correctly on a General Training Reading paper.

Writing and Speaking

When marking the Writing and Speaking modules examiners use detailed performance descriptors which describe written and spoken performance at each of the 9 IELTS bands.

笔 记 区

Writing

Examiners award a band score for each of four criterion areas: Task Achievement (for Task 1), Task Response (for Task 2), Coherence and Cohesion, Lexical Resource and Grammatical Range and Accuracy. The four criteria are equally weighted.

Speaking

Examiners award a band score for each of four criterion areas: Fluency and Coherence, Lexical Resource, Grammatical Range and Accuracy and Pronunciation. The four criteria are equally weighted.

第一章
雅思口语考试介绍

由剑桥大学考试委员会、英国文化教育处和澳大利亚国际教育开发署共同主办的雅思考试与其他英语水平考试的最大区别在于，雅思考试包括一项考官和考生一对一、面对面的口语面试。

Ⅰ. 雅思口语考试形式与内容

表1

雅思口语考试概况	
时 间	11~14分钟
考试程序	考官把考生从候考区叫入考场，考生和考官隔着桌子面对面坐着。 考试开始后，考官会询问考生的全名并要求考生出示身份证件，整个考试过程会被录音，目的在于保证考官正确地执行了考试程序。
考试形式	考试分为三个部分。首先是一般交谈(introduction)，接着是个人陈述(individual long-turn)，最后是双向讨论(two-way discussion)。 **第一部分：一般交谈(4~5分钟)** 进入考场后，考生与考官互致问候。在核对身份后，考官会问一些关于考生生活、背景等的基本问题。(具体话题可参考表2、3) **第二部分：个人陈述(3~4分钟)** 考官给考生一张话题卡(Cue Card)。(具体题目可参考表4)考生有1分钟准备时间，并可以做笔记。之后考生要做1~2分钟的陈述。考生讲完后，考官会就考生的阐述内容提一两个相关问题，由考生做简要回答。 **第三部分：双向讨论(4~5分钟)** 考官与考生围绕由第二部分引申出来的一些比较抽象的话题进行讨论。第三部分的话题是对第二部分提示卡内容的深化和拓展。

1. 第一部分

在这一部分，考官会介绍自己并确认考生身份，然后打开录音机，报出考

笔记区

试名称、时间、地点等考试信息。考生可以利用这段时间尽快让自己熟悉考场环境，稳定情绪。考官也会试着帮助考生克服紧张心理，因此一般会以十分友好的方式开始提问，如：

Good morning. My name is Andrew. Can you tell me your full name, please? Or:

What should I call you? Or:

OK, can I see your identification, please?

接下来，在第一部分的开始，你可能会被问到以下列出的至少一个话题。

表2

第一部分 开始可能出现的话题	
Your studies and job	
Studies:	subjects studied, why you're studying, things you like/dislike about your course, what qualification you will gain, etc.
Job:	main responsibilities of job, things you like/dislike about it, etc.
Your name, family and hometown	
Your name:	who gave it to you, any special meaning, etc.
Your family:	family member, location and appearance of your family home, etc.
Your hometown:	whereabouts, notable features, weather, etc.

在谈完家庭、工作或学习后，你可能会被问到两三个有关你自己或个人背景的一般性问题，这些问题可能包括下面列出的话题。

表3

第一部分紧接着可能出现的综合性话题	
兴趣爱好：	hobbies and interests, shopping and fashion, reading, music and TV, sports and exercise, etc.
地域文化：	holidays and festivals, birthday, wedding, food, punctuality, transport, etc.
语言学习：	how long, most difficult aspect of language learning, etc.

当然，这部分有时也会出现与第三部分类似的、趋于抽象性的问题，如"What do you think about fashion?" 或者 "What can be done to improve public transport?"等。但绝大部分问题都是考生相当熟悉的话题，考生应尽可能充分地回答考官的问题——即提供有效的额外信息，这样可以让考官对考生的口语能力有一个好印象。

笔记区

2. 第二部分

在这一部分，考官给考生话题卡和纸笔。考生有1分钟的准备时间去迅速筛选信息，根据话题卡上的具体问题，记下几个想要表述的重点，然后做答。接着考官会根据考生所陈述的话题，问一两个直接相关的问题作为结束。这部分话题仍然是考生所熟悉的、日常生活中常见到的。下面是一个例子：

TOPIC CARD

Describe a teacher who has greatly influenced you in your education.

You should say:

who the teacher is

what subjects he/she taught

what was special about him/her

and explain why the teacher influenced you so much.

话题中的细节问题一般遵循由表及里、由浅入深、由描述到解释的原则。考生在做陈述时首先要引出主题，为确保陈述达到规定的时间并基本符合提问要求，考生应尽量覆盖所有问题，同时又有所侧重，做到有头有尾，详略得当。考生可以在草稿纸上写下一些想法和要点。如：

Mr. Chen Li
sports
nice, national volleyball team
encourage students
interested in everyone
never give up

接下来考生可以根据这些要点做1~2分钟的发言，量化地讲，实际上就是做一个200字左右的口头作文。例如：

The teacher that really influenced me a lot was Mr. Chen Li. He was the sports teacher when I was in high school.

He was in his thirties at that time and I'd say all my classmates admired him because he was kind of a hero to us and also because he was very nice. As far as I can remember, one thing that was special about him was that he'd been on the national volleyball team. I don't think he ever actually won a medal or anything like that. But for us, just the fact that he used to represent our country was really something. Actually, he was a very good teacher, very responsible...and dedicated...you know.

I guess the thing he taught me was to have a fighting spirit. I mean he always encouraged us to do our best in sport, even if we were terrible at it. He used to say "It doesn't matter if you win or not. The important thing is to do your best and keep going." He also taught us a lot about...health...and maintaining a positive attitude towards life. And compared to other teachers, he seemed to be more

笔记区

interested in everyone. Luckily, we still keep in touch and I often go to see him on holidays.

考生说完后，考官会根据所说内容提一两个追加问题(follow-up questions)，如在所举例题中，考官可能会问：

a) Do your classmates like Mr. Chen, too?

b) How much time did you spend on sports classes every week in high school?

这些问题是一个很自然的收尾，考生不需要展开回答，简要做答即可，然后开始进入第三部分。

第二部分的话题范围可以大致分为四类，每一类的具体话题众多，而且不断有新的话题涌现，考生可能没有时间也没有必要准备所有的话题，因为同一类题目中要求用到的语言能力和语言资源是相通的，考生可以把握住它们的共性，以不变应万变。以人物题为例，不管是电影明星、邻居或者是家庭成员，虽然每个具体的个人不同，但在描述他们的时候都要用到描述、评价和解释的语言能力，也都要用到描述人的特征(身高、长相、年龄等)和性格特点的词汇和句子，因此考生只要具有了这些基本的语言资源，再精心准备几个有代表性的题目，考试的时候只要头脑冷静，反应敏捷，即使遇到没有准备过的题目也照样可以纵横捭阖。比如刚才范例中的老师Mr. Chen Li，在考场上也可以是你的邻居，或者最好的朋友。而且语言考试的灵活性在于，即使题目是让你描述一个物品(如礼物)，这并非意味着你的描述只能集中在物品本身上，你也可以顺便谈一下礼物是谁送的，从而利用上你已经掌握的描述人的语言能力和资源，而我们所讲的语言能力和语言资源是完全可以在雅思口语的第二部分打破具体话题的界限，做到融会贯通的。

表4

第二部分 常见话题

人物题

family members, friends, film stars, sports stars, neighbours, teachers, a happy / successful person, children, a character in a TV programme or a film, (wild) animals, etc.

地点题

rooms and buildings, a place you would like to visit, a natural beautiful place, a lake or a river, a shop, a supermarket, a garden or a park, etc.

物品题

a gift, an old object, an expensive thing you want to buy, a vehicle or a bike you want to have, a card or a letter, a photo, a toy, a way to relax, a special meal, a

笔记区

dish, a sport, a TV programme, a film, an advertisement, a book, a website, a subject, newspapers or magazines, etc.

事件题

sporting events, family events, a wedding, a long-distance trip, important changes, happy events in your childhood, a story you heard when you were a child, a project you finished with others, an exhibition, a cultural difference you find interesting, first day in school / at work, etc.

3. 第三部分

第三部分中考官要求考生回答与第二部分话题有关的问题，是第二部分的延伸，其问题趋于宽泛、概括和学术化。第三部分的问题就形式而言，有很多是关于回顾过去、描述现在和展望未来的，如：

How has education changed in your country in the last 10 years?
What changes do you foresee in the next 50 years?

学生在回答这些问题时应特别注意使用正确的动词时态。此外，第三部分经常考的题型还有：

做比较： How do the expectations of today's school graduates compare with those of the previous generation?

评价优缺点： How beneficial do you think it is to group students according to their level of ability?

解决问题： What can be done to solve the problems in your education system you mentioned just now?

阐明标准： What qualities are required of a good teacher?

……

关注题型的原因在于储备一些必要的句型结构和词组，比如在评价优缺点时经常会使用到的句型和词组有：

The main advantage is that...
But in my opinion the real disadvantage is that...
One thing really positive about ... is that...
However,...
On the other hand,...
etc.

笔 记 区

这些清晰的结构可以引导考生理清思路，使答案富于逻辑性。

结构具备了，考生还要具备必要的观点（idea），因为光有一个空架子绝不能算言之有物(informative)。观点可以来自于考生的常识，而考生也可以针对雅思的内容去网络上(如海外的新闻网站或搜索引擎Google等)搜集素材，或者平时多关注一些英文报纸（如*China Daily* 或*21st Century*等），以了解新时尚以及新资讯，让自己的语言素材更加鲜活。那么第三部分最常考的主题是什么呢？其实也都是时下人们普遍关心的问题，粗略地讲可以分为这四类：

表5

第三部分 常考主题

1. 科技对人类生活方式的影响

computers' effects, communication tools, Internet

2. 对待传统的态度

preserving traditions (architecture, handicraft, festivals, cooking, etc.)

the importance of cultural events

3. 社会问题及政府责任

education

environment, wildlife conservation, pollution

public transport

celebrities' role in society

the ethics and qualities of journalism

advertising

TV's effects on children and family

censorship

4. 个人情感及人际关系

family, generation gap, friendship

human nature (happiness, etc.), older people and children

gender differences

II. 雅思口语考试的评分标准

1. 雅思口语考试的四个单项评分标准

考官主要考查考生以下四个方面的表现：

笔记区

1) Fluency and Coherence 流利与连贯程度

Fluency refers to the way a candidate communicates in English. It doesn't mean the faster the candidate speaks, the better. Fluency means a steady flow of speech. Another key issue is how well ideas are put together, and what kind of structures are used to connect one idea or one sentence to another.

流利程度指考生用英语交流的方式。这不等于考生讲得越快就越好。流利指的是讲话平稳流畅。另外，考生遣词造句的能力也很重要。

2) Lexical Resources 词汇量

Lexical resources refer to the vocabulary the candidate uses. The interviewer will see if the candidate uses a wide range of or limited vocabulary in his/her speech and if he/she uses the words in the correct way or not. The interviewer also examines the flexibility and variety of the candidate's vocabulary, i.e. if he/she has different choices of words to use or has to repeat the same limited number of words from time to time.

词汇量是指考生使用的词汇。考官将考查考生使用词汇的广度、准确性、多样性和灵活性，比如，看考生是能够使用不同的词汇还是不断重复有限的词汇。

3) Grammatical Range 语法

The interviewer will be looking to see if the candidate uses English grammar properly in speech. Does he/she use the correct tense when talking about things in different time? The interviewer will also examine the variety of sentence patterns the candidate uses, i.e. if the candidate demonstrates the ability of using both simple and complex sentence structures.

考官会留心考生使用语法的准确性、时态的准确性和句式的多样性，比如考生是否能同时使用简单句和复杂句。

4) Pronunciation 语音

The interviewer will see if the candidate speaks with reasonably understandable English pronunciation and how close his/her pronunciation, intonation and rhythms are to those of a native speaker of English.

考官会注意考生的语音是否容易听懂，跟以英语为母语的人的语音、语调和节奏感的相近程度。

2. 雅思口语各成绩档次描述（评分标准）

雅思口语各成绩档次描述原文（http://www.ielts.org）见下页表格。

笔记区

IELTS Speaking band descriptors (public version)

Band	Fluency and coherence	Lexical resource	Grammatical range and accuracy	Pronunciation
9	• speaks fluently with only rare repetition or self-correction; any hesitation is content-related rather than to find words or grammar • speaks coherently with fully appropriate cohesive features • develops topics fully and appropriately	• uses vocabulary with full flexibility and precision in all topics • uses idiomatic language naturally and accurately	• uses a full range of structures naturally and appropriately • produces consistently accurate structures apart from 'slips' characteristic of native speaker speech	
8	• speaks fluently with only occasional repetition or self-correction; hesitation is usually content-related and only rarely to search for language • develops topics coherently and appropriately	• uses a wide vocabulary resource readily and flexibly to convey precise meaning • uses less common and idiomatic vocabulary skillfully with occasional inaccuracies • uses paraphrase effectively as required	• uses a wide range of structures flexibly • produces a majority of error-free sentences with only very occasional inappropriacies or basic/non-systematic errors	• is easy to understand throughout, with L1 accent having minimal effect on intelligibility • uses a wide range of phonological features to convey meaning effectively
7	• speaks at length without noticeable effort or loss of coherence • uses a range of connectives and discourse markers with some flexibility • may demonstrate language-related hesitation at times, or some repetition and/or self-correction	• uses vocabulary resource flexibly to discuss a variety of topics • uses some less common and idiomatic vocabulary and shows some awareness of style and collocation with some inappropriate choices • uses paraphrase effectively	• uses a range of complex structures with some flexibility • frequently produces error-free sentences, though some grammatical mistakes persist	
6	• is willing to speak at length, though may lose coherence at times due to occasional repetition, self-correction or hesitation • uses a range of connectives and discourse markers but not always appropriately	• has a wide enough vocabulary to discuss topics at length and make meaning clear in spite of inappropriacies • generally paraphrases successfully	• uses a mix of simple and complex structures, but with limited flexibility • may make frequent mistakes with complex structures, though these rarely cause comprehension problems	• can be understood throughout, though mispronunciation may occasionally cause momentary strain for the listener

IELTS Speaking band descriptors (public version)

BRITISH COUNCIL · idp IELTS AUSTRALIA · UNIVERSITY of CAMBRIDGE ESOL Examinations

Band	Fluency and coherence	Lexical resource	Grammatical range and accuracy	Pronunciation
5	• usually maintains flow of speech but uses repetition, self-correction and/or slow speech to keep going • may over-use certain connectives and discourse markers • produces simple speech fluently, but more complex communication causes fluency problems	• manages to talk about familiar and unfamiliar topics but uses vocabulary with limited flexibility • attempts to use paraphrase but with mixed success	• produces basic sentence forms with reasonable accuracy • uses a limited range of more complex structures, but these usually contain errors and may cause some comprehension problems	
4	• cannot respond without noticeable pauses and may speak slowly, with frequent repetition and self-correction • links basic sentences but with repetitious use of simple connectives and some breakdowns in coherence	• is able to talk about familiar topics but can only convey basic meaning on unfamiliar topics and makes frequent errors in word choice • rarely attempts paraphrase	• produces basic sentence forms and some correct simple sentences but subordinate structures are rare • errors are frequent and may lead to misunderstanding	• produces some acceptable features of English pronunciation but overall control is limited and there can be severe strain for the listener
3	• speaks with long pauses • has limited ability to link simple sentences • gives only simple responses and is frequently unable to convey basic message	• uses simple vocabulary to convey personal information • has insufficient vocabulary for less familiar topics	• attempts basic sentence forms but with limited success, or relies on apparently memorised utterances • makes numerous errors except in memorised expressions	
2	• pauses lengthily before most words • little communication possible	• only produces isolated words or memorised utterances	• cannot produce basic sentence forms	• speech is often unintelligible
1	• no communication possible • no rateable language			
0	• does not attend			

得分	流利度与连贯性	词汇资源	语法结构的范围和准确性	发音
9	• 发言时极少有重复或自我更正，偶尔的停顿也是由于在思考内容，而非搜寻合适的词汇和语法 • 发言连贯，语言中上下文流畅，联系自然而充分 • 全面而得体地围绕话题展开发言	• 面对任何话题都能灵活、准确地使用词汇 • 自然、准确地使用习语	• 自然、准确地使用多样语法结构 • 语法结构的使用自始至终保持准确，虽然偶尔犯一些英语为母语者也会犯的“口误”	
8	• 发言时很少有重复或自我更正，偶尔的停顿也多是由于在思考内容，极少情况下是为了搜寻合适的语言 • 连贯而得体地围绕话题展开发言	• 能自然、灵活地使用多样词汇来准确表达思想 • 能巧妙使用较不常见单词和习语，尽管偶尔有不准确 • 能按要求有效地变换措辞	• 灵活使用多种结构 • 大部分语句无误，极偶尔情况下出现表达不恰当，或个别简单错误	• 自始至终易于理解，母语语音对英语的影响极小 • 使用多种语音手段来有效达意
7	• 能充分展开，且不会有刻意思考的痕迹，没有语言上的不连贯 • 能较灵活地使用连接词或语言中的信号词 • 有时出现由于语言水平而带来的重复或自我更正	• 能灵活使用词汇讨论多种话题 • 能使用较不常见单词和习语，对语体和搭配有所了解，尽管有时使用不当 • 能有效地变换措辞	• 较灵活地使用多种复杂结构 • 多数语句无误，但有些语法错误	
6	• 有充分交流的意识，但有时由于重复、自我更正或停顿而导致说话不连贯 • 能使用连接词或语言中的信号词，尽管有时不准确	• 有足够的词汇来充分讨论话题，清晰达意，尽管有不准确 • 大致可以变换措辞	• 能使用简单和复杂结构，但缺乏灵活性 • 复杂结构经常出现错误，尽管这些错误很少导致交流障碍	• 自始至终可以被理解，尽管发音错误偶尔会为听者带来一点费解
5	• 通常能维持语流，但需要通过重复、自我更正或放慢语速才能实现 • 可能会过多使用某些连接词或语言中的信号词 • 能流畅表达简单语言，复杂语言会导致语言不畅	• 能讨论熟悉或不熟悉的话题，但词汇使用缺乏灵活性 • 尝试变换措辞，但未能成功	• 能使用基本的句子结构，且使用基本正确 • 复杂结构的使用有限，且通常包含错误，有时导致交流障碍	
4	• 回答时有明显停顿，语速可能较慢，时常有重复、自我更正 • 能把基本句连接起来，但重复使用某些简单连接词，语意上多有不连贯之处	• 能讨论熟悉话题，对于不熟悉话题只能表达意思，词汇的选择上时常犯错 • 很少尝试变换措辞	• 能使用基本的句子结构，或正确的简单句子，但从句结构很少见 • 错误频繁，可能导致误解	• 可以发出英语中某些语音，但总体较差，给听者带来严重理解困难
3	• 发言时停顿过长 • 连接简单句的能力有限 • 只给简单答复，时常难以表达基本想法	• 使用简单语言表达个人信息 • 遇到较不熟悉的话题词汇匮乏	• 尝试使用简单句子结构，但不成功，或明显背诵事先准备的语言 • 表达中错误很多（背过的表达除外）	
2	• 说大多数词前都要长时间的思考停顿 • 交流很少	• 只能说只言片语或事先背过的语言	• 不能使用基本的句子形式	• 语言经常无法识别
1	• 无法交流 • 语言无法评估			
0	• 考试缺席			

笔 记 区

第二章
雅思口语考试策略回顾

Ⅰ. 雅思口语考试难在哪里？

虽然雅思口语考试在听说读写四项中是最短的，只有10~15分钟，但是很多中国考生依然经常把它看成最大的障碍。笔者认为主要有以下几个方面的原因：

1. 中国学校长期以来由于种种原因在英语教学中忽视学生听说技能的培养。中学和大学的英语考试很少考查学生的听说能力，即便考，听说部分占的比重也很小。所以学生经常可以从这样的考试中获得满意的分数，却很难张口与英语本族人交流。英语被当做知识来研究而不是作为交流的工具来习得。

2. 很多中国考生不知如何准备雅思口语考试，因为它没有可以借鉴的标准答案。他们太习惯于用背好的答案去准备考试了。而雅思口语考官期望看到的是考生用逻辑清晰、意义明确的语言自然交流、表达思想的能力。考官能轻易识破考生用背好的答案回答问题的企图，并可能立刻打断考生的背诵，然后换一个新的话题要求考生回答。考生甚至会因此而被扣分。

3. 口语的提高不像其他三项技能——听、读、写那样容易见效。如前所述，口语与其说是一种知识，不如说是一种交流技能和习惯。而习惯是需要相对长时间才能培养起来的。口语和听、读、写之间最大的区别在于它不仅需要人的头脑思维，更需要身体上的训练，即你必须真正开口讲话，以准确到位的面部肌肉和舌头的协调运动来发出让对方听懂的声音。考官判断考生的英语水平时不仅看他/她说的内容，更看重他/她表达这些内容的方式。换句话说，假如两个考生的回答用词、句式完全相同，但语音、语调和节奏感不同，会给考官留下完全不同的印象，因而最后得分也会完全不同。考前突击背一些好的表达很容易做到，但要在短时间内改变一个人的讲话习惯，包括语音、语调、节奏和口音，几乎是不可能的。

Ⅱ. 为什么说雅思口试不像很多考生想像的那样难？

换一个新的视角来看待雅思口语考试，我们可能会发现它其实并不像我们认为的那样难。

笔记区

1. 雅思口语考试并不仅仅以考查学生所用的语言点为重点。语法并不是考官惟一检查的内容。更能使考官产生深刻印象的是考生讲话的流利程度。考生没有必要以牺牲流利为代价去追求百分之百的精确。要知道很多人，包括很多英语本族人都会在讲话时犯语法错误。考生不必时常停下来改正自己偶尔出现的小错误，只要这些错误没有影响到理解和交流。需要声明的是这种策略决不等于说我们可以完全忽略口语考试中的语法表现。如果考生犯的语法错误太多，特别是当这些语法错误导致了歧义或使谈话无法进行下去，同样要被扣分。另外，流利并不一定意味着说得越快效果越好。在我看来，流利就是没有太多停顿和冷场的平稳的语速。

2. 我们不妨把雅思口语考试看成与一个新朋友的闲聊而不看做考试。在竞争中决定成败的往往是人的心理状态而不仅是他/她的实际能力（不仅在语言考试中，而且在任何其他竞争中，如体育比赛）。以前考生的经验表明你越是不把它看成考试，越是处于放松状态，最后成绩就越令人满意。大胆利用你的常识，想到什么尽管随意表达，特别是当你被问到一个一无所知的问题时。记住：考官感兴趣的不是你对某个话题了解多少，而是你能否有效地表达出你的知与不知。这是一种以交流技能而不是以知识为核心的考试。

3. 有时可以用一些表示犹豫的词语来避免可能出现的冷场。常用的有：er, um, uh, and, yes, right, yeah, oh right等等。但是不能过度频繁地使用这些表示犹豫的词语，它们几乎没有什么实际含义，也只能为考生争取很短的犹豫时间。更好的选择是用一些被叫做“fluency fillers”的短语。试举例如下：

   1）I mean, you know, you see, what I mean is that等用来进一步解释先前的说法。

   例：We are wasting our time. I mean/You know/You see/What I mean is that we spend most our time not living in the moment. We are either regretting the past or worrying about the future.

   2）By the way, talking of, speaking of用来引出一个与先前所说的话有字面联系的新话题。

   例：A）My mother does most of the cooking at home. She cooks really delicious food. By the way, my favourite food is hot pot.

   B）My favourite month of the year is September, with the blue sky, fresh air and many holidays. Speaking of holidays, Christmas is coming.

   3）Anyway, anyhow表示可以回到先前提到的某件事。

   例：Anyway, to answer your last question, I do love classical music.

   4）As far as I know, as far as I can see, as far as I'm concerned表示说话者就个人而言或发表自己的看法。

   例：A lot has been lost and, as far as I can see, little has been gained.

总之，只要考生尽量放松自己，积极主动谈话，在有限的时间内最大限度地展示自己用英语交流的能力，雅思口语考试比我们想像的容易对付得多。

笔记区

雅思口语考试的情况具体细节大家都知道，其中最让考生担心的就是Part 2&3部分，其实准备这项并不难，下面介绍一下准备这部分口语测试的方法：

1. 一定要清楚地了解每个卡片的内容，包括卡片上让你描述的3~4个小标题。考生必须在Part2部分中描述出来，还有就是描述时运用的时态一定要清楚，否则肯定影响分数，因为考官对时态乱用比较敏感。

2. 每天抽出一定的时间练习，没有条件互相练习的考生可以用录音机把自己说的话录下来，然后自己给自己找错误、纠正。就这样反复练习，尽量使自己减少出现语法错误，如he /she运用不当等等。

3. 千万不要整段背诵现成的答案，因为这样即使你说的再好也不会得到理想的分数，考官可以看出来你做了准备。建议考生最好不要预先写出完整的答案，最多在每张卡片上写些关键词，根据这些提示词每天反复练习。多准备些有创意的和有个性特点的内容，但不要跑题。

还有一些细节方面的事情：谈话时如果需要停顿或思考，千万不要在词语间加上"嗯"，"啊"，"那个"等中文语气助词。应该用"well"，"all right"等英文语气词。在和考官对话的时候还要记住：

1. 眼睛不要乱看，要保持与考官的目光接触，也就是eye contact。
2. 表情不要死板，在对话中要根据谈及的内容适度表现出一些"喜怒哀乐"等面部表情。
3. 适当使用一些body language，但是不要过多。记住这是考语言而不是考表演。

还有一些琐碎的事情，不得不提一提：考口语前最好洗个澡，刷刷牙。（尤其是男生，老外最讨厌身上有异味的人了，包括口臭。）可以的话喷一点香水。女生最好化化妆，但注意是"淡妆"，千万别浓妆艳抹地去考场吓唬考官（这不是选美）。去考场的时候带点水，因为考生肯定要提前1小时左右到考场，如果在等候期间渴了的话，找水可不那么容易。

III. 雅思口语考试应试策略

雅思考试作为一种国际通用的英语语言水平测试系统，它的权威性和实效性越来越受到准备到英语国家，特别是英联邦国家留学和移民的人士的认可，雅思热方兴未艾。但与此同时，雅思考试一些不为人所熟悉的风格和特点，却使很多考生感到不知所措甚至因此失利，尤其是它包括一项考生与考官面对面直接交谈的口语考试，更使许多习惯于中国式聋哑英语的考生望而生畏。下面简要讨论一下雅思口语考试中一些简单实用的应试策略：

笔 记 区

1. 如何应对考官在第一阶段开始时的三个目的？

考官在第一阶段最初的1~2分钟大致有三个目的：

1） 有些比较随合、善解人意的考官会尽量帮助考生放松情绪，克服紧张心理。在请考生坐定后，他们问考生的第一个问题很可能不是我们所期待的："What's your name?"或"Where are you from?"之类的正式问题，而是一个似乎与考试无关的非正式的轻松话题。比如他/她会像接待来访客人一样轻松地来一句："It's a nice day today, isn't it?" "Your T-shirt looks beautiful!" "How did you come here today?"等等，跟你闲谈上一两句，待你放松之后，再进入正式的面试话题。而我们有些中国考生被这突如其来的生活话题搞得不知所措，有的竟然哑口无言，目瞪口呆，连一个善意的微笑都没有回应，心理怀疑自己是不是走错了房间……要记住雅思口语考试的目的是考查考生在英语国家用英语与人交流的能力，或者说考官看重的是你的"生存英文"(survival English)而不是你的"学术英文"(academic English)。所以这时考生的正确做法应该是顺其自然地与考官交谈，充分展现你与人顺畅自如的交流能力，既放松自己，又给考官留下一个良好的初步印象。比如：

Interviewer: "How did you come here today?"

Candidate: "I came here by bus/taxi/bicycle."

I: "It's a nice day today, isn't it?"

C: "Yes, it is. It's the best season of the year."

I: "Your T-shirt looks beautiful!"

C: "Thanks. This is my favourite one."

当然，不要期待每个考官都会千篇一律地用这种方式开始面试，正像不要期待每个考官都用非常正式的问题开始提问一样，要准备迎接各种不同的面孔和问题。考官毕竟是人，不是机器。

2） 考官的第二个目的，同时也是一个顺理成章的结果，是得到有关考生英语水平的初步印象。这一印象对于考生的最后得分至关重要。因为根据心理学测试的结果，一个有经验的面试官可以在面试开始后1~2分钟之内得出对考生评判的结论，而无需等到面试结束。在余下的时间里，考官多半都在按照自己初步结论的惯性思维，从考生的回答中有意无意地寻找符合自己所做结论的证据来进一步证实自己的结论是正确的。这是人之常情，考官也是人。其实这种思维方式不仅体现在各种面试中，也普遍存在于社会生活的方方面面。我们对于一个人或任何事物在最初接触时形成的第一印象往往是很难改变的，除非发生什么戏剧性的情况，这种印象经常是占据主导地位的。

这就意味着我们应该特别注意对第一阶段最初几个问题的回答，尽管它们都是非常简单的问题。考生绝不能掉以轻心，忽视对这些简单问题的回答。有些考生在回答这些简单问题时甚至会犯一些低级错误，给考官留下不好的第一印象，也影响了自己后面的正常发挥。例如：

I: "What do you do?"

C: "I'm talking with you."

笔记区

考官明明在问："你是做什么的？"考生却回答："我正在跟你谈话。"可以想像，考官会因这样的回答对考生产生多么不利的第一印象："这个考生连这样简单的英语都听不懂，将来怎么在英语国家生存？"

3） 考官的第三个目的更加重要：他/她在从考生的回答中寻找下一步继续深入交谈的话题。第一阶段将持续大约4~5分钟。在问了几个简单问题之后，谈话将很自然地进入某个考生回答中提及话题的细节并沿着这一方向延伸下去。这就意味着考生在回答考官最初的几个问题时要格外小心，尽量避免提及自己没有把握深入交谈的话题。因为一旦考生不小心涉及了自己不熟悉的领域，而考官恰好对这一话题很感兴趣，考生将不得不在非常不利的处境中挣扎。例如，有些考官很喜欢在第一阶段谈论考生的个人爱好和业余生活。在被问到此类问题时，有些考生为了显示自己谈话的积极态度和爱好的广泛，向考官陈述了一系列的个人爱好，其中很可能包括一些自己并不很熟悉的项目，而当考官兴致勃勃地就这一话题追问下去时，考生往往才发现自己已经陷入困境。

正确的应对方法是不仅用口，而且用心回答每个问题。在回答任何问题时，不要慌慌张张地急于切入主题，大脑中迅速思考一下这个问题可能涉及到的后续问题，尽量把话题引到自己比较熟悉而考官又可能感兴趣的话题上，而不要匆忙中为自己设下一个陷阱。比如当考官问你曾经做过哪些职业或从事过哪些业余活动时，如果你的回答是"I like singing."就可能被问到更多有关"singing"的问题，如"Who is your favourite singer?" "What is your favourite song?" "Why do you like him/her/it?"等等。这就要求考生在考前要做好相应的准备，并在考试中思维敏捷，随机应变。

2. 如何应对第二阶段的语言提示卡？

拿到卡片后的第一件事不是马上开始讲话。在正式开始讲话之前，考官将给考生一分钟准备时间，并且给考生提供一张白纸和一支铅笔，考生可以边构思边在纸上做一些简单的笔记整理思路。一分钟后，无论考生是否准备好，考官都会要求他/她马上开始就卡片上的话题讲1~2分钟。而这时很多考生还没有准备好，以至于讲得杂乱无章结结巴巴，甚至大脑里只有只言片语或一片空白，讲不到一分钟就无话可说。所以第二阶段的要害不是讲话的过程本身而是在开始讲话之前的一分钟准备是否充分到位、思路清晰、有章可循。建议考生按以下三个步骤进行准备：

1） 拿到卡片后，首先仔细审题，快速浏览卡片上的内容并迅速准确地判断话题内容。注意：浏览卡片内容要既准确又迅速，一定不要误解标题和小标题上的任何内容，否则会造成谈话跑题而丢分。比如卡片上要求考生"talk about a Chinese traditional festival"，如果考生讲的是"National Day"就不会得到任何分数，因为"National Day"是个现代节日，而不是"traditional festival"，这就像写作考试中作文写跑题一样。

2） 第二步应该是根据对卡片内容的理解迅速决定要讲的内容，这个过程一般

笔记区

不应超过15秒钟。很多考生因为这一环节耗费了太多时间而陷入困境，比如考生得到的卡片上要求考生讲一部自己最喜欢的电影，如果该考生花了30秒甚至更长的时间才最终想好要讲哪一部电影，接下来组织思路和记笔记的时间就会相当紧张。在余下的20~30秒中，考生很难有充足的时间从容地整理思路，当考官打断你的思考要求你开始讲话时，结果可想而知！

3） 第三步理所当然应该是记笔记了。不言而喻，这个过程依然要求速度，一分钟时间稍纵即逝。记笔记时应注意以下几点：

① 不要试图写完整的句子甚至短语。一般来说一分钟之内我们无法写出三个以上的完整英文句子，这是一种时间的浪费。考生需要做的只是迅速记录下自己大脑中闪现的ideas。记录的方式可以多种多样，考生可以写英文缩写，如用Am代替America(n)，也可以自己设计一套只有自己能读懂的缩写代码。总之，记笔记的方式多种多样，总的原则就是怎么快怎么来，怎么方便怎么来。

② 没有必要抛开原卡片上的提纲而另起炉灶，在白纸上重新起草一个新的提纲，这也是一种得不偿失的做法。因为考生只有一分钟的时间整理思路，这和写作文完全不同。最有效的手段应该是把笔记完全建立在卡片提纲的基础上，在一分钟之内尽量把卡片上的4点提纲扩充在白纸上。实践证明，这种方法是行之有效的，也是一分钟之内完全可以做到的。试想，如果你只有4点提纲，那么每一点要讲到15秒以上才能讲到一分钟，但如果你有多达8点甚至更多的提纲，每一点只需讲到8秒钟就可以达到目的，而且你的讲话会显得很有逻辑。

3. 如何应对第三阶段的讨论？

第三阶段是在前两阶段的基础上为了让还有潜力挑战自己的考生继续施展自己的语言表达能力而提供的机会。考官将就第二阶段的卡片话题与考生展开进一步深入的讨论，问题会变得越来越抽象而广泛。考官将根据考生的表现灵活掌握这一阶段问题的难度甚至谈话时间。一般来说，想拿到7分以上的考生必须在这一阶段有较好的表现。有关这一阶段的应试技巧不作为普通性的策略来讨论，因为只有具备了一定的语言表达能力，才能谈得上用更抽象的方式发表观点深入探讨某个问题。我们将在以后的章节中专门论述这方面的问题。对一般考生来讲，这一阶段要掌握的总的原则是避免用抽象的方式论述抽象的问题，尽量把抽象问题具体化，比如举例说明问题就是一个简单实用的办法。例证既能多占时间，又更有说服力。

Ⅳ. 雅思口语之网上淘宝

雅思口语第三阶段为two-way discussion，其间考官和考生进行4~5分钟的交谈。话题总的来说是围绕第二阶段的题目展开的，比如说如果第二部分要求考生描述他/她喜欢的一个房间或公寓，那第三部分的问题会紧紧围绕住宿和生活方式这样的主题。由于问题有了广度和深度，回答起来也就不是那么容易，有些

笔记区

问题想必考生用中文都没有考虑过，更别说用英文来讨论了。因此在准备第三阶段时，有必要先了解问题的风格和类型。一般而言，第三阶段的题目通常包含描述变化(中国住房近20年的变化)、做比较(大学生活和中学生活)、做预测(将来交通方式会有何发展)、提出解决方案(如何解决环保问题)以及陈述个人意见(网络对阅读习惯有何冲击)等。就主题而言，题目涉及衣食住行、科技文化；就深度而言，关于同一话题的题目也有深浅之分，比如说同样是“public transport”，考官可能会先问 “What kind of public transport do people around you use?”，然后再过渡到 “What can the government do to improve public transport?”，很明显，两个问题的难度不同。雅思口语的这种话题多样、深度递增的出题特点，让很多考生觉得准备起来无从下手。很多人会考虑购买市面上的参考书，背诵上面的答案，实际上这个办法很不可取。原因有二：其一，答案千篇一律，会引起考官反感；其二，答案本身存在问题，很多就是中国人自己编写出来的，在用词和答题角度上带有很深的中国人思维的痕迹。那么怎样才能准备一些很个性化但同时在语言上和思维上又很地道的答案呢？其实上网淘资源是一个很好的解决方案。比如就以“public transport”为例，看看如何一“网”打尽。

关于公共交通的话题在雅思中时常考到，如果考生对这个大话题下的相关词汇、句型和观点有比较全面的把握的话，那么无论考官问与此相关的何种话题，考生都可以轻松应对了。而这些内容在网上都可以找到最地道的英文资料。考生要做的，只不过是利用网上的搜索引擎(比如说Google等)去查询。

第一步，将关键词输入搜索引擎。尽量多输入关键限定词，如“encourage public transport”或者“improve public transport”，以便缩小查询范围，使查询结果更符合题目的要求。

第二步，如图所示，经过搜索，共找到了2,090,000项符合要求的查询结果。(晕!)考生当然没有必要逐一浏览所列网站，其实查询结果中的头两页里就已经

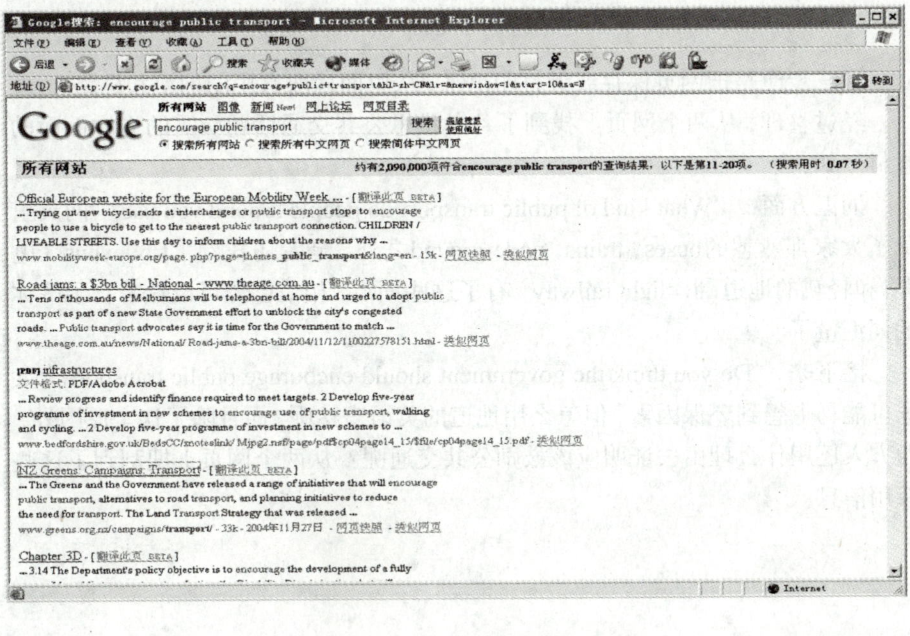

笔 记 区

可以找到宝贝了，大家只要稍稍读一下每个网址下的介绍内容，看哪些网站跟鼓励发展公共交通看上去关系密切，然后打开即可。经过比较，笔者发现有两个网页上的内容完全可以涵盖公共交通的各个方面。它们分别是：

http://www.transport2000.org.uk/campaigns/PublicTransport.htm

http://www.edinburgh.gov.uk/CEC/City_Development/ Transport_and_ Communications/Local_Transport_Strategy/consultleaflet3.html

其中一个如下图所示。

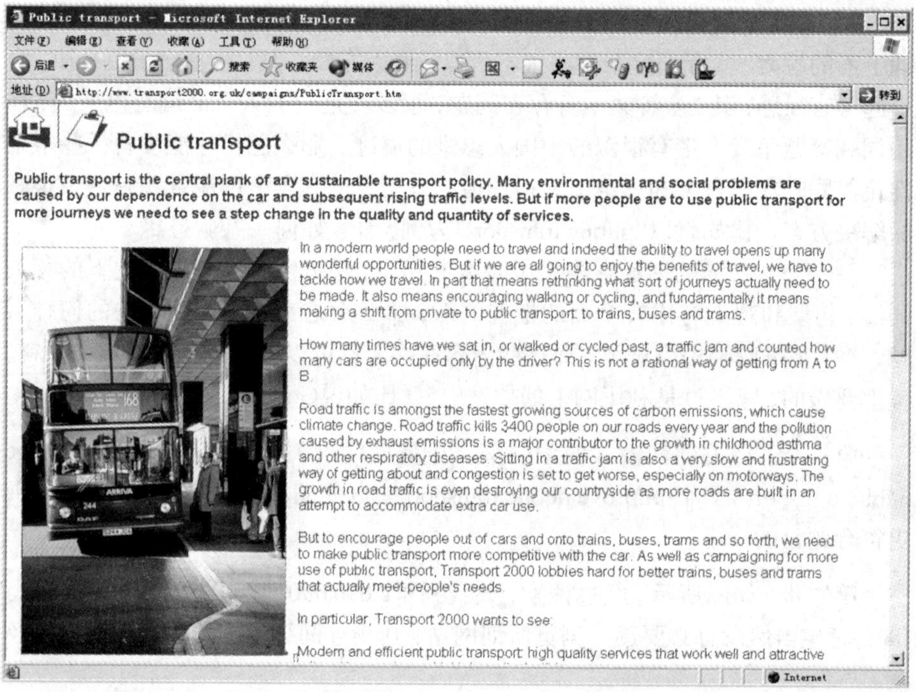

第三步便是把网页保存或者打印出来，从里面摘取有用的词汇和思路。

经过整理，从两个网页上找到了备考雅思公共交通话题所需的方方面面的素材。如：

词汇方面，“What kind of public transport do people around you use?”网页里除了大家都熟悉的buses，trains，underground之外，笔者还找到了trolleybus（电车）和轻轨的地道翻译light railway。有了这些词汇，相信已经可以让考官了解你的词汇量了。

接下来，“Do you think the government should encourage public transport?”大家可能马上想到环保因素，但怎么用地道的英语表达呢？而且除了这个原因外，西方人还用什么理由去证明应该鼓励公共交通呢？从两个网页上搜刮到了这些有用信息：

笔 记 区

Too many people are killed and injured on our roads. Even more suffer from the effects of transport pollution. Lack of exercise, associated with car based lifestyles, is a growing health problem. Globally, transport pollution is the fastest growing contributor to climate change, which could have serious consequences in the long term.

原来除了环保的原因外，西方人还考虑到了交通事故和健康的原因。

当然，从网上得到的最大收获是找到了回答“What can the government do to improve public transport?”的最地道的答案。对于这个问题，中国考生想到的可能是“政府应该造更多的马路”、“改善服务”、“降低票价”等答案。这些回答也还可以接受，但西方人的思路是什么呢？一起来看一下：

- make transport more accessible to people with disabilities and those with low incomes
- maintain the road network in good condition
- priority for public transport: We need more bus lanes and priority traffic lights that let buses through first.
- modern and efficient public transport: high quality services that work well and attractive rail and bus stations with high quality facilities

这样的回答岂不是更符合西方人的思路？答案第一条所体现出来的对弱势群体的关怀岂不更能引起西方考官的共鸣？而且语言也是那么地道。

如此这般，关于“公共交通”的话题便解决了。雅思第三部分中难度较大或涉及到西方价值观的问题，比如说“research using animals”、“bio-engineering”等，也可以在网上找到不错的答案。即使是涉及中国传统文化的问题，如“What do you think are the features of traditional Chinese architecture?”，考生也可以在Google上键入“features of traditional Chinese architecture”进行搜索，看看西方人写的东西，而不必搜肠刮肚去找中文资料，然后翻译成英文。笔者经过查询，找到了下面这个网站：

http://www.houstoncul.org/culdir/arch/arch.htm 内容是“Traditional Chinese Culture in Taiwan：Architecture”，从网址上看应该是美籍华裔编写的，所以语言很地道。内容上，文章讲到了“平衡和对称”的原则，“木结构框架”以及“四合院”等等，考生完全可以借鉴。

由此可见，网络上丰富的英语资讯加上强大的搜索引擎，使得互联网成为了巨大的英语语料库。因此，考生们在备考雅思或者学习英语过程中如果遇到词汇匮乏、思路狭窄、资源短缺等问题，不妨试一下网上淘宝，相信会有惊喜收获。

笔 记 区

V. 雅思口语考试各阶段复习规划

培训前	1. 收集口语考试资料，了解雅思口语考试的模式和特点。 2. 在对口语的话题有所了解之后，可以开始系统地收集相关语言素材，建立自己的语汇本，按照专题(如城镇描述、教育话题等)收集词汇、词组、句子以及好的段落及文章。 3. 平时可多阅读英文报纸、杂志等，如从“*21st Century*”(《二十一世纪报》)上获得一些最新的体育、娱乐和英语学习资料，从“www.economist.com”(《经济学家》杂志的网站)上获得一些很好的政治、经济评论文章。 4. 如果在准备的过程中遇到很棘手或感觉无从谈起的话题，如“What are the benefits of keeping animals in a zoo?”可以将问题的关键词如“benefits of keeping animals in a zoo”输入搜索引擎网站(如Google)，便可以检索到关于这个话题最地道的英文素材了。 5. 考生可养成每天定时大声诵读英语的习惯，时间可设定为每天30分钟，诵读的内容要简单易懂，最好有native speaker的配音，这样考生可以模仿其语音、语调。 6. 通过看情景喜剧(如“*Friends*”等)或看英文电影来提高口语也是不错的办法，但切记不要只看热闹，应该“精看精听”，甚至后来可以做到为该影视作品配音。 7. 时间充裕的话，可集中一段时间(如1~2个月)改善自己的发音，尤其是元音或由于地域原因自己无法分辨清楚的因素。可考虑使用市面上的语音教材，并请英语专业的同学或老师帮助自己纠音。
培训中	1. 继续坚持口语素材的收集，在培训过程中可以更加有针对性地扩展跟雅思相关的词汇和表达法。 2. 按照老师的要求，课前将本节课要讲的话题进行预习，课后完成作业，这样收获才会最大。 3. 如果可能的话在班上找一位同学做学习伙伴，两人可以一起备考。具体形式有：两人设定题目交谈；两人同读一篇取自杂志或报纸的短文，然后口头总结并讨论；分工找资料等。 4. 如果是为期较长的培训班（如周末强化班等），学员应尽量在培训期间就将口语第一部分的问题准备完，第二部分应掌握授课老师所讲的经典例题，第三部分应掌握常见的论证结构，并能熟练讨论常见主题(如科技对生活方式的影响、社会问题与政府职责等)。
冲刺	1. 将口语第一部分的问题分成4组，每天找固定时间大声回答，并录音，请英语专业的同学找出发音和语法错误。 2. 第二部分至少精心准备15个话题卡，内容涵盖人物、物品、地点、事件等主题，并关注考前近半年的口语话题卡。 3. 考前两周自己制作10套完整的口语模拟题，包括一、二、三部分，每天模拟2套。找同伴或者外国人练习模考4次，或参加新东方提供的口语模考。

笔记区

第三章
雅思口语考试常考问题和卡片话题

Ⅰ. Part 1 常考问题及答案

Confirmation Questions

1. Good morning, my name is Jake. Could you tell me your full name please?
2. And what shall I call you?
3. Can I see your identification, please?
4. Does your name have any special meaning?
5. Do you work or are you a student?

Studies Questions（for Academic Module Students）

6. What is your major?
7. Why did you choose your major?
8. How do you like your major?
9. What do you like most about your studies?
10. Is there anything you don't like about your studies?
11. How do you like your life in the university?
12. Is your university a good place to study in?
13. What do you think of the training you got in the university?
14. How was your high school experience?

Work Questions

15. Where do you work?
16. When do you go to work everyday?
17. How do you get to work?
18. What do you do for a living?
19. What are some of your responsibilities? I mean, what does your job involve?
20. Tell me about a typical day at work. What do you do on a daily basis?
21. How do you like your job?

笔 记 区

22. What do you like most about your job?
23. Is there anything you don't like about your job?
24. Which part of the day do you like best?
25. What made you decide to get into this field?

Hometown Questions

26. Whereabouts is your hometown?
27. Let's talk about your hometown or village. What kind of place is it?
28. Could you tell me something about your hometown?
29. What kind of landscape surrounds your hometown?
30. What are the main tourist attractions in your hometown?
31. What are the people like in your hometown?
32. What places in your hometown do you like best and tell me why?
33. What places in your hometown might a visitor be interested in visiting, and tell me why?
34. Do you think your hometown is a good place for a young person to live?
35. What are the advantages and disadvantages of living in your hometown?

Accommodation

36. Tell me about the kind of accommodation you live in.
37. What are the advantages and disadvantages of the kind of housing you live in?
38. Which do you prefer, a flat or a house?
39. Which floor do you live on, and what are the advantages and disadvantages of living on that floor?

Family

40. Can you tell me something about your family?
41. What do your family members do for a living?
42. What do you and your family like to do together?
43. Do you prefer big families or small families? What do you think are the advantages of big families and small families?

Hobbies and Spare Time

44. What kind of hobbies do you have?
45. How did you become interested in your hobby?

笔记区

46. What do you do in your spare time?
47. Do you like to be with a group of people or alone when you're free?
48. How do you spend your weekends?
49. How do you spend your free time?
50. What kinds of things do you like doing when you're not working?
51. Do you like doing these things with a group of friends or by yourself?

Reading

52. What kinds of books do you like to read in your spare time?
53. Do you like reading books and newspapers?
54. Where do you like to read books?
55. Do you discuss the books you read with friends?
56. Is reading popular in your country with young people?

Sports

57. What is your favourite sport?
58. Why do you like it so much?
59. What sports are played in your country?
60. What is the most popular sport in your country?
61. What are the sports facilities like in your hometown?

Films and TV

62. Do you often go to the cinema/theatre?
63. Which cinema do you often go to?
64. Do you prefer to watch film in the cinema or at home?
65. Do you like to watch alone or with your friends?
66. What kind of films do you like?
67. Who's your favourite film star? Can you describe him/her to me?
68. Do you often watch TV? What's your favourite programme?

Music

69. How often do you listen to music?
70. What kind of music do you like?

笔 记 区

Clothing Questions

71. What kind of clothing do you like best?
72. What kind of clothing is popular in China?
73. What kind of clothing do children usually wear?
74. What does traditional clothing in China look like?
75. How do older people feel about younger people's clothing?

Future Plan Questions

76. What sort of accommodation would you most like to live in when you get to England?
77. What problems or difficulties do you think you may have in Britain/Canada/Australia?
78. Can you imagine what life in Britain/Canada/Australia will be like?
79. What do you want/intend to study?
80. Which university are you going to study at?
81. Why did you choose this university?/Could you tell me why you chose to study at (name of university)?
82. What are your plans in Britain/Canada/Australia/New Zealand?
83. What are you going to major in?
84. What kind of differences in the cultures are you expecting between China and New Zealand?
85. What do you intend to do after you graduate?
86. Are there any special places you want to see in Canada? What are they?
87. What kind of things do you want to do in Canada that you can't do here?
88. What are your goals in life?

Foreign Language Studies

89. How long have you been studying English?
90. Do you think English is important for China?
91. What do you think of English?
92. What is most rewarding about learning a foreign language?
93. What do you think is the best way to study English?
94. What aspect of English do you find the most difficult?

Weather Questions

95. What is the climate like in your hometown?

笔 记 区

96. What is the weather like in Beijing?
97. How would you compare the climate in your hometown with other cities?
98. What are the advantages and disadvantages of the weather in your hometown?
99. What is your favourite type of weather in your hometown?

Food Questions

100. What kind of food and dishes do people eat in your hometown?
101. What is the main food in China?
102. In what ways has the diet of people in your country been changing?
103. How has your diet changed?

Festival Questions

104. Tell me about the biggest traditional festival in your country./ What's the biggest traditional festival in your country?
105. What do you do during the Spring Festival?
106. Can you describe one of the main festivals celebrated in your country?

Changes Questions

107. What changes have taken place in your hometown in the last 20 years?
108. Has your life changed in the last 10 years, and if so, in what ways?
109. Is there anything you'd like to change in your life?
110. How different is your life from the lives of your parents?
111. Has tourism changed China very much?
112. Has the transport changed over the past 20 years in China?

Travells and Holiday Questions

113. Do you enjoy travelling?
114. What do you usually do on your holidays?
115. Is there anywhere you would particularly like to visit on your holidays? Where and why?
116. Let's talk a little about travelling and transport. For a long trip, how do you prefer to travel?

笔 记 区

Transport

117. Which type of transport do you usually use in your hometown?
118. Which type of transport do you prefer for travelling around?
119. What's the traffic situation like in your hometown?

Buildings

120. Does your hometown have a lot of modern buildings or are they mostly traditional?
121. Which buildings do you prefer to look at?
122. Could you describe the traditional architecture of your country?

Birthdays

123. How important are birthdays in your country?
124. How do Chinese people celebrate their birthdays?
125. Do you like to celebrate your birthday with your parents or with your friends?
126. What do children get for their birthdays in your country?
127. Which is the most important birthday for a Chinese?

参考答案

Confirmation Questions

1. *Good morning, my name is Jake. Could you tell me your full name please?*
   My full name is Huang Qi Guang.
2. *And what shall I call you?*
   Most people call me Xiao Huang.
3. *Can I see your identification please?*
   Yes, here is my identification.
4. *Does your name have any special meaning?*
   Yes, my name does have some special meaning. My family name means "peace", and my first name means "strong one". My English name was given to me by one of my high school teachers, and it does not have any special meaning really.
5. *Do you work or are you a student?*
   a. I'm a student. I'm doing computer science in Beijing Institute of Technology.

笔记区

b. I work for a large European car maker. I work on car design. In fact, I run the Design Department.

Studies Questions (for Academic Module Students)

6. *What is your major?*

   I major in Accounting, which is part of the School of Business at my university. I mainly study the international accounting system as it relates to foreign trade.

7. *Why did you choose your major?*

   Because I've always enjoyed working with computers, and I was always good at math and logic. I was fortunate to have a computer in my home when I was in high school, and I spent quite a lot of time just playing around on the computer. My parents bought me all sorts of books on computer programming, and I just started to read them and pick up the ideas in them.

8. *How do you like your major?*

   a. I enjoy it, actually. I didn't know that much about it before I studied it, but I'm glad I chose it because it suits me a lot. My father actually suggested that I major in Accounting, because he thought that I'd enjoy it, too.

   b. I don't like it at all. I wish I could switch to a different one, but it's next to impossible to change majors. I just hope that when I get a job, I won't have to do a lot of work related to my major.

9. *What do you like most about your studies?*

   I just like learning the principles, and I like solving problems successfully. I also like getting to know my classmates, and working with them.

10. *Is there anything you don't like about your studies?*

    Generally I like my subjects, but I hate the examination system. There are too many examinations, and most of the time we have to memorize lots of things in books. I'm not very good at that and I find it's a waste of time and energy. Other than that, I quite enjoy my time at school.

11. *How do you like your life in the university?*

    a. I don't like it very much. The dormitory's very crowded, the food is tasteless and my teachers aren't very inspiring. When I was a high school student, I was looking forward to university life so much. I'm quite disappointed, because it's really not what I expected.

    b. I like it a lot. Sometimes it is a little hard to live in the university, but I have made many good friends and I enjoy my major. It was hard at first to live apart from my parents, but I think that it has been a good change for me. I am much more independent and more able to deal with troubles on my own. My courses are mostly interesting too, so I'm glad that I chose the major I did.

笔 记 区

12. *Is your university a good place to study in?*

Oh, sure. The university is quite a prestigious one, famous for its teaching quality. But what I like best is the library, which is said to have the biggest collection of books on horticulture. I can always find something exciting when I study in the library.

13. *What do you think of the training you got in the university?*

a. I think most of my courses will be helpful in the future. My university has tried very hard to keep up to date with the latest developments in our field. There were some compulsory classes that I didn't like, such as politics and history, but overall, I think I was provided with a pretty good education. I don't think it's possible to learn everything you need to know about a future career, but I'm satisfied my courses have given me a good start.

b. I don't think it was very good. There were some compulsory classes that I had no interest in. Also, our facilities were not very modern, so there were many things we couldn't do.

14. *How was your high school experience?*

a. I had a good high school experience because I was at a good school, and I made so many good friends there. I think I was lucky to have good teachers.

b. I think my high school experience was not a happy one because I seemed to always be under a lot of pressure, and for some reason I always seemed to have bad luck. When I got to university my luck started to improve.

Work Questions

15. *Where do you work?*

I work in the main office of Motorola. It's near the Lufthansa Centre, by the third ring road and Liangmahe road in Beijing. I've been there since 1995.

16. *When do you go to work everyday?*

I am required to get to work at 9:00 o'clock, but sometimes I get there at 8:00 o'clock, or even earlier.

17. *How do you get to work?*

I drive a car. I own a Santana car, and each morning I have to fight through the traffic. Sometimes I wonder if having a car is really worth it.

18. *What do you do for a living?*

I'm an engineer. But my day-to-day work involves quite a lot of management. In fact, I'm in charge of the Beijing branch of Motorola, and have a dozen or so engineers working under me to handle the technical side of the work.

19. *What are some of your responsibilities? I mean, what does your job involve?*

I'm a sales manager. I'm in charge of overseeing sales operations for all of

笔 记 区

northern China, including Beijing. I have about 40 employees under me who are the regional sales representatives.

20. *Tell me about a typical day at work. What do you do on a daily basis?*
Most of the time, I sit behind a desk and answer phone calls. It's not a very active job, but I do enjoy it most of the time, except when I get a phone call from a very angry customer. Sometimes, they just want to shout at someone, and because I'm the first one to answer the phone, I get the full vent of their anger.

21. *How do you like your job?*
I enjoy it very much. It does have its ups and downs, but really it's quite a good job. I enjoy the people I work with too, which really can make or break a job. We work very well together and can trust each other to do our fair share.

22. *What do you like most about your job?*
  a. My job is challenging and interesting, and I think that the best thing about it is the satisfaction I get from solving problems. Each time I manage to make things go smoothly, I get a great sense of satisfaction.
  b. I guess I like the pay. I know that sounds cold, but in fact my job is very routine and so I just feel that at least the pay gives me some satisfaction.

23. *Is there anything you don't like about your job?*
  a. I think the worst part of the job is all the unnecessary bureaucracy that exists to do everything. I just wish that there could be simpler routines and not so many steps to everything.
  b. I think the worst part of my job is the long hours that I'm sometimes required to work. I think it should be designed so that I can be allowed to go home on time every night.

24. *Which part of the day do you like best?*
Going home from work! Well actually I should say stepping into my flat and greeting my baby daughter who is now about 2 years old.

25. *What made you decide to get into this field?*
I didn't really plan to be a teacher at first, but my parents encouraged me to go into teaching. At first I really hated it, but after a while I got used to standing in front of a room full of students. I enjoyed my classes and the challenges of teaching, so that's when I knew that teaching was the right profession for me.

Hometown Questions

26. *Whereabouts is your hometown?*
Zhengzhou. It is located in Henan province, which is in central China.

27. *Let's talk about your hometown or village. What kind of place is it?*

笔 记 区

My hometown's a small place, just outside of Beijing. It takes about an hour to get to there. The people there are mostly farmers, but a lot of the young people work in Beijing. It's a quiet place and I like it.

28. *Could you tell me something about your hometown?*

a. Well, it's quite big and it's the capital of Shanxi province. The population's about 6 million and it's famous for its historic sites, especially for the Terracotta Warriors. Xi'an used to be the capital of China, and it's the beginning of the famous Silk Road.

b. Okay. Well, my hometown is Beijing and I live just outside of it near the 4th ring road. As you probably know, Beijing's the political and cultural centre of China, and it's quite a historical place as well. It's huge—about 12 or 13 million people live in it now—and it seems to be getting bigger every year.

29. *What kind of landscape surrounds your hometown?*

a. Harbin's right near the Song Hua Jiang River, and it's kind of in a flat area, with mountains in the distance.

b. Qingdao's a coastal city near the sea, so the main landscapes are the beaches and bays. There are also some nice hills nearby.

30. *What are the main tourist attractions in your hometown?*

There's the Great Wall and the Forbidden City. These are the two that are most well known. They are also symbols of China. They attract most visitors, but there are quite a lot of other famous sites as well.

31. *What are the people like in your hometown?*

They're usually very friendly, but a bit conservative. People still hold onto a lot of old customs and traditions, which is what I mean by conservative. But I think people there are very hospitable and kind. If you ask someone for directions, they'll always try to help you out, or find someone else who can.

32. *What places in your hometown do you like best and tell me why?*

I like the Temple of Heaven best because it's very beautiful. It has a lot of space and there are lots of really nice and old trees there. In the early morning, it's very peaceful. The older people practise their *Tai-ji*, while the younger children just run around and play. I like there a lot.

33. *What places in your hometown might a visitor be interested in visiting, and tell me why?*

I'd recommend the Great Wall, Summer Palace, and the Forbidden City. Those are the most famous places in the city, and I think they best represent Beijing.

34. *Do you think your hometown is a good place for a young person to live?*

a. Yes I do, because it's got a lot of opportunities and the entertainment facilities are quite good. You can get a decent job here if you have some skills, and you

笔记区

can make a lot of good friends if you have a good personality.

b. No, I think if you're young you'd be better off going to a bigger city with more opportunities. I think my hometown is more suitable for an older crowd, who enjoy a more peaceful life. Younger people get bored with the way things are here.

35. *What are the advantages and disadvantages of living in your hometown?*

I think the biggest advantage is that it's a place where you can find a good job with a good salary, if you try very hard. Also, the people are quite kind and generous. The main disadvantages are the traffic and pollution problems. If you stay in my hometown you will know that these are the two things that everyone here hates the most.

Accommodation

36. *Tell me about the kind of accommodation you live in.*

I live in a two-bedroom apartment with my parents. The apartment's not big, but we've made it very comfortable to live in. We live on the third floor, and there's no lift in our apartment. The highest floor is the sixth floor, so whoever lives on the sixth floor has to climb up and down everyday.

37. *What are the advantages and disadvantages of the kind of housing you live in?*

Let me think. The biggest advantage? I guess it would be the convenience of it. I can do anything I want. As for the biggest disadvantage, some people might say the space, but I think the biggest disadvantage of living in a flat is that you never really get to know your neighbours.

38. *Which do you prefer, a flat or a house?*

Well, it depends on the condition that they are in. I'd probably have to say a flat, because you don't have to worry so much about maintaining it.

39. *Which floor do you live on, and what are the advantages and disadvantages of living on that floor?*

I live on the 1st floor. The advantage is that it's easier to get to, because you don't have to climb any steps. The bad thing is that it's a bit noisier, although we don't have to put up with too much noise from downstairs, since there is no downstairs.

Family

40. *Can you tell me something about your family?*

I have three brothers and no sisters. Both of my parents are still alive, and are still working. My grandparents on my father's side are both alive too, though my mother's parents have already passed away. I am also married...I got married two years ago.

笔记区

41. *What do your family members do for a living?*

My father's retired, and my mother's still working as a nurse at the Xie He Hospital. My father used to be a city inspector. I have no brothers and sisters.

42. *What do you and your family like to do together?*

I guess we mainly just talk about a lot of things and then watch TV together. My parents and I like to visit people together. Sometimes we go shopping together, but to tell you the truth I prefer doing that by myself.

43. *Do you prefer big families or small families? What do you think are the advantages of big families and small families?*

Well, big families are probably good for the children, because there are so many people to play with. But I think that big families also create a large burden for the parents and it's difficult for each child to receive the attention he or she deserves.

Hobbies and Spare Time

44. *What kind of hobbies do you have?*

I'm a big basketball fan, even though I'm not very good at playing basketball myself. I love to watch the NBA on TV whenever I get a chance. I also play ping-pong and volleyball whenever I can.

45. *How did you become interested in your hobby?*

Since I was young, my father has always involved me in different activities. My father is a ping-pong coach in a high school. So I always have a chance to follow him when he coached. When I was in the school, I got a chance to play with other students in other sports. So that's how I developed an interest in different sports.

46. *What do you do in your spare time?*

I like to play on the computer and surf the Internet. Once I get on the Internet, I find that time really passes very quickly. Before I know it, several hours have passed and my back and neck are aching. I also like to go for walks and read novels on ancient Chinese history.

47. *Do you like to be with a group of people or alone when you're free?*

I like being with a group of people. It's livelier and I feel more at ease, especially when I feel that my friends are also having a good time.

48. *How do you spend you weekends?*

I usually sleep in on Saturday morning if I can, study in the afternoon in the library, and go out with friends in the evening. On Sundays, I like to go shopping and just spend time walking around outside if the weather is nice. If I don't have much money, I still like to go window-shopping, and I get almost as much pleasure out of that!

笔 记 区

49. *How do you spend your free time?*

I attend training courses in the evenings. However, as a mother, I also take my son somewhere on the weekend. For example, I may drive to the suburbs or the countryside around Beijing and go fishing, swimming or mountain climbing. I enjoy family life very much.

50. *What kinds of things do you like doing when you're not working?*

I'm kind of an indoor type of person, so I guess I like reading most. I'm interested in reading all kinds of books and newspaper or magazine articles, especially those on current issues. I just want to be informed of what's going on in the world.

51. *Do you like doing these things with a group of friends or by yourself?*

I prefer being with my friends and family. I'm kind of an outdoor type. I like to go swimming or play badminton with my family or friends during weekends or holidays. If I have a longer vacation, I usually travel to further away places all over the country.

Reading

52. *What kinds of books do you like to read in your spare time?*

I like reading biographies of interesting people. I like these because they teach me something and also I find that other people's lives are sometimes even stranger than the lives of people in fictional stories.

53. *Do you like reading books and newspapers?*

Yes, I like to read *21st Century* and *China Daily*. I usually read as much as I have time for, which is sometimes quite a lot. Both of these newspapers are in English, and I find that it really is a good way for me to practise my English.

54. *Where do you like to read books?*

I suppose it depends on the book. If it's just a normal novel, then I guess I'd rather read it at home in my room. But if it's a nonfiction, informational book, I guess I'd rather read it in a library.

55. *Do you discuss the books you read with friends?*

Yeah. If there's something interesting in them. For example some of the things people say in the biographies make good quotes and I like talking about these people to others.

56. *Is reading popular in your country with young people?*

No, I'd say that it's getting less popular. There are just so many other things to do that we don't really have to rely on books that much for entertainment. I think TV is the main reason. It's just easier to watch a show than read a book.

笔 记 区

Sports

57. *What is your favourite sport?*

My favourite sport is basketball. I've been playing it regularly for about a year, and I'm quite crazy about it now.

58. *Why do you like it so much?*

Basketball is fast and it's a bit more exciting than playing other sports like football. I love the NBA, so that also makes me more interested in the sport as well.

59. *What sports are played in your country?*

Ping-pong and basketball are probably the most popular sports. China has a very large following of basketball fans. And I think this is partly due to Yao Ming, you know, the Chinese player who plays in the NBA in the States.

60. *What is the most popular sport in your country?*

I'd have to say that football's really the most popular sport in China. There are literally millions of crazy football fans. Whenever there's a match on TV between China and another country, you can hear loud cheers and shouts all around the city whenever China scores a goal, and loud groans and moans when the other country scores.

61. *What are the sports facilities like in your hometown?*

Beijing has a lot of modern indoor facilities offering bowling, tennis, swimming, and other things. But, it's too expensive for most Chinese, and you have to belong to the club in order to use the facilities. There aren't very many sporting facilities that are free and open to the public.

Films and TV

62. *Do you often go to the cinema/theatre?*

a. Yes. On Friday nights, I usually go and watch whatever's playing. It's kind of a family tradition that I started when my son was young.

b. No. I'm not really interested in the theatre. I'd much rather read newspapers and watch TV than pay for the theatre.

63. *Which cinema do you often go to?*

There's a cinema just around the corner from my home. It's called the Poly Plaza Cinema. It's probably one of the largest cinemas in Beijing, so they always play the most modern films. And, the ticket price is still fairly reasonable.

64. *Do you prefer to watch film in the cinema or at home?*

Oh, it's hard to say. I know it's cheap to buy a DVD and watch it at home, but you definitely get better picture and sound quality in the cinema. So on the whole, I

笔记区

like to go to the cinema to watch a film.

65. *Do you like to watch alone or with your friends?*

In most cases, I'd like to watch a film with my friends. The reason is that after watching the film, we can talk about it and I think it's a very good opportunity for discussion, an opportunity to learn.

66. *What kind of films do you like?*

I definitely like comedies best. I don't see why I should pay money to be sad or scared, so I really don't like sad films or horror films at all. I just like to laugh, and I like movies that can put me in a good mood.

67. *Who's your favourite film star? Can you describe him/her to me?*

I like Leonardo di Caprio. I first saw him when he starred in *Titanic*. He's very handsome...blond hair, blue eyes. He has this look about him that makes him seem very sad, but at the same time hopeful. I have his posters all over my room at home.

68. *Do you often watch TV? What's your favourite programme?*

a. No, I hardly watch TV at all. I don't find any programme interesting. I think it's just a waste of time to watch TV.

b. Yes, I like watching the news and I enjoy watching some of the serial TV shows that come on. But I have to keep up with them, which is a bit hard since I don't have a lot of time to watch them these days.

Music

69. *How often do you listen to music?*

Everyday. As soon as I get home I usually play something. I've also got a walkman that I use, and so I often put it on while travelling on the bus because I can't stand all the noise of the traffic.

70. *What kind of music do you like?*

Definitely classical music. I have nearly every famous classical work ever recorded. I could sit for hours in a room with my stereo turned up, just listening to classical music. I've also attended several concerts here in Beijing, where world famous orchestras have come to play the great works of Mozart, Beethoven, Chopin or other composers.

Clothing Questions

71. *What kind of clothing do you like best?*

My favourite kind of clothing is very shiny, dark clothing. I like wearing very interestingly designed clothing, and I like wearing clothes that are suitable for nightclubs.

笔 记 区

72. *What kind of clothing is popular in China?*

Right now a lot of people are wearing the Zhong Shan Zhuang. It's a style of clothing that is actually quite old, and was worn by Sun Yatsen. I've seen quite a few people wearing it these days. Young people are wearing more and more brand-name clothing.

73. *What kind of clothing do children usually wear?*

Most of them have to wear school uniforms while at school. When they get home they change into all kinds of clothing. It's hard to say what particular style they like. Every child is different.

74. *What does traditional clothing in China look like?*

Well, if you're talking about ladies, the traditional clothing for wealthy ladies was always the Qi Pao. It is long and is decorated with simple designs and made of silk. The men usually wore long shirts with big buttons.

75. *How do older people feel about younger people's clothing?*

I think most of them don't really like the clothes. They think they're too revealing or just too flashy. I think they believe the girls are dressing too boldly these days.

Future Plan Questions

76. *What sort of accommodation would you most like to live in when you get to England?*

I think I will try to live in an apartment shared with other students—something like a one-bedroom or a two-bedroom apartment. I was told living in room and board is more expensive than living in an apartment. Besides, I prefer to cook my own meals, so living in a dormitory or room and board is out of the question for me.

77. *What problems or difficulties do you think you may have in Britain/Canada/Australia?*

I will probably have some trouble with English at first. I heard that once you get used to using English all the time, it gets a lot easier to pick it up. I suppose I'll also need to learn how to do things in Canada. For example, I won't know how to buy a subway ticket and use the transport system, mail a letter, open a bank account, and other things. I think that it's pretty normal to face these troubles when one first arrives.

78. *Can you imagine what life in Britain/Canada/Australia will be like?*

I have seen many pictures of Canada. I'm looking forward to the fresh air and beautiful scenery. In some ways I can just picture myself there. But, I've never been to Canada before, so what I picture now, I'm sure, is not even close to what it will actually be like. Even though some of my friends have already immigrated to

笔记区

Canada or are there studying, I can only get a partial glimpse of what it will be like. I'm looking forward to the adventure!

79. *What do you want/intend to study?*

I plan to study Business. Hopefully at thc master's degree level. I've heard that if I can get an MBA from a university in the West, my chances of getting a good job in a joint-venture company are very good. If I can't get into Business, then I hope to study Computers. Business is really my first choice, though.

80. *Which university are you going to study at?*

It's a small university in eastern Canada called Mount Allison University. It has a very beautiful campus, but it's quite remote. The nearest town is at least an hour's drive away. It'll be quite a change from living in a big city, but I'm looking forward to the peace and quiet.

81. *Why did you choose this university?/Could you tell me why you chose to study at (name of university)?*

The London School of Economics is especially famous for Business and Economics. I think it's the best place for me to specialize in Finance and Banking, and the university has a good reputation among employers here in China.

82. *What are your plans in Britain/Canada/Australia/New Zealand?*

a. I plan to study at Monash University, and get my Masters in International Trade. That should take me about 4 to 5 years to complete.

b. I plan to immigrate to Canada. I have a few friends who can help me there. I am a petroleum engineer, so I think it should be easy to find work in Calgary.

83. *What are you going to major in?*

I want to major in Mass Media Communications. I am interested in this area and I think it is something I can do quite well.

84. *What kind of differences in the cultures are you expecting between China and New Zealand?*

That's a good question. To be frank, I'm not sure, but perhaps I think the way of life there may be more formal. The pace of life I've heard is a bit slower, so I'll have to try and keep myself from getting bored.

85. *What do you intend to do after you graduate?*

I plan to return to China and get a good job or if I have further opportunity, I hope to do some further study in my field once I complete this degree. It's really hard to say what I'll be doing after my studies, because I think that many doors will open to me once I complete a degree in Canada.

86. *Are there any special places you want to see in Canada? What are they?*

I want to see the Rocky Mountains in British Columbia, and I also want to visit

笔 记 区

Quebec. I have heard so much about the beauty of the Rocky Mountains. Also, I heard Quebec is quite different than the rest of Canada. Some of my friends told me that it's like visiting Europe. Even though I don't speak French, I think it will be a very interesting place to visit. Eventually, I hope that I can drive across Canada and really spend time getting to see all the famous sites.

87. *What kind of things do you want to do in Canada that you can't do here?*

I want to buy a car. In China it is so hard to buy a car. There are all kinds of restrictions. Even though I've had my driver's license for more than a year, I still haven't had much opportunity to drive. Many of my friends bought a car once they arrived in Canada. It's quite funny actually, because many Chinese are eager to buy their own cars. Another thing I want to do is to visit my former English teacher who lives in Vancouver now. I met her in 2002 when she taught me English at my university. We've kept in touch until now, so I hope I get a chance to meet up with her again.

88. *What are your goals in life?*

My short-term goal is to improve my English and go abroad to study. My long-term goals include adjusting to a new country, getting a good job, having a family, and eventually owning my own business. I have a lot of goals in life, but some of them are really just dreams. I mean, I don't think I'll ever be able to attain them all.

Foreign Language Studies

89. *How long have you been studying English?*

Hmm...let me see... that's hard to say. I started in middle school and so I guess you could say about 9 years in total. But it's been kind of "off and on".

90. *Do you think English is important for China?*

Well, I think it will help us become better at business and diplomacy. For the nation, it will just make us easier to deal with, and I think we will have fewer problems, when we engage other nations. You know, I believe that language problems are often the main cause of misunderstandings.

91. *What do you think of English?*

I think it's a tough language, frankly. Maybe not the toughest language, but I think there are lots of things that make it confusing. It seems to be a language that's easier to pick up if you're just listening and using it regularly.

92. *What is most rewarding about learning a foreign language?*

Communicating. When you can communicate successfully, it makes all that hard work worthwhile. I love just talking with my foreign friends, and if they understand me I feel quite proud.

笔记区

93. *What do you think is the best way to study English?*

I don't know. I mean, I've tried all kinds of ways. I suppose the best way is to use it regularly and to try and memorize a lot of different words and expressions, but I guess you need a lot of persistence for that.

94. *What aspect of English do you find the most difficult?*

Well, that's difficult to say. I guess it's the grammar. I mean, it's simple enough to study the rules, but when I try to produce it I always seem to make mistakes. If I write the sentences I'm OK, but whenever I try to say them I seem to make mistakes.

Weather Questions

95. *What is the climate like in your hometown?*

It's generally very hot in the summer, like about 40 degrees Celsius. In the winter, it's cold—about minus 14 degrees Celsius. Spring and autumn are both mild and pleasant, with temperatures ranging from around 12 to 25 degrees Celsius. Oh, summertime is extremely humid as well.

96. *What is the weather like in Beijing?*

In general, it's pretty dry. Winter is a bit cold. It is dry and windy, with a bit of snow. Spring is short and a bit windy. Summer is hot and a bit more humid, and temperatures can go as high as 30 degrees, so it can be kind of uncomfortable in the summer unless you have air conditioning. Fall is probably the best season—it's very comfortable—not windy, and neither too cold nor hot.

97. *How would you compare the climate in your hometown with other cities?*

Well, there are definitely places that have a milder climate. My hometown's weather is a little bit uncomfortable for some people in summer and winter. There are places where the weather is quite stable all year round. On the other hand, there are some places where the weather's even worse, like in Daqing.

98. *What are the advantages and disadvantages of the weather in your hometown?*

Advantages and disadvantages? That's a difficult question to answer, let me think for a second. Well, I guess the main advantage is that it's dry, so we don't have to worry about too much rain, and the winters are not too cold like in some other places in northern China. The disadvantage is that it can get windy here, and when there is a sandstorm, well, that can be terrible to put up with.

99. *What is your favourite type of weather in your hometown?*

Actually, I've never thought about that. I guess it would have to be a sunny but not too hot day. It would be warm, like the kind of weather we get here in Beijing during autumn.

笔 记 区

Food Questions

100. *What kind of food and dishes do people eat in your hometown?*
Most people in Changsha like spicy dishes because it's quite hot and humid there, so we need to eat a lot of chilies to help us adapt to the weather. Many people say that in all of China people in Changsha eat the spiciest food.

101. *What is the main food in China?*
Well, I'd say it's rice, but I think there are areas where rice is not that important. Each major area in China might eat rice in different quantities, but I think its still the biggest food and probably will always be the top one.

102. *In what ways has the diet of people in your country been changing?*
Well, we tend to eat more convenience foods now, especially fast food from restaurants like McDonald's and Chinese fast food places. Also, I'd guess we are now eating a lot of dishes regularly that we thought were big luxuries about 20 years ago.

103. *How has your diet changed?*
I don't think it has changed that much. I still eat the same things as I ate when I was a child. I guess the main change is that I have more time and money to go out for dinner.

Festival Questions

104. *Tell me about the biggest traditional festival in your country. / What's the biggest traditional festival in your country?*
Definitely the Spring Festival. I suppose it's somewhat like Christmas in western countries. Spring Festival is the only time when all families gather together and stores and business are closed for several days.

105. *What do you do during the Spring Festival?*
I usually go back to my hometown and spend a week in my parents' home. We eat delicious food, visit family and friends, and watch TV. I also like to contact my high school friends and see how they're doing and what they're up to. We give each other presents and we buy ourselves new clothes to wear for the New Year.

106. *Can you describe one of the main festivals celebrated in your country?*
National Day, which is on October 1st, is a big holiday. We get seven days off and there are a lot of fireworks displays. There are large flower pictures and other types of flowers decorating the city, and some of the larger cities hold parades.

Changes Questions

107. *What changes have taken place in your hometown in the last 20 years?*
Well, I'm pretty young, but my parents always complain that my hometown's

笔记区

traffic is much worse, and they say that prices are a lot higher. But I think on the positive side, life is better, houses are in better condition and there are much better shops and cleaner conditions in the restaurants.

108. *Has your life changed in the last 10 years, and if so, in what ways?*

I think my life has changed. It's a bit more comfortable than it used to be, because my parents have more money than they used to have. I think I am a bit more responsible than I used to be, and not quite as carefree.

109. *Is there anything you'd like to change in your life?*

Yes, my dependence upon my parents. Right now I'm quite dependent on them for money, so I hope I can be more independent in the future and one day be able to support them instead of their always supporting me.

110. *How different is your life from the lives of your parents?*

It's very different. I have had many more opportunities and a much more comfortable life than they had. I remember my father telling me stories about having just one egg to eat each week, and that was the highlight of his week. I can't really imagine life like that, so I'm grateful that I have a better life than my parents did. I appreciate their hard work to get us to this point in our lives.

111. *Has tourism changed China very much?*

Yes, very much in the last 20 years. Each year we are getting more tourists coming to China since the open door policy. People see more foreigners, and are used to the sight of them now. China is becoming more cosmopolitan, and people are getting to know more about the outside world.

112. *Has the transport changed over the past 20 years in China?*

Yes, a lot. We used to have very few bus lines years ago. Most people would use their bikes to get to and from places in the city. But now in big cities there are more bus lines, so it's a lot more convenient. Some cities also have subway lines, and that makes things faster. There are also more taxis in cities, and more people are using them as a mode of transport.

Travells and Holiday Questions

113. *Do you enjoy travelling?*

Yes, very much. I've been to most of the major cities in China, and I've also travelled to Thailand and Singapore. I think the more I travel, the more I want to travel. I just like seeing how other people live, and it's really amazing to learn about different cultures—much more exciting than just reading about them in a textbook.

114. *What do you usually do on your holidays?*

During my holidays, I try to catch up with friends and go out together

笔记区

somewhere. That's the only time I can relax and do something I enjoy. Other than that, it's really difficult because I am always busy with my work, and sometimes I have to work overtime.

115. *Is there anywhere you would particularly like to visit on your holidays? Where and why?*

a. Yeah, I guess the best places to me are beaches. You see, I really like beaches because I just like watching the water come in and I love riding up and down on the waves as they come into the shore. So places like Qingdao and Dalian are great places to me.

b. Yes, I'd love to visit Xinjiang if I have a chance. Xinjiang is in the western part of China. The people there are mostly minorities, and I've seen the landscape in some pictures. It's incredible. If I travel to Xinjiang, I'll take a train so that I can see the landscape throughout the journey.

116. *Let's talk a little about travelling and transport. For a long trip, how do you prefer to travel?*

In my country, if it's a long trip, I prefer taking a train. Not only is it more economical, but also the time has shortened tremendously in the past few years. Air travel is more expensive, and I don't think it's worth the extra cost.

Transport

117. *Which type of transport do you usually use in your hometown?*

I use the bicycle. It's fast and cheap and I can always trust it to get me to places in the same amount of time.

118. *Which type of transport do you prefer for travelling around?*

Trains are better because they don't encounter any traffic jams, whereas sometimes in the bus, we get stuck in traffic. Also, it is always difficult to get on buses during peak hours, whereas with a train you have a better chance of getting a seat during peak hours.

119. *What's the traffic situation like in your hometown?*

It's quite bad now, and I think it's getting more and more serious. The big problems are too many cars and not enough space. I think that building more roads sometimes just adds to the problem because people just buy more cars.

Buildings

120. *Does your hometown have a lot of modern buildings or are they mostly traditional?*

Well, that's an interesting question, because it depends where in my hometown. The downtown area has mostly modern buildings, and you'll see a number of

笔记区

skyscrapers. Outside the city centre are a few of those spread throughout the town, but there aren't too many nowadays.

121. *Which buildings do you prefer to look at?*
Well, I love the old-style buildings with the steep roofs and balanced style. I like all the symbol designs on them too. But to be frank, I think we need to concentrate on replacing those older buildings that were built 20 or 30 years ago, because, in my view, they are just eyesores.

122. *Could you describe the traditional architecture of your country?*
Firstly, the buildings are made of wood or bamboo instead of stone or metal. Secondly, they are very high and always have curved eaves. Thirdly, the traditional buildings have doors and windows that are adorned with paintings.

Birthdays

123. *How important are birthdays in your country?*
I think they're very important in China, especially for children and old people. A birthday party is not only a celebration. It's a time for family reunion.

124. *How do Chinese people celebrate their birthdays?*
The celebrations vary according to different age groups. For young people like me, usually we invite our friends to eat out and then we go to a pub or something to have fun. For older people like my grandparents, the party is more elaborate.

125. *Do you like to celebrate your birthday with your parents or with your friends?*
Because I live away from my parents, I usually have a birthday party with my classmates and my friends. It's great fun!

126. *What do children get for their birthdays in your country?*
Oh, lots of different stuff. Candies, cakes, toy guns, teddy bears.

127. *Which is the most important birthday for a Chinese?*
I guess it's the 18th one, like in other countries. It's the time you become an adult. From then on, you have to take responsibility for your actions.

笔 记 区

II. Part 2&3 最新话题汇总

人物题

1. OLD PERSON 老人
2. TEACHER 老师
3. FILM STAR 电影明星
4. SPORTS STAR 体育明星
5. CHARACTER IN TV OR FILM 影视角色
6. HAPPY/SUCCESSFUL PERSON 开心/成功的人
7. NEIGHBOUR 邻居
8. CHILD 孩子

地点题

9. FAVOURITE ROOM OR APARTMENT 喜欢的房间/公寓
10. NATURAL BEAUTY 自然美景
11. HISTORIC PLACE 历史古迹
12. LAKE OR RIVER 江河湖泊
13. GARDEN OR PARK 花园
14. SHOPPING CENTRE 商店

物品题

15. TOY 玩具
16. BOOK YOU READ 读过的书
17. CLOTHES OR JEWELRY 衣服首饰
18. VEHICLE OR BIKE 交通工具
19. NATIONAL PRODUCT 国产货
20. BOOK YOU WANT TO WRITE 想写的书
21. WORK OF ART 艺术品
22. HANDICRAFT 手工艺品
23. SPORT 体育
24. WAY TO RELAX 放松方式
25. NEWSPAPER OR MAGAZINE 报纸杂志
26. FILM 电影
27. TV PROGRAMME 电视节目
28. ADVERTISEMENT 广告
29. WEBSITE 网站
30. PHOTO 照片
31. EXHIBITION 展览
32. (WILD)ANIMAL(野生)动物
33. POPULAR GAME IN CHILDHOOD 儿时游戏
34. SUBJECT 科目

事件题

35. LONG-DISTANCE TRIP 长途旅行
36. ENJOYABLE VISIT 友好的拜访
37. PROJECT 跟人合作的项目
38. CULTURAL DIFFERENCE 文化差异
39. IMPORTANT CHANGE 重要变化
40. WEDDING 婚礼

笔记区

一、人物题

1. *Describe an old person who had an influence on you.*
You should say:
who the person is
when you first knew him/her
what kind of person he/she is
and explain why he/she has influenced you.

I think my father has the biggest influence on me. He used to be an editor working for *The Beijing Youth Daily* but now he is retired at home. He's over 60 years old but looks smart. He's a little bit overweight, has a pleasant face, and always gives the impression of being someone who is very easy-going and nice. Indeed my father is the most kind-hearted person you would ever want to meet and he's very popular in the neighbourhood.

I guess my father has taught me a lot about the most important things in life. For one thing, he taught me to live a healthy lifestyle. He likes exercise very much and on Sundays my parents and I always go for a walk in the Fragrant Hills in a suburb of Beijing. He has kept doing this for almost 10 years. Can you imagine? At first, I didn't quite like it. It is a drag getting up so early on Sundays, isn't it? But very soon I got used to it and began to enjoy it actually. For another, my father has taught me a lot about optimism. He got through a lot of hardships to become an accomplished editor. He's not the kind of person that gets upset easily. I guess what I've learnt most from him is to maintain a positive attitude towards life, no matter what happens.

Further questions

1. What are the differences in attitudes between the young and the old toward life in China?
Oh, it's a very tough question. I believe there are quiet a lot of differences. Let's take marriage for example. My grandparents' generation seemed to gain security through marriage. They got married early. But nowadays, young people like me are much more concerned with developing as individuals. Usually we try to get a career going before we get married and start a family.
2. What is the main problem for China's old people?
That's hard to say. As far as I see it, I don't think there is enough entertainment for old people. My grandfather retired a few years ago. Every morning he goes to a small park in the neighbourhood for a walk. But other than that, there are not other options for him. I hope the government could set up more leisure centres for people like my grandfather. They need to communicate with their peers and they're entitled to this kind of city service as well.

笔记区

3. What's the attitude of the government toward old people?

Well, basically the government is very much concerned with the welfare of the old people. This can be seen from the many policies it has produced in the interest of the older people in fields like pension, medical care, etc. I can see that the government does not consider this age group simply as a liability, but as a kind of resource, with their experiences and wisdom, that can bring benefits to the society as a whole.

4. What aspects of society are not good for old people?

As I mentioned earlier, it seems there are not many public facilities where old people can exercise, talk to each other, and meet new people. But I guess there are other problems as well, like the pension scheme and medical care. Oh, there's one more thing, family planning also gives rise to serious problems as well. It seems there are not enough young people to support an increasing number of aging population.

5. Are there any influences that old people bring to your family?

Sure, first of all, old people set up positive, or negative role-models for younger generations. They can influence other family members in terms of interests, personality and things like that. My grandfather likes painting very much and partly because of this all my cousins are keen on painting as well. Of course there are practical things too. For example, the old people can help with the childcare, which is obviously a relief for young couples that both work.

2. *Describe a teacher who had a great influence on you.*

You should say:

who the teacher is

what subject he/she taught

what's special about him/her

and explain why the teacher had a great influence on you.

The teacher that really influenced me a lot was Mr. Chen Li. He was the sports teacher when I was in high school.

He was in his thirties at that time and I'd say all my classmates admired him because he was kind of a hero to us and also because he was very nice. As far as I can remember, one thing that was special about him was that he'd been on the national volleyball team. I don't think he ever actually won a medal or anything like that. But for us, just the fact that he used to represent our country was really something. Actually, he was a very good teacher, very responsible...and dedicated...you know.

I guess the thing he taught me was to have a fighting spirit. I mean he always encouraged us to do our best in sport, even if we were terrible at it. He used to say "It doesn't matter if you win or not. The important thing is to do your best and keep

笔记区

going." He also taught us a lot about...health...and maintaining a positive attitude towards life. And compared to other teachers, he seemed to be more interested in everyone. Luckily, we still keep in touch and I often go to see him on holidays.

Further questions

1. What makes a good teacher?

   Well, different people have different ideas on this issue. But as far as I am concerned, a good teacher should be patient, responsible and knowledgeable.

2. What is the most important quality of a good teacher?

   Of course different people value different aspects of a good teacher. As to myself, being inspiring is the most important quality of a good teacher. Good teachers should be those that bring hopes to their students. They encourage and motivate their students to think on their own, act on their own and take adventures. As a result, they usually bring out the best in their students.

3. What are the differences between good teachers and bad ones?

   Good teachers inspire students to study while bad ones ask students to obey orders. Good teachers are close friends while bad ones are bossy leaders. Good teachers make students eager to know more while bad ones make students fed up with studies.

4. What factors are the driving force for people to become teachers?

   To be frank, it is really hard to tell. The answer varies from case to case. Some do it for money. Some do it for fun. Some do it for a sense of achievement. Some do it to make a long-held dream come true.

5. Why do some people choose to be a life-long teacher?

   Maybe they do it because they think they find true happiness in giving. Helping others to grow up and giving them suggestions and advice seem to be a great cause. They want to contribute their life to such a cause.

6. What are the difficulties the teachers will confront?

   The difficulties may arise from many aspects. We are living in a world of the explosion of knowledge which makes it necessary for teachers to upgrade their knowledge all the time. Therefore the teachers must spend a lot of time and energy to improve their own qualities all along. Meanwhile students are getting increasingly critical. They want qualified, inspiring and learned teachers rather than somebody that just teaches something in the textbooks.

7. Did you ever act as a teacher?

   Yes. As a matter of fact I used to teach in a university in Qingdao. I taught English. It was really an unforgettable experience. I got along very well with my students. We had a lot of good moments together.

8. What types of schools are there in China?

   There are many kinds of schools in China, such as primary schools, junior high

笔记区

schools, senior high schools, vocational and technical schools, colleges, universities and graduate schools.

9. How do single-sex schools and mixed schools differ?

Students in single-sex schools can be more focused on their studies while their peers studying in mixed schools are distracted by relationships between boys and girls. Mixed schools can provide a sound environment in which children's mentality can grow up healthy. By studying in such schools, they learn to deal with people of the opposite sex and know how to make friends with different types of people.

10. Between single-sex schools and mixed schools, which is better?

I don't think there is an easy answer to this question as too many factors are involved. The roles of students, parents and schools all need to be considered. But there is something to be sure of. That is, single-sex schools often provide a more academic environment while mixed ones provide a more colourful and exciting atmosphere.

11. What kind of schools would you like to send your children to study?

Mixed schools, definitely. I want my children to grow up with a healthy mentality. I will encourage them to make friends of both sexes. As women and men constitute the whole world, my children need to, and must acquire an understanding of how people of different sexes behave. Otherwise their life would always be incomplete due to the lack of knowledge of the other sex.

12. What do you think of the private schools and public schools?

Private schools are usually better positioned to provide a high-quality teaching faculty, equipment and facilities while public schools, funded by governmental revenue, sometimes may find it hard to do so. As a result, private schools' doors are only open to the students who come from rich families while public schools absorb students regardless of their families' financial standing.

3. *Describe a film star in China.*
You should say:
who the person is
when you first knew him/her
what the person does?
and explain why he/she is famous.

I want to talk about a male film star: Ge You. He is one of the best actors in China. I knew him from a TV series. At that time I was only a primary school student, and he had already been very famous.

After several successful TV series, he embarked on a new career in films, which brought his fame onto a new stage. Till now, he has won many awards, international

笔记区

and domestic alike. For example, in 1993 he earned the award of best actor in the Cannes Festival. His domestic awards include best actor of the Baihua Award and the Golden Rooster Award, etc.

In my opinion, there are two reasons contributing to his success. The first one is his characteristic appearance. Actually he is not as handsome as most other actors. The prominent feature of his appearance is his bald head. There is not a single hair on his head. This becomes an advantage to his career because he plays in comedies most of the time. It adds a humorous element to his acting. The other reason is his excellent acting skills. He is a very gifted actor. In fact, his father is also a good actor. Maybe he inherits part of his talent from his father. He believes that a truly excellent actor is capable of every character and is very strict with himself. He has tried nearly all kinds of characters: editor, taxi-driver, gangster, thief, etc., all of which are vividly illustrated by him. His talent is acknowledged by the society. Ge You is regarded by many people as the one who can represent the acting quality of China.

Further questions

1. Through what way do we know celebrities?

   I think mass media is the most important channel through which we know those celebrities. They are always the focus of newspapers, TV, radio and magazines. Nowadays, Internet offers us a much easier access to the information of famous people. Sometimes our friends and family members like to talk about their favourite celebrities with us, which provide another way for us to know them.

2. Will we be influenced by them?

   I think it depends. For some teenagers who have not quite grown up, they tend to be easily influenced by the celebrities they like. They take them as role models. They may imitate their voice, hairstyle, dress style and their behaviours. But as for most adults, I do not think they can be easily influenced. They make judgments according to their own value system. Compared with teenagers, they have a much clearer idea of what they want and what they should not do. Instead of simple imitation, their behaviours are usually consistent with their value system.

3. What are the advantages and disadvantages of being a celebrity?

   Bing a celebrity means the society has recognized your achievement, which means they have established a kind of social status. Celebrities hold privileges, resources and people's admiration in their hands. They make money much easier than ordinary people. Those are all the advantages. But they have acquired them at the expense of their private life. They are forever in the focus of limelight. Meanwhile, the public have almost zero tolerance toward the celebrities' mistakes. They are not allowed to fail the public's expectation. Once they make a mistake, even a trivial one, it will be exemplified and spread far and wide. No wonder that some celebrities complain that they would rather be ordinary people.

笔 记 区

4. What will you do if you become famous one day?

Well, first of all, I will satisfy all the wishes of my parents. After so many years' hard work, they deserve all I can give them. At the same time, I will pay back what the society has given me. Nowadays, many teenagers look to celebrities in search of role models. Thus I want to set a good example for those who love me. Meanwhile, charity is another field that I want to take part in. Through this, I can extend my help to those I do not know but in dire need.

5. What happens to the celebrities' children?

First, obviously they do not have to worry about money. In that case, they can fully develop their interest without financial problem. They are able to afford many things that children from ordinary families never dream of. But like their celebrity parents, they are also sought-after objects of media. Therefore, unlike their peers, they do not have a normal environment to grow up. What's worse, celebrities are too busy to take good care of their children. They cannot spend much time with their children. So to those children, what they gain is based on their sacrifice of some important parts of their childhood.

6. Why do many people want to be well-known?

It is very natural. Everyone wants their achievement to be recognised. The title of celebrity gives people a sense of self-fulfillment. Being well-known is a sign that their identities and status are socially acknowledged. Meanwhile, this title will bring huge profits to individuals, financially and socially. They gain lots of advantages and privileges as well as earn considerable amount of money. So many people will seize any chance that will make them well-known.

7. Why are people eager to know the privacies of celebrities?

To me, it is a kind of human nature. People are born with this sense of curiosity. The shining images of the celebrities on TV or other kind of mass media arouse the public's curiosity to know more about them. They want to have a full picture of those public figures. If people are really interested in a person, they want to know everything of him, especially what he is like in everyday life.

4. *Describe a sports star you admire.*
You should say:
who the person is
what he/she does
what is special about him or her
and explain why you would like to meet him or her.

Though I'm not very keen on sport, I do have a sports star who I admire a lot. The name of the man is called Liu Xiang.

This athlete from Shanghai is a well-known track man who has successfully

笔记区

achieved champion in the 110 metres hurdle race in the 2004 Olympics Games. He finished his race in 12.71 seconds and that evens the world record.

Actually, Liu Xiang is not only my admired hero, virtually every Chinese who has seen his performance in the game is deeply impressed. In recent years, Chinese athletes have successfully gained international recognition for their outstanding performance. However, there haven't been many breakthroughs on the track field, and that's why I admire Liu so much. He has achieved the record which is said to be impossible, creating a miracle in front of a world of spectators. It was the first time that a Chinese, a yellow-skinned man, broke the dominance of black people on the track field. In a greater sense, his achievement is not only our Chinese pride, but the pride of all yellow-skinned people. Well, another interesting thing of Liu that amazes me is that besides being a successful athlete, he also sings well. In fact, some entertainment companies even claim that he surely possesses the potential to be a pop star. Being such an interesting capable young man full of drive, Liu definitely is my hero.

Further questions

1. How do you appreciate the advantages of doing sports?

   I think doing sports has three main advantages. Firstly, it's a very active way to relax. I find it very effective to play basketball whenever I'm tired of working. Secondly, doing sports can make people healthy. Now many people take medicines to loose weight, but scientists are suggesting that the best way to loose weight is to do sports. Lastly, doing sports like football or basketball can cultivate the team spirit and help develop the ability to cooperate. These points are what I consider advantages of doing sports.

2. In the place where you live, what kind of sport do people usually do?

   Well, I'm a boarding university student, and in my university, students do different sports. There are several basketball courts and they're usually occupied by players in the afternoon. Volleyball and tennis are also very popular among my peers. There are also lots of people who are fond of playing badminton and I'm among them. My hope is that one day we can have an indoor badminton court, because the windy weather in Beijing usually makes it hard for us to play outside.

3. Do you think it is reasonable that the sportsmen are paid so much?

   I think it's reasonable. I think whatever the vocation is, the salary of a person should be in accordance with his or her social value. One thing I want to make clear is that sportsman is a kind of profession, and their salaries are earned not granted. Sportsmen doing the sports in front of spectators is like actors performing to an audience. Their work has a huge economic effect. Therefore I think sportsmen are paid what they ought to be paid. It is absolutely reasonable.

4. Do you think that sports stars should be eligible to earn money by shooting

笔 记 区

commercials?

Yes, I think so. I think everyone has the freedom to shoot commercials. It's groundless that sports stars are deprived this right simply because of their identity as sports stars. Actually, I don't see any negative impacts for sports stars shooting commercials. They're adults who are aware of their behaviours. It is unlikely that the stars have a poor capacity to figure out what they should do for the good of their further development. I consider this issue a private thing and I respect sports stars' own choices.

5. *Describe a character in a TV programme or in a film you like.*
You should say:
who the character is
when you first saw the TV programme or film
what kind of person the character is
and explain why you like this character.

I think many people in China have watched this film: Forrest Gump. The hero in the film— Forrest Gump—must have impressed me a lot.

The first time I saw this film was in my senior high. Forrest Gump is a mentally retarded person. His IQ is lower than that of an ordinary person. But out of everyone's expectation, he becomes a rich and famous fishing tycoon in the end.

It is a typical American-dream style of film. But this is not the reason why I like the film. This character is so attractive to me because of a sentence he always bears in mind: life is like a box of chocolates; you never know what you gonna get. This is what his mother, who is his only relative, tells him before she dies. It is these words that make him believe that no matter what difficulty faces him, life will be better in due time. When I heard that line, tears welled up in my eyes. At that time, my whole life was centred on the entrance exams. Heavy peer pressure and fierce competition made me feel that I was in the middle of nowhere. His words as well as the whole movie reminded me that one day I could also get something wonderful from this chocolate box—life. This injected new motivation into my study.

Someone may laugh at me because I turned to a mentally retarded person for encouragement. But sometimes, aren't we too wise to overlook the truth in life?

Further questions

1. What kind of film star is popular now?

The film stars with beautiful or cute faces are still very popular. But now a new kind of film star is on the rise—those who are gifted and have their unique styles. For example, Clint Eastwood, the lead actor in Bridge of Madison County. He is famous for his excellent acting skills and talent in writing and directing films. He

笔记区

won the 2005 Oscar Award, though he is in his 70s. This kind of film stars is not only popular among audiences, but also deeply respected by them. This is the new trend of film stars: you do not have to be good-looking, but you'd better have something different from others.

2. Is there more and more violence in film or TV?

Yes. I think so. This is one of the issues that film and TV have raised. Some film companies deliberately produce films featured by violence in order to attract a particular audience, such as young people who are fond of extreme and adventurous films. This is true of some TV series. Meanwhile, more violence appears in TV news, for example the report of clashes between Iraq police and insurgent groups. Some advertisements contain violence too. On the whole, more and more violence is accessible to people, through film and TV alike.

3. What kinds of people like to see action films?

I think action films find its largest audience among young people, especially young males. They welcome the films with few conversations and much action. This has something to do with their group character. Young males are full of energy. They love quick-paced films and derive great visual enjoyment from watching action films. Also, people who believe that fighting is the best policy are also action film fans. They can identify themselves with the characters in the film. Some of them go even further to imitate those characters.

4. What will future films be like?

Well, this is a rather extensive topic. First of all, films in the future will have more varieties to cater to the tastes of different audience groups. Secondly, more and more advanced technologies will be employed in the producing process, such as digital technology. This will make the film-making much easier. Therefore, maybe ordinary people can produce films of their own. Also films that can reflect future social problems will come out. For instance, as globalization is accelerating, civilization and culture clashes are unavoidable. In the foreseeable future, more films will centre on this theme.

5. Do you like a film that is made with digital technology?

Yes, I do. Digital technology enables the director to make what is in his mind into reality. It can break down the traditional limit on film production. The film directors can create some non-existent characters or settings according to their need. That's how some famous and widely loved films were produced, such as Matrix and Star Wars. Digital technology offers more fantastic visual enjoyment to us.

6. What kind of characters will people admire in the future?

To my understanding, in the future, people will admire those characters that are ordinary people. They will be less fascinated by those heroic characters because they are too far away from people's everyday life. On the contrary, the small characters will come into prominence. Those characters in the films are just like

笔记区

ordinary people in real life. In the films, they have their own character weakness and are troubled by problems that people usually have in their lives. By watching films, the audience can relate themselves to those characters. Sometimes they may get encouragement from the characters. So in the future, this kind of characters will be more and more popular.

7. Is there any difference between the characters that men admire and those women admire?

I think the major difference is that men prefer female characters while women pay more attention to male characters. This difference results from the sexual appeal. Most heroes and heroines are very good looking people. But there is not much difference other than this one. Both men and women admire brave, dynamic, generous and capable male characters. At the same time, both of them adore those female characters that are kind-hearted, considerable and gentle. It is human nature—always admire people with something they do not have.

6. *Describe a happy/successful person you know.*
You should say
who the person is
why the person is happy/successful
and how you know this person.

Well, I think my teacher Mr. Wang is the happiest person I've ever known. He teaches English Literature in the university where I am studying now.

I guess he has very good reasons to be happy. First of all, he has a very fulfilling family life. Mr. Wang has two lovely daughters. Once he took them to his office and guess what! The two girls made his office into a mess but Mr. Wang was still quite cheerful. He always tells us that his daughters are the best gifts he has ever received in his life. Second, he loves his job. He loves teaching and believe me, he knows how to teach. He breathes life into the subject he's teaching. English Literature could be boring but he has the magic to make it fun. There's quite a lot of exciting discussion going on in his class.

But I believe the real source of his happiness is a love of life and a thankful attitude towards life. He's definitely not the richest man, nor is he the most talented. But he's quite contented with what he has now. I mean his family, his colleagues, and his work.

Mr. Wang is the most popular teacher among the students in the English Department. He's also my hero, too, because he taught me more than English Literature. He also taught me that happiness does not come from outside. It comes from within.

笔 记 区

Further questions

1. Do you want to be successful?

   Yes, both in material terms and in spiritual terms.

2. How do you think about success/happiness?

   For me, happiness is simply a matter of attitude. It's not about money or social status. Happiness /success is about service, character, integrity, honesty, loyalty, commitment, truthfulness, being trustworthy...doing your best for yourself, your family and your friends.

3. Can you be successful without money?

   Sure, it depends how you define success. There are many people who are not rich but who live up to high ethical standards.

4. What are the advantages and disadvantages of being famous?

   Let me see. I think when one becomes famous, he/she can easily get more wealth, and more satisfaction out of life. They can gain recognition from their peers and have access to more opportunities and resources. But on the other hand, they will have to pay a high price as well. For example, they can't spend much time with their family. Some of them may get very depressed because of the stress in their work.

5. Why do most people want to be well known?

   As I said before, once you become a celebrity, you will reap a lot of benefits, which an ordinary person can't even imagine.

6. How do film stars affect your life?

   I think they have influence on us in every way. Language, fashion, music, or even our diet. But apart from that, they become role-models for us, especially teenagers.

7. Why do ordinary people want to know about famous people's private affairs?

   I guess this is human nature, isn't it? If you are interested in a person, you will be curious about their hobbies, lifestyles and so on.

> 7. *Describe one of your neighbours.*
> *You should say:*
> *where he/she lives*
> *how you got to know him/her*
> *whether you often see him/her*
> *and explain whether he/she is a good neighbour.*

I'd like to talk about my neighbour, professor Wang, who has lived next to us for about ten years.

He used to be my father's colleague and really looks like my father. He's not very tall, about 170 centimetres at most I think. It is very easy to recognise professor Wang

笔 记 区

because he is bald on top and wears a pair of big glasses, which makes him look very professional and knowledgeable. He's very nice, friendly and easy-going. When you have problems, he is the person you should turn to for he is intelligent and ready to help.

Now we don't see each other very often as I went to college in another city a few years ago. But I visit him whenever I go back to my hometown.

I guess for me he is the best neighbour that one can have. He has influenced me a lot in learning English since my childhood. You know, in the 1980s when very few people had TV, he was given one by a foreign friend. Every Sunday morning, I would go to his family to watch a very popular English language teaching programme named Follow Me. Apart from that, he often encouraged me when I felt bad or did a bad job on an exam. I still remember he told me that as long as I had tried, it did not matter what result I got on the college entrance examinations. I wish I could become a professor like him in the future.

Further questions

1. What is the difference between friends and neighbours?

   It's a little difficult to tell the difference between friends and neighbours. As far as I am concerned, I would tell my friends about my secrets and share my happiness and sorrow with them. However, I rarely do so with my neighbours. Furthermore, your neighbours live next to you and may help you whenever you need them while a friend might live far away from you.

2. Do you think it's important to get along well with your neighbours?

   Of course. We should love our neighbours because we are a community.

3. How can you keep a good relationship with your neighbours?

   Well, it's not difficult. You just treat them as your friends. You could visit them from time to time, taking a bottle of wine or something with you. And I am sure that they will do the same in return. If you have made a few dishes, why not ask them to your dinner? This would be a good way of keeping a good relationship. Besides, it would be a great idea for you and your neighbours to take a trip together. There's nothing better to know each other than exploring new places.

4. How do people communicate with others at present?

   Great changes have taken place in the past several decades. For example, ten years ago, we liked to pay a visit to relatives and friends during Spring Festival while now people prefer to exchange New Year greetings via e-mails, cards, or text messages. Another example is that in the past, Chinese people were interested in showing their hospitality and friendliness by sending some home-cooked food to their neighbours while now people prefer to eat out even when friends visit.

笔记区

8. *Describe a child you are familiar with.*
You should say:
his or her name
how old he/she is
and what his/her hobby is.

I would like to talk about my nephew, Sun Zheng. He is about 5 years old, big eyes, very lovely kid, and always causes problems, you know, like most other children at his age.

He has interests that you would normally expect a five-year-old could have. He likes toy guns, snack food, presents, and beautiful girls as well. But the thing he likes best is cartoons. He's fascinated by the stories and the characters. I guess his favourite is the Big Windmill programme on CCTV 1, a sort of collection of cartoons of various kinds, with two adorable hosts. My nephew is keen on that programme and every time he comes back from the kindergarten, the first thing he does is to pick up a pack of corn chips and turn on the TV and sit in front of it, waiting for the programme to begin. Sometimes he even discusses the stories with his parents, who, every now and then, are quite impressed by his wild ideas and sometimes plausible arguments.

Anyway, like many other kids of his age, the little naughty boy grows up very happily.

Further questions

1. Who are happier, children nowadays or the ones 20 years ago?

   I'm not very sure but I guess 20 years ago children were happier. Of course at that time kids didn't have KFC or Pizzahut. They didn't have elaborate birthday parities or sophisticated toys. But they didn't have to pass various English exams, either. I think even though children nowadays have easy access to all those luxuries, they have to face more challenges as well.

2. What do you think of adolescent education in China?

   It's OK. But there's too much rote learning and duck-feeding. Traditionally, the classroom in China is teacher-centred rather than student-centred. Though there has been much improvement, there's still something wrong. I think apart from academic subjects, schools should provide training that develops other dimensions of personal growth.

3. What are the effects of pressures exerted by teachers and parents?

   Obviously both parents and teachers have great influence on children. In China today, there are still quite a number of teachers and parents who set too ambitious, if not unrealistic goals for their children. Too much pressure can only stifle their interest in studies.

4. What do you think of the problem that parents overindulge their children?

笔记区

I think it's a serious problem in China. The rise in the living standard only makes matters worse. Take my cousin for example. He's the only child of his family and everyone centres around him. The biggest problem that may arise is obviously children like my cousin don't have the opportunity to learn to survive independently, which is an essential skill in an ever-changing society like China. Another problem is that they may become too self-centred to care about other people.

二、地点题

9. *Describe your favourite room or apartment.*
You should say:
where it is
how long you have lived there
what rooms and furniture it has
and explain why you like it.

My favourite apartment is my 2-bedroom apartment in Haidian District where I have lived 4 years. I don't have much furniture inside—two bookshelves, one table, one desk, a few chairs, two couches and a bed. My apartment is the most appealing to me for a few reasons:

First of all, I have a large living room which is consequently multifunctional. It naturally serves as a place to receive guests, but at the same time, it is also my private gym in which I do exercises to lose weight while watching TV. In addition, it is my café and dining room as well.

Secondly, my soft and comfortable bed contributes a lot to my fondness for my apartment. As everyone knows, people spend a lot of time sleeping which is very important for the recovery of energy. As a result, bed selection should be done carefully. I chose a reasonably soft and large bed so that I can spread out fully while I am resting.

Of course I have only listed a few of all my reasons, but I am sure you have already felt how much I love my apartment by the couple of points I said above.

Further questions:

1. Do you live in the city or in the countryside? What are the advantages and disadvantages of both areas?

I live in the city and I love the modern lifestyle. I know it's very quiet in the countryside but it may be quite inconvenient when it comes to shopping, entertainment, and eating. Of course, living in the city has its downsides, too. But

笔记区

overall, I think I am a city person.

2. What is the difference between an old house and a modern house? Which one do you prefer? Why?

I'm not an expert on architecture but since there are many old houses in my hometown, I think you can easily tell the differences if you compare them with the newly-built ones. First of all, it's the materials. Old houses usually have a wooden frame structure whereas the modern ones are built with concrete and steel, which makes them more sturdy. Second of all, the old ones do not have the modern facilities like central heating, security system, etc., I mean the things you can easily find in modern houses and skyscrapers. Personally, despite the modern amenities, I still prefer the old ones because they can give you a feeling that you are back home.

3. Should the state provide cheap housing for low-income earners?

I feel it's really the responsibility of the government to provide housing, just as they should provide education, and ideally, health services. That's one of the reasons why we pay our taxes.

4. To what extent does climate determine the kind of house we build?

Well, in my view, climate probably has quite a lot to do with the way we design and build our houses. For instance, in countries where it snows a lot, you find houses built with a steep roof...so that the snow can't settle on the roof, and...you know... damage the roof. But in warm climates the houses are often build with a verandah to keep the sun out of the rooms and to provide a cool place to sit.

5. What will the houses in the future be like?

It's hard to imagine but one thing is for sure. I believe the houses in the future will be environmentally-friendly and energy-saving. For example there will be some kind of equipment that can transfer solar energy into electricity in every house. The electronics in it will depend on such energy instead of electricity provided by a power plant.

6. Should we preserve old buildings?

It depends. I think we should do everything to protect buildings of historical interest like the Palace Museum or the Suzhou Garden. The reason is that they are our cultural heritage, and they provide us with a gateway to understanding Chinese architecture.

10. *Describe a naturally beautiful place where you can relax.*

You should say:

where it is located

what kind of place it is

what you can do there

and explain why it is special to you.

笔 记 区

I want to talk about Fragrance Hill, which is situated in the northwest of Beijing. It is within splendid surroundings twenty kilometres from the city centre. Although it is a little bit far from where I live, it is very convenient for me to go there, I just take a bus near the school and I don't have to change to another bus halfway.

It is a beautiful natural scenery that is famous for its maple trees prevailing over the whole area. Many people go there for the purpose of climbing and exercising. Last time I went there with my classmates before the National Day Holiday, we enjoyed ourselves very much with the sightseeing and the fresh air that we seldom have nowadays in the city. I have never climbed a hill or mountain before that. It was my first time to have a try and I felt very excited, especially when I reached the top of Fragrance Hill, namely the Gui Jianchou.

Standing on the top of the hill, I felt as if I were standing at the top of the world. It made my mind more open and I could try to reflect on my life experience and think about the things happening around me. It really made me feel relaxed and peaceful.

Further questions

1. What is dangerous to natural places?

   I think there are two points that are endangering those natural places. First of all, many places are being polluted. The water pollution, the air pollution and the white pollution, ect. Secondly, many natural places are far from the city centre where most people live and work. Due to the long-distance, many people prefer to visit some places of interest near home. Without many people going there, the natural places may not get enough money for maintenance, thus get deserted. I think that is something that we definitely do not want to see.

2. What kind of pollution is the public most concerned about?

   I think many people are concerned about the water pollution in China. For one thing, we are suffering from water shortage and many people are wasting water and not aware of the fact. Meanwhile many small factories let the chemicals go into the rivers without restrictions. It has caused severe water pollution in many areas.

3. What is your attitude to the environment?

   I believe environmental protection is a necessity as well as a duty for everyone. China has long been advocating sustainable development, which means that the development of this generation will not cause damage to that of the next generation. And I think that is a good thing for us to do.

4. What can you do for the environment?

   I think we can do many things. Although we cannot launch some big projects to prevent the environment from getting polluted, at least we can do some small things that can beautify the surroundings, such as the recycling of waste paper, newspapers and batteries, not wasting water or electricity, etc. We should change our lifestyle before it is too late.

笔 记 区

5. What is different from your grandparents' views on the environment and yours?

   I don't think my grandparents care so much about the environment as we young people do. In their time, there were no environmental problems, at least not so severe as it is now. As the country develops, there are many problems during the process. And there is a lot of information about this heated topic. We are more familiar with the issue and more aware of the current situation. And that's why we are more concerned about environmental protection.

6. Why do you think people like to go to natural places?

   Modern people are faced with too much pressure and competition from all sides in terms of work, study, and relationships. They find it a good way to relax themselves by going to those natural places and enjoy the beautiful scenery and fresh air. It is a good way for them to temporarily forget all the troubles in life. There is nothing to worry about but relax. They get more refreshed and better prepared for the work or study afterwards.

7. Do you think people should be charged to go to natural places?

   I think it is necessary. The government may need the money to maintain those places and to improve the conditions, so that people can better enjoy themselves there. And I think it can help effectively regulate the place.

11. *Describe an interesting historic place.*

You should say:

what it is

where it is located

what you can see there now

and explain why this place is interesting.

The Temple of Heaven is one of the most interesting historic places I have ever been to.

Located in the southern part of Beijing, it is China's largest existing complex of ancient sacrificial buildings. Believe it or not, it is three times the area of the Forbidden City.

There you can see The Altar of Prayers for a Good Harvest, standing on a round foundation built with three levels of marble blocks. There is also the famous Echoing Wall enclosing the Imperial Vault of Heaven. One interesting place is the Centre of Heaven Stone that echoes when a visitor speaks loudly when standing on the stone. Nearly everyone who visits The Temple of Heaven likes to try it.

I think it is an interesting historic place because the design of the temple reflects the ancient mystical Chinese perception of things. For example, because the number nine was considered the most powerful digit, many things are designed in multiples of nine. The Temple of Heaven is where the Emperor came every winter to worship

笔 记 区

heaven and to pray for a good harvest. A bad harvest could be interpreted as his fall from heaven's favour and threaten the stability of his reign. Now the temple is a place where many people do exercises in the morning. This is a great change of role for The Temple of Heaven.

Further questions

1. How do people in your country feel about protecting historic buildings?
   People have begun to realize the importance of protecting historic buildings. Historic buildings are a precious heritage of significant historic value that reflect the culture of a people with a 5,000 years' history. People feel the necessity to protect historic buildings because they are tired of the identical, block-like, unfriendly concrete skyscrapers.
2. Do you think an area can benefit from having an interesting historic place? In what way?
   Sure. I believe an interesting historic place passes on the culture of its people. It inspires people's interest in history. People learn history while visiting these places. It also serves as a good example to promote people's consciousness of the need to protect historic places. Historic sites are also good resources for tourism. Local people can benefit a lot economically if a site attracts many tourists. But the premise is that people have to protect it.
3. What do you think will happen to historic places or buildings in the future?
   As our country is under large-scale construction, many historic places or buildings may be torn down. Some may disappear due to neglect of protection and repair. Though some people have begun to realize the importance of protecting historic places, it is still not an issue that draws great attention from the general public. In addition, we have little policy support or enough money for the protection of heritage sites. When people realize what they have lost, it is too late.
4. You mentioned history. How were you taught history when you were at school?
   History was a subject that we had to learn because there were history examinations to pass. We just read lots of books and listened to the teacher. This is mostly a passive way of learning. We were told to remember historic figures, events and other facts. We learnt mechanically, though we were not really interested in those numerous facts. And we were given little chance to analyze what lay behind historical events.
5. Are there other ways people can learn about history, apart from at school?
   The Internet is a quick and convenient way to access abundant information, and also vivid pictures, but the information may not be well organized. People feel at a loss dealing with too much information. I think one good way to learn about history is watching serious historic newsreels. Visual images can inspire people's

笔记区

interest in learning. Historic places and cultural relics are things that can teach us a lot about history. People often feel they have gone back in time when they visit historic places.

6. Do you think history will still be a school subject in the future?

I guess so. But I hope it's taught in a much more interesting way than it is nowadays, and isn't just the boring and compulsory reciting of historic facts. It is going to exist as a school subject because the younger generation should know something about what happened to our nation and the world in the past. They observe present reality better if they learn about history. There are many other ways to learn history, but we have to admit that school is the place where history can reach the largest number of young people. The subject should inspire interest in the past, not stifle it.

12. *Describe a river, lake or sea which you like.*

You should say:

what the river, lake or sea is called

where it is

what the land near it is like

and explain why you like the river, lake or sea.

Well, let me tell you a bit about the Sea River. It's very famous among the locals, and flows right through Tianjin. It is called Sea River because it is larger than an ordinary river, like the sea is.

The Sea River to the locals is like the Yellow River to the Chinese people. It is of great importance to the city, and is a major reason underlying the development of the city. The whole city grew around the river. In the past, there were many villages along its banks and the people there mainly relied on fishing and boat building. I can imagine how simple and uncomplicated their lives were. But nowadays things have changed greatly. The villages are gone, and hundreds of skyscrapers and other buildings have taken their place. And the Sea River got severely polluted. It used to be our major source of drinking water. But with more and more industries dumping their waste into the river, the pollution got worse and worse. The government and local people have realized the seriousness of the situation, and have done a lot to clean up the river and prevent it from being polluted again.

There are many beautiful parks and gardens alongside the river now, so the Sea River is taking on a new face, and it's much prettier.

Further questions

1. What do people enjoy doing when they go to rivers, lakes or the sea? Why do you think these activities are popular?

笔记区

I think first of all, people enjoy beautiful scenery. Many people love to stroll along the beach or river bank, or just sit there and relax, looking at the water. And of course there are more energetic things that a lot of people enjoy, like scuba diving and surfing. In winter, people enjoy skating on frozen rivers or lakes.

2. Apart from relaxation and excitement, can you think of any other benefits people get from activities they enjoy in water?

Well, there's the sense of achievement. And of course, swimming and surfing are great exercise. Those old people who go swimming all year round always seem to look much younger than they are.

3. Do you prefer swimming in a swimming pool to swimming in the sea, or in a lake?

Oh, I much prefer the sea, but not when it's too cold. In Tianjin, I often go to the beach for a swim. But that's impossible when I'm at university, so I have no choice but to use the pool.

4. Can you think of any advantages or disadvantages of going to the sea or to a swimming pool?

Well, the first thing is that many people don't have easy access to the sea, so they have no choice but to go to a swimming pool, or a lake or river if there's one not too far away. So that's a big advantage of swimming pools—they can be built almost anywhere. And you can swim all year round in most of them: you don't have to worry about the weather. But sometimes they get too crowded, which is a disadvantage if you want to swim laps. Our university pool has lanes for serious swimmers that people can't use for just splashing around in. Disadvantages of the sea? Let me think. Yes, there's the question of safety. Swimming pools employ people to make sure no one drowns. A lot of popular beaches have lifeguards, which make things safer, but there's still a much greater chance of getting into trouble in the sea than in a swimming pool. Because swimming pools don't have strong currents that can pull you out to sea, or jelly fish or sharks. But I still prefer swimming in the sea to in a swimming pool.

5. How important is it for a town or city to be located near a river or the sea?

In the past, towns or cities located near a river or the sea, I mean with a natural harbor, developed faster and earlier than other places. A major reason is the convenience of transport. Look at those cities along the east coast of China. They are much richer and more developed than the cities in the middle and west of China, and of course are closer to international markets, so they were where traders from other countries as far away as Africa came. And before the railways were developed, ships were the only way to move large quantities of goods. So towns or cities near a river or the sea became important ports. Actually, I've forgotten about the Silk Road, which for centuries was obviously the only way to transport, mostly luxury goods like silk and spices, between landlocked areas of China and Central Asia, even Europe. What do they call camels? "Ships of the

笔 记 区

desert", that's it. But they have mostly been replaced by rail and road transport.

6. You spoke earlier about water pollution. Do you think there are any problems with shipping in this regard?

   Well, I don't know a lot about it, but I have read, and seen a few things on TV, that some irresponsible ship captains just throw their waste oil and other rubbish straight into the sea. I guess they don't want to pay for it to be treated properly when they get to port. But with satellites and things like that it's getting easier to spot ships doing this, and probably, at least I hope, the captains and crews are becoming more aware of environmental protection. I know many countries have really heavy fines for ships that pollute in their territorial waters.

13. Describe your favourite park or garden.

You should say:

where it is

what you see

and what you do in the park.

OK, I am going to talk about a small park near where I live. It is a very quiet and lovely place.

The park is within walking distance from the apartment building I live in. The park is a square-shaped one. The best part of it is an open-air patch of land in the middle, which may serve as a dancing ball in the evening, attracting quite a lot of old people from around the park. In the southeastern corner of the park, there's a small piece of land with pebbles on it, where people can walk on barefooted. It's very much like a massage for your feet and it feels good. My mum loves that! But what I like best is the sports facilities in one corner of the park. Every morning when I get up, I usually take a walk in the park and do a bit of exercises. A fresh start, isn't it!

Of course, there are other reasons I like this park. It is also a very good meeting place for the neighbourhoods around it. The busiest time in the park probably is the morning. There are quite a lot of people and a lot of talking and laughing, which is quite good I think. Because nowadays many people have a very busy lifestyle. They don't even have time to talk much outside of the office. The park provides a fantastic opportunity for people to talk and to get to know each other.

Further questions

1. Is it necessary to have your own garden?

   It isn't necessary but it would be lovely if I could. It would be a wonderful place for BBQ, wouldn't it?

2. What would you use a garden for?

   First of all, I would plant some trees and flowers. Gardening can be a great way to

笔 记 区

relax, you know. Second, a garden would be a good place where I can read, listen to music or simply take a nap.

3. What is the influence of parks on our life?

   Parks can be perfect getaways in cities. Plus, it is said they are also good for the urban ecosystem 'cause they can absorb heat and green-house emissions.

4. What do people often grow in the garden?

   In China people often grow various flowers like chrysanthemum and lilies. I guess if I had a garden, my mum would definitely grow a lot of vegetables. She used to do that when she was a child.

14. *Describe your favourite shopping centre.*

    You should say:

    what it is

    where it is located

    what you can buy there

    and explain why you like it.

I'm not quite keen on shopping actually, so I don't know much about those fancy department stores in Beijing. If I have to go shopping, it's for daily necessities like food and shampoo, and things like that. The supermarket where I do most of my shopping is Carrefour, a French chain supermarket, I suppose.

It's located in the Zhongguancun Square, not very far from the place where I live. It's within walking distance.

As I told you, I go to Carrefour mainly for things I need every day. Carrefour has everything you could expect of a big supermarket: rows and rows of shelves, full of beautifully-packaged stuff. You can get anything you need.

I quite like this supermarket. First, it takes only five minutes to get there. You can hardly like one that takes you an hour at least simply to get there. Second, Carrefour has everything you need. It's like a one-stop thing. You don't have to buy grocery in one shop and CDs in another. It's quite convenient, especially for those like me, who don't want to waste a lot of time shopping. There's another reason why I like it. There're quite a number of fast food restaurants and bookshops near the entrance. So if I feel tired, I can have something to eat or pick up a book and have a nice cup of coffee. I like that.

Further questions

1. Why are there a lot of big stores?

   As competition is fierce in modern society, shop owners are trying every means to cut costs in order to get greater profits. The mode of operation employed by big stores could guarantee this and thus more big stores appear.

笔记区

2. What are the main differences between small stores and big stores when you go shopping?

There are a lot of differences between small stores and big stores. Big stores provide a greater variety of goods while the choices are limited when you go shopping in a small store. In addition, big stores make more ads than small stores and prices are lower in big stores than in small stores.

3. Do you think small stores will disappear in the future?

Well, it's hard to say. You know, small stores have their own advantages. For example, it is easier to run a small store than a big one for it occupies less space. The investment could be smaller and the risks are lower.

4. What do you think is the best way to advertise?

TV or newspaper I suppose. Both of them are the most popular mass media among people. TV commercials could provide a vivid image of the stores while newspapers carry more information.

5. What are the differences between men and women when they go shopping?

Well, women like window shopping. They rarely make a sudden decision to buy something and are interested in comparing prices at different places. As for men, what they are concerned about most is the quality and how soon they can get it. As a result, men usually go directly to the store and make the purchasing decision as long as they think the products are of good quality.

6. What do you think of on-line shopping?

Well, the most important advantage of Internet shopping is convenience. People usually do online shopping from their homes or offices to save the time and the hassle of going to the mall. The disadvantage of on-line shopping is that the computer image of the products can hardly compare with piles of racked and shelved clothes that can be touched for quality and tried on for comfort.

7. What do you think of the use of credit card?

First of all, there's the advantage of convenience. You don't have to carry around cash. And they are good for organizing your finances. If you charge everything each month, you' ll have a complete record along with your checking account of where your money went. However, one huge disadvantage to credit cards is that because it's so convenient, it is easy to make purchases and start buying things that you cannot pay for.

笔 记 区

三、物品题

15. *Describe a toy that you have received which is very important to you.*
You should say:
what the toy is
who gave it to you
why the person gave it to you
and explain why the toy means so much to you.

The toy I am going to talk about is very special to me. It is a doll I used to play with for quite a long time.

My parents gave it to me when I was four as a birthday present. I consider it as special because it was a very high-tech doll at that time and I was very proud of it. It would cry if I hit it or accidentally dropped it. But when I put a kind of dummy into its mouth, it would immediately stop crying. Next time I let go of the dummy it would laugh happily. Sometimes it would make some noises like a real baby.

It brought a lot of fun into my childhood. At that time, not many kids had this kind of doll and I liked to show it to my friends in the kindergarten. It made me a star among the children. Of course sometimes we would play with the doll together. It is the first present that my parents bought me and it means a lot to me. Although it can cry or laugh no more, I still keep it. And every time I see it, I remember the happy times playing with it and the smile on my parents' face.

Further questions

1. What are the differences between the toys which boys like to play with and those girls like to play with in your opinion?
   Usually, boys like to play war games with model guns, shouting at and killing their enemies. Boys are fascinated with video games. They like to collect sort of game cards and compete with each other. Boys like to play the games that we girls often regard as somewhat violent. On the contrary, girls like to play quietly with their dolls, with each other or alone. Girls like to play house. Someone acts as the father, and another one acts as the mother, with a doll as their child. They have some small things serving as the house, the car, and so on.
2. What role do the toys play?
   First of all, children consider the toys as their companies. Since the introducing of the one-child policy, every family should have but one child. People don't live together with other relatives as they used to do and parents are often out working. Therefore, they are often left alone at home. In this case, toys are very important to children as a kind of companion. Secondly, many toys are made to develop

笔 记 区

children's intellect and interest, thus lay the foundation of their future study and work. Those toys are designed to train children's ability and to exercise their hands and the whole body even.

3. What kind of toys do Chinese children usually play?
Boys like to play with toy guns, toy cars and robots with remote control. They like to play gameboy and video games. Meanwhile, girls like to play with dolls and they like to play house with their peers. Many children nowadays are fascinated with computer games. Computer to them is like a toy, not a tool any more.

4. Has there been any change for the last 20 years?
Yes, definitely. Firstly, children have more choices now. There are millions of kinds of toys they can choose from. Secondly, the quality is becoming better and better. And the toy manufacturers take into consideration the safety of their products. Thirdly, more and more toys are serving as a tool to train the children's ability. Children can learn things while they are playing with the toys.

16. *Describe a book or story you read when you were a child.*
You should say:
what the book's name is
who gave it to you
what it was about
and explain what influence it has had on you.

Well, I would like to tell you something about *The Children's Encyclopaedia*, or literally, *The One Hundred Thousand Questions*. I read it when I was a kid.

I got this set of books as a birthday gift from my father when I was 6 years old.

As you will guess from the name, the set of books covers many areas that a child might be curious about. It taught me about geography, biology, chemistry, and physics. Of course, at that time I wasn't able to distinguish the difference between the subjects, but the books attracted me so much as a collection of the natural mysteries in my eyes. I loved these books and read them whenever I could. Never before had I been so attracted to a set of books. Besides reading the books, I also carried out the experiments mentioned in the books. Until now, I can still remember the feelings of satisfaction when I had first lit up a light by connecting wires and batteries.

This set of books has had a great impact on me. It proves that my frequent access to the books not only cultivated at a very early age my interest in natural sciences, but also helped me build strong experimental skills through the hands-on experience. Yes, *The Children's Encyclopaedia* definitely is the set of books I liked reading most when I was a child.

笔记区

Further questions:

1. When do Chinese children usually start reading? Reading what books? Why?

   I think if I'm right, Chinese children, like children of other countries, generally start reading at four or five. For them, parents usually select easy cartoon books as they can draw children's attention and they're easier for them to understand. Later, there are plenty of choices for children: books of Anderson's tales, easy Chinese poems, and so on. These are among children's favourite.

2. What games do Chinese children usually do to help them read?

   Well, I think in many kindergartens and schools, children are often invited to do role play and acting to help them read. They can make reading interesting and will help children have a better understanding about the stories.

3. What do you think of starting to read at a very early age? Is it good or bad? What do you think are the ways to solve the negative impacts if you think there are some?

   It's hard to give an absolute "Yes" or "No" answer to this question. Starting to read at a very early age can be highly appreciated if it is carried out smoothly and properly. It is widely known that the early intellectual development is crucial for a child's growth. Therefore, proper amount of reading for young kids is very welcome. However, this shouldn't be overdone. After all, people should have laughter and happy memories besides books. So I think if properly managed, starting to read at an early age is good for children.

4. What do you think of the Internet's impact on reading?

   The Internet has influenced reading significantly. Before, people read things printed on paper such as books, newspapers, letters and so on. Now, people have abundant access to electronic information. We read through the computer screen: PDF files, emails, on-line downloadable newspapers, etc. This has not only brought us great convenience, but also saved us lots of paper. Well, I'm satisfied with the changes the Internet has brought to our reading habits, though there is still space for improvement on Internet reading.

5. Do you prefer the traditional way of reading or on-line reading?

   I think I prefer both of them. There are different aims for different reading. If I'm to read for a recreational purpose, I would choose to have a book in my hands, sitting comfortably, and enjoy the book in a relaxing way. However, if I'm to read for a paper task, I would choose on-line reading, because software is capable of finding the exact information I would like to find in an e-book. That is obviously much more convenient than searching information through index. Therefore, I think, it really depends on the actual situation to decide which one to choose.

6. Through what way, do you think, can make people enjoy reading?

   My advice for this problem is to read what you like and what you are familiar

笔记区

with. There is an old saying that interest is the best teacher. Interest, as I see it, is the most important factor for readers. Only by having an interest, can people have initiatives to read on the relevant topics. Therefore, to begin with the most interesting topic will help people enjoy reading.

7. Will the way people read change in the future? What kind of changes will there be?

I expect there will be changes in the way people read in the future. As the Internet is developing rapidly, in the near future, e-books should be much more popular than they are today. It is possible that on-line reading will replace the printed books, becoming the most important source of reading. I also expect the advent of audio-text books so that it is more convenient for people to read. At that time, people will be able to listen to the books when they drive to work or do exercises. That is quite a fancy picture.

8. What kinds of books do people prefer when they are at different ages? What will you prefer reading when you are old?

Well, I suppose people do have different preferences over books when they grow. Young people like me may enjoy reading adventure stories. Middle aged people will have preferences over love stories. I guess when people grow older, they may like reading stories they read when they were young. It's like a kind of nostalgic state of mind I think. To me, I think when I become old, as I've just mentioned, I'll probably re-read the old books to refresh the good feelings and happy memories.

17. *Describe the clothes/jewelry in your special occasions.*

You should say:

what it is

who bought it for you

on what occasions you wear it

and explain why you wear it on such occasions.

It is an Esprit jean mini-skirt I bought for myself as a birthday gift in the first year of my college life.

I wear it on my birthdays, of course. I need to keep the special moments when I am still young enough to wear a mini-skirt. Since I have fallen in love with playing tennis, I usually wear it when playing tennis with my friends on a summer afternoon. Mini-skirt, beautiful sunshine, energetic girls, all these convince me that we are young and we can enjoy every minute of our life. Besides, girls like to show their slender legs, and a mini-skirt is the best choice. When invited to an informal party, wearing a mini-skirt makes me feel like a princess, especially when a boy asks me to dance.

I feel confident when wearing my skirt, so every time I am hosting a school

笔记区

ceremony, I wear it. Though everybody is looking at me, all my nervousness will be gone. I believe confidence, youth and passion are the spirit of Esprit jeans. When I feel low, I will walk alone on the campus in my mini-skirt, thinking about happy memories.

Further questions

1. Talk about the style of a kind of clothes.

   Clothes worn by hip-hop singers are now quite popular among young people. This kind of clothes looks special for its large and loose style. The colour of the clothes is simple, mainly black and white. It emphasizes the unique character of a new generation and stands for a street culture which is passionate and dynamic. Young people declare their identity by wearing this kind of clothes.

2. Do you think the clothing is more important than before? Why?

   Yes, it is much more important than before. Clothing is not for the simple purpose of keeping warm any more. It is something people wear to show their status, character and taste. People care about what to wear on different occasions because they believe dressing properly will leave a good impression on others. Some people even say that we are what we wear.

3. What type of clothing do you wear in different occasions?

   Basically, I prefer clothes of simple styles such as jeans and T-shirts when I am on the campus or with my friends. But when attending parties or formal get-togethers, I will choose dresses and high-heeled shoes. We'd better wear a suit or a white blouse when we go to work because it looks efficient and capable. Girls are usually dressed in a lady-like way when with their boyfriends.

4. What information can you find in another person's clothing?

   We can read a lot from a person's clothing because the way people dress reflects in a way their personalities, tastes and attitudes towards life. People who are confident and passionate usually wear colourful clothes. Those who dress in an avant-guard style care about life style and are sensitive about fashion. Brand name zealots emphasize tastes of life and usually expect a lot from life.

5. What is fashion? What are the differences between men's fashion and women's fashion?

   Fashion is a life style about optimism and brightness. Everyone can have his or her own unique and wonderful understanding of life, thus forming his or her view of what is fashion.

   A car is the symbol of a man. For men, cars are the fashion that they are ever after. Social status, personal achievement and male dignity are what they pursue, so they will probably define fashion from these aspects. While for women, fashion is something that can add to their female charm. Latest fashions, perfumes and cosmetics are always at the centre of their attention.

笔记区

6. **On what occasion will people change their type of clothing?**

   People favour clothing that they have been used to. They change their type of clothing on the occasions that they think important to them. They want their styles of clothing to be considered proper and be recognized by other people. People especially care much about what they wear when in front of people they have a crush on. That's why it takes such a long time for girls to choose clothing before meeting Mr. Right.

7. **Do you like fashionable clothes or traditional clothes?**

   I am in favour of fashionable clothes because they make me feel part of the youth world. Fashionable clothes pass us the newest trend of the fashion world. We have very beautiful traditional clothes, but they don't seem to fit me.

8. **Talk about traditional clothes in China. Why people like to dress in traditional clothes? Is there any special meaning?**

   We have traditional clothes such as Sun Yat Sen's uniform, cheong-sam. Both of them are perfectly designed and convey unique Chinese culture. Sun Yat Sen's uniform, with four pockets, was designed by our great leader Sun Zhongshan. Cheong-sam is the favourite of Chinese women because it best exposes the beauty of oriental women. It is almost the symbol of Chinese women. People like to dress in traditional clothes because they feel special wearing them. This is something only for Chinese. Besides, there is a "return to the ancients" movement in the fashion world. So the traditional can be the most fashionable.

9. **Talk about advantages and disadvantages of policemen in police uniforms.**

   Policemen in uniform look professional and trustworthy. The uniform gives a sense of security and stateliness. But it is unfair for policemen to wear the same clothes all the year around. It tends to be uncomfortable.

18. *Describe a vehicle or bike you want to have.*

    You should say:

    what it is

    what features it has

    when you can buy it

    and explain why you want to have it.

Well, I like cars, and I hope that one day I can have my own SUV which is made by BMW.

One thing I expect on my SUV is that it could be equipped with GPS so that it can offer me advice on the most convenient driving route during rush hours. Since I'm a crazy fan of music, and I would like to enjoy my favourite music while I'm driving, I hope that my SUV will have a state-of-the-art audio system. I'm sure driving in that kind of SUV will be a fancy thing to do. About why I'd like to have an SUV, I think

笔 记 区

there are two reasons. One is that it is much more comfortable to drive in an SUV than in a sedan, because it offers more legroom. As much of a tall man as I am, extra legroom is very important for me. Another thing that attracts me to have an SUV is that it is safer to drive in a relatively large vehicle. After all, safety is a most important concern for many drivers.

Well, about when I can buy one, I don't think that will happen in a short time. As I know, SUVs have average higher prices over sedans and they do have a large consumption of petrol which will also cost quite a fortune, so I guess when I'm able to have an SUV, I'll probably be in my forties.

Further questions

1. How do you come here in the morning?

   I came here this morning by taxi. It's quite convenient...only took me seven minutes or so to arrive. I always choose to take a taxi on important occasions like today. Well, of course, it costs much more than going by bus.

2. How many kinds of transport are there in China? What efforts does the government make to improve public transport?

   Well, there are many kinds of transport: city bus, underground, railway, airplane, coach, ship and so on. People choose different transport means in accordance to their need. About the efforts to improve public transport, in Beijing, I think the government has invested a lot of money to optimize the underground train system. The city bus system has also improved a lot. Now we have more bus routes to choose from, and there are more buses running on the streets to meet the demand from the public.

3. Would you please make a comparison between the status quo of transport and the situation in the past?

   Now in megacities like Beijing, Shanghai, and Guangzhou, we have wider streets and more flyovers than before. Further, new ring roads are built one after another to relieve the pressure in city centres. However, despite these efforts, traffic pressure doesn't seem to be relieved, because everyday, there's a large number of new cars flowing onto the streets. Compared to the past, now we have a much heavier pressure on transport. I think that's the most apparent change in transport.

4. Describe the advantages and disadvantages of saloon cars.

   Saloon cars provide people with an easy and convenient way to travel at a low cost. With the development of the public transport system, it is possible to get to most places in the city by saloon cars, without worrying where to park your car. However, during rush hours saloon cars can be very crowded, and sometimes, because of the traffic congestion, people have to wait for a long time for a bus to come. These are what I consider disadvantages of saloon cars.

笔记区

5. Do you like riding a bike? Is it safe? How about driving a car?

Yes. Like most Chinese, I do ride a bike. In the past, particularly when I was young, I enjoyed riding a lot. However, as I'm growing older, I have gradually lost the interest in riding. There are two main reasons. Firstly, it's dangerous to ride since we Chinese often ride without helmet protection, and in many places, lanes are not separated for automobiles and bikes. Secondly, it saves energy to take a bus especially when going to far places. Of course, I like driving a car most. If I were rich enough, I'd definitely choose to drive.

6. **Some people prefer short excursions while some choose long-distance travel. What's your advice for travellers?**

My advice for travellers is not to forget to enjoy the beauty around you while you're taking time and money visiting distant places. I don't think that only by travelling to far places can offer us a better holiday experience. Actually, time and expenses don't allow many people to travel far often. In this sense, short excursions have their advantages. They're convenient and cheap. Actually, there are lots of beautiful sites around Beijing, and I do think them fine destinations for excursions.

7. **What do you think of walking? What kind of people do you think like walking?**

I find walking a very easy and effective exercise to keep the body healthy. According to a report, proper amount of walking exercise can be beneficial to our heart and lungs. About what kind of people like walking, I guess they're the people like me who find doing sports too hard. I wouldn't like to get myself too tired from exercising. For me, walking is much easier and doesn't require a lot of strength.

8. **What kind of car do you want to buy if you have enough money?**

Well, provided that I'm wealthy enough, I would like to by a Bentley sedan. When I was in secondary school, I read an article about Bentley cars. I was deeply attracted to these cars because many parts of them are delicately hand-crafted with luxurious materials. Bentley cars are not mass-produced, and that's what I value most. I believe this will make the driving experience with Bentley unique.

19. *Describe a national product.*

You should say:

what it is

where it is sold

how the product is advertised

and how useful the product is to the people in your country.

The national product I'd like to talk about is the Lenovo laptop computer. Lenovo Company first introduced personal computers to Chinese households. In

笔记区

2005, it acquired IBM's Personal Computing Division and became one of the leading computer companies in the world. Now Lenovo notebooks are sold worldwide, with its sales headquarters in New York, Paris, Beijing and Sydney. It has become one of the Chinese national products that can represent the Chinese national industry.

Lenovo notebooks do not use TV advertisements as much as other products to enlarge its publicity. Large advertising boards put up in the business centres are one of Lenovo notebooks' strategies to advertise themselves. This is because many types of Lenovo notebooks are made to cater to the needs of businessmen. Another strategy is to sponsor sports. In 2004, Lenovo became a worldwide partnership of IOC to support the Olympic Games. Thus now the symbol of the Olympic Games—the five interlinked rings—can be seen on Lenovo notebooks. Since the 2006 Winter Olympic Games, Lenovo notebooks will be used by judges, and IOC officials. This means anyone who watches Olympic Games will see Lenovo notebooks. No TV advertisement can achieve this effect.

Lenovo notebooks are our national pride. They offer us high quality products with relatively low price compared with foreign brands of notebooks. Thus this product accelerates the computerization of Chinese households, which makes us keep in touch with the most advanced technology.

Further questions

1. Is it necessary for governments to take control of advertisement?

   In my opinion, governments should regulate advertisement. When advertisement is used properly, it can provide people with useful information and a kind of visual entertainment. But nowadays, it has been abused. Some advertisements interrupt TV programmes frequently. Some are in poor taste, containing sexual and violent elements. Some fake advertisements mislead and cheat consumers. So I think governments should get involved to guarantee the high quality of advertisement.

2. What influence does advertisement have on people?

   Every coin has two sides. So does advertisement. It provides the most direct, comprehensive and detailed information. We get to know about many household goods from advertisement. Sometimes many people use job advertisements to find jobs. Artistic advertisement offers pleasant visual enjoyment. But some advertisements are in low quality. There is too much violence and sexual elements in advertising. Fake advertisements are filled with empty promises, which cheat and misguide people. Some of them may even threaten people's lives.

3. What do you think an advertisement should pay attention to?

   The first thing an advertisement should consider is that it must make sure all the information it contains is the virtual truth. Exaggeration or false information should not be allowed to exist in any pieces of advertisement. Second, advertisement should be of high quality and made artistically. Violence and sexual

笔记区

elements must be expelled from the content of advertisement. Next, advertisement is not necessary used solely for commercial purpose. It can also educate the public, advocate for higher moral standards and call for people to act upon them. To this extent, advertisement cannot only provide information but also serve as an instrument to create a better social environment.

4. What influence does advertisement have on children?

Children spend a lot of time watching TV, so they are inevitably influenced by the content of advertisement. They are easily guided by advertisements. Thus they will ask for whatever is advertised on TV, which becomes a big headache for their parents. I do not deny that they can learn something through advertisement, such as songs and words. But nowadays, violence and sexual elements in advertisements are great concerns of their parents. Children may get a distorted picture of the world. Some of them may even try to imitate those negative things, which is very dangerous. So children should be guided by parents when watching TV.

5. Why do many Chinese like to spend so much money on brandname things?

First, I think they do this because now they can afford that. When people get rich, they will pursue a higher quality of life. Brandname items must be famous for a reason, such as quality, style and taste, thus they can satisfy those people's needs. Of course, they have to pay more for them than on things with ordinary quality.

Well, another reason is that famous brands are a symbol of status in China, like watches and cars. People want others to know that they are rich enough to buy those things, which will indicate their status. In other words, they are kind of enslaved by vanity. Sometimes this type of consumption is a waste of money.

6. Could you name several famous Chinese brands?

There are quite a number of famous brands in China. For example in the sportswear industry, there is Li Ning, a brand named after one of the first Chinese gold medalists in the Olympic Games. And in the home electronics industry, there are Haier, Changhong and other big names.

20. *Describe what kind of book you would like to write (e.g. textbook, history book, story book).*

You should say:

what kind of book you would like to write

what you would write in your book

and what kind of people would read your book in your opinion.

The book that I'd like to write is something like an autobiography.

It's interesting to put down the things one has experienced and the places one has

笔 记 区

visited. That is something unique and distinguishes one from another. I would write about my life, about the heart attack I got when I was a child, about the growing pains I suffered, the love I gave and received. I would write about my friends, my family, the cities I've been to. Because it is exactly these events that formed my character and made my life full of stories. It feels good to share with others your story or your experiences.

My book is meant mostly for family I'd reckon, for my children, or even my grandchildren to learn about my story, my happiness and sorrows. That's gotta be fun and of course meaningful doing this, I mean writing the book. I don't want to write anything boring that one has to cram for before exams.

Follow up

1. When would you plan to write it?

   I've actually started writing a diary and I got some articles published in some journals.

2. Do you like writing?

   Yes, very much. For me it's a good way to relax and looking back on the past.

Further questions

1. What is the most important quality about a writer?

   It all depends on the nature of the books he/she wants to write. For instance he/she has to be faithful to the facts and objective if one wants to write a textbook or history book. You've got be serious about writing that kind of stuff. As for fiction writers, they should be imaginative.

2. Why do people choose to write for a living?

   I guess early last century writing was the only possible means of making a living for women. Nowadays many choose to write out of their personal interests. What's more, they can get paid for their interest. Isn't it good?

3. What kind of difficulty would a writer face?

   Instability, financially, I guess, especially for freelance writers. The lack of inspiration is also terrible, writers usually come up with bottlenecks when they want to write something.

4. What do you think of libraries in your society?

   They're quite important nowadays though I admit in the past when knowledge was not fully desired, many libraries were torn down and many books burnt to ash. In this new era, such things won't happen again. What's more, libraries are not only a place of serious learning but also a great place to have fun and entertain oneself.

5. How can libraries encourage people to read/learn more?

   In many ways, but the most significant one is it is in the libraries that one can have

笔记区

free access to new books of vast varieties. Books are by no means inexpensive these days, and you don't know which are the ones you want to buy and keep them for second reading. While for other books you just want to scan through some pages and put them back on the shelves.

6. What do you think of the government spending money on libraries for the general public?

I totally agree that government has many other issues to be concerned with while the budget is usually limited. But spending on libraries is always a wise choice, because it never does harm to a nation if its government encourages its people to learn more.

21. *Describe a work of art.*

You should say:

what it is

where you saw it

what it is about

and how you like it.

Honesty, I'm not very keen on painting or sculpture, so this is really a tough topic for me. But if you ask me to talk about a painting, the one that comes to my mind first is the Mona Lisa, an oil painting by the famous Italian Renaissance artist Leonardo da Vinci. You've heard of this masterpiece, haven't you?

Well, actually, I've never seen the original painting, which is said to be on display in the French Loovre Museum. I remember the first time I saw it was when I was in primary school. It was a reproduction in the book on art history.

The picture is really amazing. The painting shows a woman looking out at the viewer with an "enigmatic smile". When you look at Mona Lisa, no matter where you stand, you find her looking at you and smiling at you.

My arts teacher told us that the Mona Lisa is perhaps the most famous piece in art history and is, perhaps, the most widely known portrait in the Western world. It's so different from the paintings of Chinese style. My teacher also told us that you could learn a lot about other cultures from painting, which I believe is quite true. I think while I'm studying in the U.K., I will sure go to Paris to have a look at the original painting.

Further questions

1. What kind of paintings do Chinese people like?

It's hard to say, but traditional painting like landscapes, ink and wash painting, and calligraphy are quite popular.

2. What can you learn from western paintings?

First of all there are the practical things like painting techniques and skills.

笔 记 区

Secondly you can also learn a lot about western culture and religion.

3. Some paintings are very expensive, but people still want to buy them. What do you think?

   I'm not very keen on paintings so I don't quite understand why some paintings are sold for an astronomical price. But maybe beauty is in the eyes of the beholder.

4. What can you get from painting as a hobby?

   It's a great hobby and like any other hobby, it gives you great pleasure and you can get tremendous satisfaction. And it is a kind of escape, too.

5. Should painting (arts education) be part of school curriculum?

   Oh definitely. I think painting should be included in the school curriculum. You know children can learn so much from painting. They learn to concentrate...to focus...and to observe carefully, which can help them with the academic subjects.

22. *Describe something you made by yourself.*

You should say:

what it is

when you made it

how you made it

and explain why you made it.

I want to talk about a wallet I made while I was a child. It was made of paper, actually. As a Child, I dreamt of having a lot of adult luxuries that my parents wouldn't buy, so the only way out was to make them.

Once, I made a paper wallet with front and back covers and a lot of small bags in the middle by cutting paper and gluing them together. So I could carry paper notes, coins, and even a photo separately in different layers. Plus I got a built-in notebook for taking notes, getting phone numbers. I even stuck some index cards inside the front cover for reminders and to-do lists. It folded up like a square and looked totally uncool, but I was proud to have it as a child.

I made it then only for fun and also to show off, but now I think it helped with my creative development. Until this day, my mum still keeps it for me. It's one of the best memories of my childhood.

Further questions

1. How can children benefit from making crafts?

   Crafts can be great fun and are also very useful. They include sewing, knitting, making things for your home and more. These crafts can make children creative and imaginative and develop their manual skills to work out interesting and beautiful things. It also develops their special interests and skills.

笔记区

2. **Is a creative mind important?**

Yes, I think so. Creativity is an essential quality required for future success. It doesn't matter what industry you are working in, we all need a bit of creativity. Like, I am a teacher, and I need a bit of creativity to make my class fun.

3. **Are there any differences between things made by hand and those by machinery?**

Sure. First of all, if we are talking about a handicraft like a kite or a sculpture, then the one made by hand will probably be sold for a higher price than the one made by machines because it involves much more effort and a bit of creativity. Second, I don't know what you think about this, but personally, I think hand-made things are better quality than machine-made things, and therefore are more endurable.

23. Describe your favourite sport.

You should say:

what it is

what clothes or equipment it involves

and why you like it.

Whenever I am faced with the question about my favourite sport, my answer is always the same: jogging. It has accompanied me for nearly three years and I hope I can keep this habit as long as possible.

It is said that the afternoon is the best time for exercise. When I am free in the afternoon, I will put on my comfortable clothes and running shoes, and then go jogging.

There are several reasons why I love jogging. First of all, it is very easy to do. Unlike basketball or football, which require a particular place, jogging does not have a strict demand for a place. I live on the university campus, so usually I jog on the playground or simply on the campus road. Second, I do not have to pay a lot of attention on the exercise itself. I can always enjoy the beautiful scenery around the playground as long as I want. Next, jogging is a very good exercise for mental relaxation. After jogging for about 20 minutes, I will reach a point where all my troubles and pressure seem to disappear. At that time, I keep telling myself deep in my heart that it is so good to be alive; everything will be OK; enjoy your life! Generally speaking, I jog 45 minutes in a run. When I stop, physically I am a little tired, but psychologically I feel refreshed. This is the major reason I love jogging.

To me, jogging is not merely my favourite sport. Now it has become a very important part of my life.

笔记区

Further questions

1. Why some people do not like sports?

   In my opinion, the major reason is that those people regard sports as an extra burden. They have not realized the importance of sports to their health and life. Some people are simply too lazy to do exercise. Lack of time is their usual excuse. There are also people who feel too ashamed to do sports, either they are overweight or afraid of being laughed at.

2. What kind of sports do Chinese people like? Why?

   I think the most widely loved sport is Ping-Pong, which is considered as the national sport of China. Traditional Chinese exercises are still chosen by people. For instance, Shadow Boxing is still very popular, especially among the seniors. As China is more than ready to absorb good things from abroad, sports are also one field. Nowadays, many imported sports, such as Yoga, are widely practised by young Chinese.

3. Should government support sports?

   I think so. Doing exercise is a very good way to improve people's physical condition. How often people practise and what kind of exercise they do is an important indicator of their quality of life. If government supports sports, more public facilities will be offered and more people will realize the importance of sports.

4. Why young people like some dangerous sports, like Bungee even if some have injured or lost their lives?

   Young people are always fond of exciting experience, which offers an outlet for their energy. They are proud of being adventurous. Another reason is that nowadays, young people are facing heavy pressure from family, study or relationships. Dangerous sports can serve as a channel through which they can let go of the pressure, even if it only lasts a very short period.

5. What is the difference between young people and old people in their attitudes towards sports?

   I think there are quite a lot of differences. For old people, the most important thing is to keep good health and fully enjoy the rest of their life. For young people, however, good health is not the only thing they are concerned with. Experience is also a concern. That's why many young people are quite interested in extreme sports and outdoor sports.

6. Compare the advantages and disadvantages between indoor and outdoor sports.

   Every coin has two sides. Both of them have advantages and disadvantages. For indoor sports, it does not require too much about the weather, and there are better facilities offered. But sometimes it is too crowded in the gym, especially on holidays. Thus the air is stuffy and people cannot get enough room to practise. As

笔记区

for outdoor sports, the air and room are relatively better than that of in the gym. But people cannot practise when the weather is bad. Meanwhile, the facilities cannot match those in the gym.

7. Should tobacco companies be allowed to sponsor sports activities?

I do not think tobacco company sponsorship is a good idea. It is true that sports, especially that need a large sum of money, such as the Olympic Games, need commercial sponsorship. It allows organizers to provide better conditions for the athletes and to publicize this activity. But if tobacco companies are among the sponsors, this activity is actually advertising for these tobacco companies, which is not in line with doing sports. Anyway, organizers can always find other sponsors besides tobacco companies.

8. What do you prefer, exercise alone or on a team?

I think it depends on what kind of exercise you are doing. Some sports like basketball, football, and Ping-Pong need more than one person to practise. There are also sports that are very tiring so people can encourage each other when in difficulty. While some sports, for instance jogging or fishing, require a comparatively quiet situation. So it is better to practise them alone.

24. *Describe your favourite way to relax.*

You should say:

what it is

where you like to relax

what you do exactly

and explain why you like this type of relaxation.

My favourite way to relax is to listen to country music. After a long day's work, I need light and sweet music to relax myself.

Usually, I will turn on the radio while taking a bath. On weekends, I would like to spend my day on a sofa, reading fashion magazines while listening to American country music.

I especially appreciate country songs by John Denver. Whenever I listen to his famous song *Take me Home, Country Roads*, I feel being taken back to my childhood and the small town where I shared happy memories with my friends. Music is something that can purify your mind, while country music can always bring out those memories of good old days.

When I listen to it I feel relaxed because it seems that I live in a world where there are nice people, clear streams, fresh air, vast farmland, country roads with plenty of daisies and beautiful sunshine. All the pressure, panic and anxiety due to the fierce competition of a quick-paced society disappear. Listening to country music makes me think that life is beautiful and comfortable and it refreshes and prepares me

笔记区

for a new day.

Further questions

1. How do people around you relax?

   Many of my friends do sports which they believe can refresh themselves. Sports make them forget all the trouble at work. Some prefer to watch movies while others read comic books and novels, among which *Harry Potter* is the most popular one. Sometimes, a lavish dinner can also relax and satisfy us because we need to give ourselves a treat for hard work.

2. What are the differences in ways of relaxing between men and women?

   I think most men do not like to expose their pressure. They may ask several friends out to pubs to have a drink and let the alcohol take away all the trouble of life. Some of them may choose to do sports. Both are silent ways to relax. Women tend to share their feelings. For them, talking with families and friends about their worries or anxieties is the best way to relax.

3. How do most people relax themselves? Why they choose it?

   I guess most people will choose to sleep when they need to relax. There is nothing better than a good sleep after a hard day's work. People feel depressed not only because there is pressure but also because they are tired. A good sleep can give your body as well as your mind a good rest.

4. What are the traditional ways to relax for Chinese people?

   Greatly influenced by the religion of Buddhism which emphasizes the quietness of the soul, a lot of Chinese people like quiet ways of relaxing, among which meditation is a good one. Playing chess, fishing, having tea and Shadow Boxing are all ways of relaxing favoured by Chinese people.

5. What are the differences between pressures people are undergoing now and that they underwent 50 years ago?

   50 years ago when there was not sufficient supply of commodities and basic needs of daily life, people struggled to feed their families. Material inadequacy and poor living conditions caused a lot of stress. The pressure people are undergoing now is basically anxiety caused by fierce, sometimes even cruel competition. In a quick-paced society, people have to work hard to maintain a decent life and not be left out by the changing world. But maybe some pressure is added by people themselves. They expect too much from life.

6. What do you think is the importance of relaxing?

   Relaxing is very important because we all need to recharge ourselves with energy and prepare ourselves for the coming days. It is also out of a necessity to keep a healthy mind as well as a healthy body.

7. Talk about your view of pressure and why there is so much of it in our life.

   Pressure comes from every aspect of our life. We take responsibilities of the

笔记区

society and the family. We seek jobs in an increasingly shrinking job market. We expect a better life so we press ourselves to work harder than ever. For many young people, pressure also comes from relationships. They need to make a relationship last longer, and sometimes they get hurt. They try to perfect themselves in front of the opposite sex.

8. People always try to be more successful than their friends. Is it one of the many causes of pressure?

Definitely. This is called peer pressure. People compare themselves with their friends because they don't want to be the weaker one. It is understandable that everyone wants to be important in life. They feel threatened when they are surpassed by their peers.

9. In what way do you think pressure will develop in the future? How are we going to solve it?

We will face new pressures in the future. As new technologies come out, there must be a group of people feeling anxious. They are afraid that they can not keep pace with modern technologies. In the job market, more and more work originally done by people will be taken by machines, so it is more difficult for people to find a satisfying job. What we can do is to arm ourselves with knowledge and do not panic. And believe we can find new ways to relax and make life easier.

10. What kind of pressure will people come across when they go abroad?

People are under pressure when they are in a new environment when there are no friends, no family members to turn to. Pressures also come from language barriers, culture shock, totally different life styles and values. They feel panic because they suddenly lose their identity in a new social background.

11. Who chat more online, men or women?

Generally, men like to play online games and search new information when surfing on-line, while women prefer to chat in an online chat room because women like to talk. Women like to imagine romantic things which might not exist. But since cyber love is not new to us nowadays, I think more and more men and women participate in online chatting.

25. *Describe a newspaper or magazine you like to read.*

You should say:

what it is

when and how often you read it

which section you like most

and explain why you prefer this newspaper/magazine to others.

The newspaper that I like to read is *21st Century*. Under the supervision of *China Daily*, it is an English newspaper which greatly benefits English learners.

笔 记 区

I began to subscribe to this weekly newspaper when I was in high school, and I kept reading it for several years. It was a happy moment for me every week I received it. Since it is designed for young people, mainly students, it is a very colourful newspaper.

The newspaper is divided into several sections. Apart from sections such as news, sports, business and science, it also includes space for a whole page of the entertainment section which is about the latest fashion, campus life, forum, and language lab. The entertainment and the science sections are my favourite. The entertainment part provides us pictures and brief essays about western super stars. The science section introduces very cute new electronic inventions and other inventions that are close to our daily life.

I prefer this newspaper because it combines language learning and the timeliness of news perfectly. It is more like a newspaper specifically made for our generation. The information it provides is just what we are interested in. Fashion, models, movie stars, this newspaper seems built for a throbbing youthful world.

Further questions

1. Do you often read newspapers or magazines? Which sections do you like best?

   For me, reading newspapers or magazines is a daily necessity. I need to know what is happening around the world. I like sections talking about fashion, life style and travelling. I am also interested in new breakthroughs in science.

2. Have you ever done something for your favourite newspaper or magazine?

   I think if you buy a magazine, you read it and you introduce new information it conveys to people around you, then you have already done something very important for the magazine.

3. What are the differences between newspapers and magazines? What are their advantages and disadvantages respectively?

   Newspapers are much stricter than magazines on the aspect of timeliness of the information they provide. That is why most newspapers are dailies, while magazines are usually weeklies and monthlies. The second difference is that reports in newspapers should be comprehensive but brief, and the information should be precise and views objective. Readers get a great deal of information by reading newspapers. Magazines usually focus on one aspect of life and go deep into it. Readers get pretty much information on one issue. And newspapers are usually cheaper than magazines.

4. Which group of people prefers reading newspapers? Why are they willing to buy newspapers?

   Elderly people who are not used to other access of information such as Internet or TV prefer reading newspapers. People who have flexible work places may prefer

笔记区

newspapers because it is more convenient.

Some people are willing to buy newspapers because they are cheap but they provide comprehensive information.

5. What are the differences between newspaper reporters and magazine reporters?

Newspaper reporters work on a flexible but busy schedule. They need to get the first-hand news, so they are the witnesses of many great events. They provide facts but little personal opinions. They have to be really quick in piecing together information. Magazine reporters pay more attention to the significance of a certain event but not the timeliness. They are allowed to work out an article during a relatively long time span, but they have to dig deep into an event. Magazine reporters only need to focus on one topic. For example, a reporter for a travelling magazine only needs to write things on this aspect.

6. How to be a good journalist?

The most important quality of a journalist is to be highly professional. That means a good journalist should be objective and not be influenced by his or her own opinion. A good journalist is supposed to be honest and sensitive to new information.

7. Do news agencies have the right to report everything? Can they criticize the government? Do they need to be restricted?

They can report everything as long as things reported are the truth. Newspapers are not only tools to provide information but also tools to promote social equity and reveal the dark side of society.

They can criticize the government if there is something for the government to improve. But they have to be restricted because we can not make sure everyone in this profession performs legally. It is people in this profession that should be restricted but not the news industry.

8. Do you think that newspapers will lose many of their readers in the future? Why?

Newspapers will lose some of their readers as more and more people realize the efficiency and convenience of getting information from the Internet. Besides, the popularization of broad band will further distinguish the advantage of the Internet. Although there are many people sticking to the traditional way of getting information and the newspapers are making efforts to be more attractive, the Internet will snatch many readers from newspapers.

9. Will Internet take the place of newspapers and magazines?

No, never. The development of the Internet may have a great impact on newspapers and magazines, but it will not take the place of them. The Internet provides more efficient and abundant access to information, but many people do

笔记区

not trust what is posted on line. And people are curious but alert about this virtual cyberspace. In some ways, newspapers and magazines are more convenient than the Internet. For example, people read newspapers or magazines when using public transport on their way to work, but it is impossible to surf on line when people are in a hurry. Besides, reading newspapers and magazines is a more healthy and natural way.

26. *Describe a film.*

You should say:

the name of the film

when and where you saw it

what the story is about

whether it is a happy story or a sad one

and explain why you like it.

The film I would like to introduce to you is known to a lot of people I suppose. It is an American film called *TITANIC*.

I've seen it at least four times and the first time I saw it was in high school, and that was the year 1999. I saw it at home on a rented DVD because that's much cheaper.

The film tells a love story on the famous giant ship TITANIC, which unfortunately sank on her virgin voyage. The main characters in the story are Jack and Rose. Rose is a daughter of a deceased English patrician. However, the harsh fact is that her father does not leave any asset for her and her mother to survive on. The only thing she inherits from her father is the noble status. To survive, she was engaged to an American business man who she didn't like. Then on the TITANIC, Rose meets Jack and they fall in love. But in the end, only Rose survives the accident.

I regard this film a very delicately made tragedy. I like it because the director created a very good stage, the TITANIC, as the background of this bitter story. Through the mischance of the people on the ship, I gain deeper insights into the misfortune of Jack and Rose. Under the tragic atmosphere set by the director, the story becomes moving, touching, and particularly impressive.

Further questions

1. Which film has impressed you most so far?

Last summer, I saw a very excellent American film called *Cold Mountain*. The story is originally written by Charles Frazier, and is shot by Director Anthony Mingeller. It is a touching one telling how a Confederate soldier makes his way back to his hometown, Cold Mountain, to find his love during the Civil War. The

笔记区

film has a very thought-provoking plot and my insight into the story is that wars change people in a way we can hardly imagine. Until now I can still feel the shock the story has brought to me, so I find this film the most impressive one so far.

2. What kind of film do you like?

I like science fiction. As a young man, I'm crazy about science fiction. From a very early age I began to read science fiction novels, therefore it's not a surprise that science fiction films usually attract my attention. These films attract me not only because of their exciting plots, but also for their amazing special visual and audio effects. *Star Wars, Artificial Intelligence, Jurassic Park*, etc., all of these are my favourite films.

3. What kind of film do you think is more popular in China?

Well, I'm a big fan of films and usually read reports about them. It appears to me that in China, comic films usually have a better performance in the box office. For instance, works from Feng Xiaogang, a comic director, usually gains ground among audiences of different age groups. I'm not going further to analyze the culture behind this fact, but I guess this is mainly because of how average Chinese identify the aims of films—to entertain ourselves. Probably this is also the same in foreign countries.

4. What's the difference between children's tastes and adult's in films?

I think when choosing a film to see, young people may usually pay more attention to the visual effect attractiveness, while adults will place more value on the content of the film. Another difference is that youngsters, because they are more exposed to western culture, tend to like western movies, while at the same time, adults often like watching Chinese films. A very good example is that Hollywood films are very popular among the youth, and Chinese films often have a larger adult market.

5. Do you prefer to see a film at home or in a cinema?

Well, as for me, two factors will influence me on choosing whether to see a film at home or in a cinema. Firstly, I often choose to see a film in a cinema when it requires visual and audio effects. This is particularly true for high-tech films. As for literary films, I often watch them at home, simply because it's a fine place for quiet meditation and appreciation. Another important factor preventing me from going to the cinema too often is the expensive price. To me, a student whose monthly budget is rather tight, seeing a film in a cinema is still a luxury which can't be enjoyed too often.

6. Is cinema important in China?

I think yes. It is the fact that the advent of the DVD has to a great extent reshaped people's habit of enjoying films and it has created huge losses for cinemas. However, cinemas in China still have a large consumers' market, and they play irreplaceable roles in the film industry. Actually, accompanied by the improved

笔记区

living standard, more and more Chinese begin seeing films in a cinema, and the growth of the audience remains steady. Cinemas are now important in China, and I believe their importance will continue to increase in the future.

7. What's your opinion on film stars?

Well, I like seeing films but unfortunately I'm not a fan of film stars. It is usually the gist of the theatrical trailer rather than the particular film star whom I favour that attracts me to go to the cinema. After all, unlike other people, what I enjoy is the character in the film not the person who plays the role. However, I think the influence of the artists can never be overlooked, because they can be very influential on the results at the box office, which is considered highly important for the film makers.

8. What's the difference between Chinese stars and international stars? Which are more popular?

In my opinion, the difference between Chinese stars and international stars is not on themselves but on their audience. Empirically speaking, Chinese stars have a larger market here in China and they have a diversified audience body, while for foreign stars, they have less audience and the young people account for a significant portion of their audience body. Cultural difference and the language barrier I think are the two major causes for this phenomenon.

9. Who do you think is the most famous foreign star in China? Why?

Well, it's really hard to say who is the most famous foreign star here in China. Personally, I favour the Academy Award winner Nicole Kidman. I value her because she's good at body language and she can skillfully interpret the different roles she plays. About other people's favourite, I think it has a lot to do with the audience's age and film choice. Since people have preferences over different kinds of foreign films and have limited access to them, it is reasonable that for the Chinese audience, there is no one foreign star that can be singled out as the most famous.

10. Do you see any changes in today's actors or actresses?

Well, it's hard to say. Certainly, I can see clear distinctions between today's artists and the artists of the past decades. They are different in the styles of acting. Seeing the films shot 20 years ago, it is quite easy to find that the Chinese actors or actresses were performing in quite an exaggerating way than people are doing today. Today's artists are much more natural both in their body language and delivery of lines. As for me, I appreciate the later style, and I believe it fits the taste of the majority of today's audience.

11. What is the most important condition for an actor or actress to succeed?

In my opinion, the most important quality to guarantee the success of an actor or an actress is the talent in acting. There are different vocations. Some vocations merely require people work hard to succeed, while some other vocations, at the

笔 记 区

same time, also expect people to have talent in doing the job, and I think acting is the kind of work that falls into this category. I find acting a very special vocation because without born talent, I wouldn't expect the success of an actor nor an actress no matter how hard he or she tries. This may sound strange, but it's really how I feel.

12. What's your view on the violence in films? Why is there so much violence in them?

To tell the truth, though I'm fully aware of the negative impact caused by the violence in films, I'm neutral with this social phenomenon. Yes, it's true that violence in films has indirectly led to lots of social violence, but I don't think films are to be blamed for. Rather, the people who are involved in social violence should be criticized for their incapacity to discern right and wrong. About why there is much violence in films, I think it's because films are shot to satisfy people's need to recreate, and many people do have a certain interest in watching violence, so in order to gain business profit, I feel it is justified for filmmakers to convey violent shots in the motion pictures.

27. *Describe a TV programme.*

You should say:

what the name of the programme is

when you watched it

what it talked about

and explain why you like this programme.

Artist is an evening talk show well-known among Chinese people.

I watched this programme for the first time about two years ago. By that time, this programme had been on TV for one year and was very famous already. Every Friday evening at nine fifteen, you can definitely find me sitting in front of the television, waiting for the programme to begin. But now that I live on campus and without a television in the dormitory, it is a pity that I cannot watch it on Fridays any more.

In each episode, the programme invites one artist or two to share with the audience their career and life experiences. They can be singers and dancers, photographers and directors, actors and actresses, and so on. *Artist* is a stage. It offers us a full depiction of the stars. It tells the audience the stories that are behind the success of the famous figures—the hardships, the tears and the happy moments as well.

This programme makes us feel that those stars are ordinary people like each one of us. They, too, have experienced hard times. They, too, have made mistakes and suffered from them and then drawn lessons from them. Thus, it shortens the distance

笔 记 区

between the audience and the stars. They look more like real people. That is the most important reason why I like it so much.

Further questions

1. What are the differences of the night programme? And is there any difference between the past and the present?

   I think people tend to be more emotional and sentimental at night. So the night programmes appeal more to their emotions. They are inclined to be slow-paced and quiet. Generally speaking, there are fewer noisy programmes, such shows with lots of action or concerts.

   As the economy develops and China becomes more open to the rest of the world, the night programmes are improving as well, in terms of variety and quality. In the past, there were fewer night programmes and they did not last long into the night. At present, there are more and more night programmes being put on television to enrich people's lives, especially people who are inclined to sleep late.

2. What influence do TV programmes have on children and older people?

   For children, I think TV programmes definitely have great influence on them. As children, they have limited access to the society. The major means for them to get to know the world is through TV programmes, especially the programmes designed for children. They have great influence on children in terms of arousing their interests, shaping their characters and helping them to know more about the society.

   For older people, the TV programmes first serve as a kind of company, especially for those who live alone. They always keep the television on, feeling as if someone is talking to them and they do not feel lonely. Secondly, the programmes keep them in touch with the world and they will not feel left out by the society.

3. How are TV programmes developing in China?

   They are developing very fast in terms of variety and quality. They are developing with the nation's rise in the world. Many programmes made in foreign countries are coming in while those produced in China are going out. Now we can even watch English programmes both produced in China and exported from foreign countries.

4. What is the current situation of modern cinema in China?

   I'm not optimistic about the situation of modern cinema in China, because more people prefer to watch DVDs at home alone or with friends. Although they offer facilities of high quality, many cinemas are reported losing money. The situation is that the DVD industry is flourishing and there are too many pirate DVDs that the cinema seems to be unable to compete with them.

5. What do you think of the situation that many people watch DVDs instead of

笔记区

going to the cinema?

I think the situation is understandable. Personally speaking, I prefer watching DVDs at home to going to the cinema. Firstly, I can watch DVDs alone or with my friends instead of sitting in a cinema where I cannot speak loudly and cannot move as I like. Secondly, I can pause in the middle when I have to answer the phone or go to the bathroom without missing any part of the film. And I can rewind or repeat some parts which I am interested in to see more closely and clearly.

28. *Describe an advertisement that you have seen and that interested you.*

You should say:

when and where you saw it

what it was about

what you felt about it

and explain why you found the advertisement particularly interesting.

I want to talk about an advertisement for a shampoo from Clairol.

It goes like this: "Do you want to know how in fact Sleeping Beauty woke up?" says a sexy male voice. Then Sleeping Beauty comes into sight. She is lying in her bed, sleeping soundly. Suddenly she smells something, and then wakes up and goes directly towards a pond with an open bottle of Clairol shampoo near it. She is obviously fascinated by the fragrance when she uses the shampoo to wash her hair. The next scene is of the Prince coming and Sleeping Beauty is back in her bed with her beautiful and fragrant blond hair down to the shoulders. This is the end of the advertisement and we can imagine that the Prince will kiss Sleeping Beauty to wake her up and they will live happily ever after. But we know that what actually wakes her up is not the kiss but the shampoo.

I feel this advertisement is very creative and original. It shows the prominent feature of the shampoo—fragrance to good effect. It rewrites a very famous fairy tale and gives it a new meaning. I like the hair of Sleeping Beauty in particular, for it is very smooth and attractive after the washing. And I think it is very successful because many of my friends bought this shampoo because of the advertisement.

Further questions

1. How does advertisement influence people?

   On one hand, it offers a lot of information about a certain product or brand. It leads the trend and direction of purchase. Besides, good advertisements can also be considered as a form of art. On the other hand, there are some fake advertisements. Those are the advertisements which contain false information. In other words, they lie in the advertisements. When people buy things because of

笔记区

the false advertisements and then realize they have been cheated, they may lose confidence in other products. If this kind of thing continues to happen, it would cause a vicious circle. And another thing, some advertisements involve sex or violence which may have a bad effect on children.

2. What do you think advertisements should specifically pay attention to?

Honesty is the best policy and it should be the first element taken into consideration in the advertising business. They should not exaggerate or lie about the effect of the product in the advertisement. And it should consider the influence the advertisement has on children. They should eliminate those scenes which are not suitable for children to watch.

3. Do advertisements bring great influence to the children and their parents? Why?

Yes. Advertisements supply children and their parents with information and keeps them in touch with the latest trends and fashion. But some scenes in the advertisements are not suitable for children to watch, such as the ones involving sex or violence. These kinds of advertisements certainly have a bad influence on children. Sometimes children want to buy a certain product after watching its advertisement and their parents have to buy it. This may lead to children getting the bad habit of purchasing and wasting money. They may think that they can get whatever they like. But if their parents do not buy them the thing that they like, it may cause tension between the two generations.

4. Why are many Chinese people willing to pay a lot for brandname products?

First of all, the living condition is getting better. People are richer than before and able to pay for the expensive brandname products. Secondly, brandname products are of high quality and offer good after-sale service. To some extent, brandname products show their status. It makes them feel good to show off in front of people.

29. *Describe a useful website you have visited.*

You should say:

what the website was

how you found the address for this website

what the website contained

and explain why it was useful to you.

Well, the first website that comes to my mind is Goggle, one of the most famous search engines in the world.

It's the first website I've ever known and also the most frequently visited. I got its address because it was contained in my computer, from this you can see how influential it is. It is just like the root of the tree for the global Internet, starting from

笔 记 区

here you can reach to all kinds of information. Open it, the front page is simple, well-designed and informative, and then fill in the blank with what you need. In a few seconds, the whole world is on your computer screen.

It's useful to me in the beginning because it's not complicated, like an ATM machine. It's useful to me now because, um, it's like a bus with no conductor, you can go anywhere and won't lose your way home. For example, when you want to find some materials for your thesis, you can go to Google because it's more brief and efficient than libraries. There are also flaws about Google—sometimes the search result is not accurate enough and some of them are even unavailable. Basically Google is a miracle.

Further questions

1. What effect has the Internet had on the way people generally communicate with each other?

   Quite a lot, I think. For example, I'm now far away from my parents, but they can see me and talk to me simultaneously on MSN or Skype, and we do not feel that far away geographically anymore. Compared to the telegraph years, it's a shocking change already.

2. Why do you think the Internet is being used more and more for communications?

   Once again take myself for example. Remember when people are expecting a very important letter, they have to wait for days or even months? But now through Internet, E-mail, or even QQ, it's a matter of seconds. And we have 6 girls in our dorm, and there are 5 lap-tops! From this number you can clearly see why we all think the Internet is being used more and more for communications.

3. How reliable do you think information from the Internet is? Why? What about the news on the Internet?

   Whether the information is trustworthy I think should be judged by different situations. Because people hide their identities on the Internet and speak freely for they are not supposed to be responsible for his or her remarks. About news I have not considered it much, actually all forms of media have false information, not only the Internet. But I think choosing a big website with credit would reduce the possibility of getting wrong news information.

4. Why do you think some people use the Internet for shopping? Why doesn't everyone use it in this way?

   Well, the reason is simple. It's so convenient, you know, you can do shopping anywhere at any time, in your office and at home. But still, many people do shopping not simply because they are running out of daily necessities or clothes. For them, shopping is great fun. That's why there are still a number of people who are not keen on Internet shopping.

笔 记 区

5. What kinds of things are easy to buy or see online? Can you give some examples?

I suppose things which are rarely seen on the market or only can be bought in foreign countries, or digital products. For example, my friend bought a Barbie which has been limitedly produced on the Internet from the U.S. at a sky-high price, and she cried when she received the Barbie for she dreamed about it for so long.

6. Do you think shopping on the Internet will be more or less popular in the future? Why?

Definitely it will be more prosperous in the future. For its priorities are clear to be seen: efficiency, quickness and convenience. And as the credit system is growing gradually here in China, we can foresee that Internet will be more popular in the future.

30. *Describe your favourite photo.*

You should say:

what it is about

when and where you took it

who took it for you

and why it is important to you.

OK, I'm going to tell you something about a photo I like very much. The photo was taken on my commencement almost ten years ago. In that year we graduated from high school and as part of the commencement ceremony, all the graduates of Class 1990, as well as the teachers who had ever taught us during the 6 years, gathered in front of the admin building and had this photo taken.

Of course, the guy who took the photo was a professional photographer. It was no easy task to put 300 people in one photo. So there was quite a lot of shouting and arguing and laughing. Everyone was cheerful and looking forward to the days to come.

A few days later, everyone got the picture. I framed it and nailed it to the wall in my bedroom. The reason why it is important to me is that it always reminds me of my fellow classmates, with whom I spent one of the best parts of my life. Though we don't contact each other as often as we used to, we still think of each other. You know, we threw a party during the Spring Festival and most of the Class 1990 showed up. It was really a happy occasion and we decided to have a photo taken again this year, which was the 10th anniversary of the commencement. I can't wait to see it!

笔 记 区

Further questions

1. What role do photos play in your life?

   Oh, my photos are part of my life. A photo album is like a record of one's life experiences, isn't it? It can be a collection of your best memories, like the places you've been to, the people you love, and the happy occasions you have.

2. What do you think of the role of photos in the mass media?

   Honestly, I can't imagine a newspaper without photos or other graphic illustrations. Photos in the mass media sometimes can say more than words or comments.

3. Why do people take photos?

   Generally speaking, people take photos because they want to remember that occasion. Photos can be a permanent record of our life experiences.

4. Where do people often take photos?

   If you like to take photos, you will do it anywhere anytime. But mostly, people take photos when they are visiting some historical sites or scenic places.

5. When do people often take photos?

   People take photos on happy or important occasions, like a graduation ceremony, birthday parties, wedding receptions, or the birth of their children.

31. *Describe an exhibition (museum) you attended.*
You should say:
when you saw it
where it was
and what you saw in the exhibition.

I'm going to talk about the "Spirit of Yimeng Mountain", an exhibition I saw in summer last year. It was one of the three exhibitions to mark the 60th anniversary of the War of Resistance against Japanese Aggression. The exhibit was run at the National Museum of China.

The show consisted of three parts, namely, Red Earth, Respectable People and Great Achievements.

Yimeng Mountain areas, now mostly Linyi in southeast Shandong, was the political, military and cultural centre of the province during the war. More than half of the local population joined the force, over one million supported the military troops, and many gave their lives in the fighting.

A variety of showpieces including photographs, videos and sculptures were also on display.

I think what I learned from it is a love of peace. The exhibit tells us what humanity suffers during war times. People die and millions lose their homes. We're not afraid of wars, of course. When we have to fight, we will fight. But we do hope to

笔 记 区

make war a history. And I think that's part of the reason why this exhibition was run.

Further questions

1. What do you think are the functions of museums?

   The main roles of museums are to preserve the past, to educate, and to broaden horizons. One of the museum's primary roles is to offer life-long opportunities for people of all ages to learn about themselves, each other, and their environment through the museum's collections.

2. What should the government do to attract more people to visit museums?

   Well, there's a lot the government can do. For example, cut ticket prices, give free tickets to students and hold special shows. Also, the government could increase investment and strengthen publicity by making more advertisements on TV or in newspapers.

32. *Describe your favourite (wild) animal.*

You should say:

what it is

how you know about it

what it is like

and explain why you like it.

My favourite animals are dogs. They are said to be one of the brainiest animals in the world. They can help people in many ways. They can lead the blind, sniff out drugs and even rescue accident victims. Helpful as they are, most of the dogs are not very big. Oftentimes, dogs I see stand no more than half a metre and weigh no more than 200 pounds. I like dogs very much. They can usually read the emotions of their owners. They can tell whether their owners are happy or upset just by judging from the owners' voice. In addition, dogs are very loyal to their owners. Stories abound in which dogs saved their owners at the cost of their own. Indeed, they are humans' pals. I love them.

Further questions

1. Do you have a pet? What is your point of view on raising pets? Can you talk about its advantages and disadvantages?

   Yes, I have raised a dog for three years. Her name is Huanhuan. As far as I am concerned, raising pets is usually a delightful experience but it may also bring some troubles. On one hand, raising a pet gives people a chance to learn how to love and be loved by another creature. In addition, a pet can always keep its owner companied so that the owner will not feel lonely. On the other hand, however,

笔 记 区

raising pets can give rise to several problems. For example, dog waste or cat waste on the street of a community is neither pleasant to the eye nor good to the environment. Plus, too many barks or miaows can produce another source of noise pollution.

2. What do Chinese think about raising pets?

In my opinion, most Chinese love to raise pets. As a nation that has a history of over 5,000 years, the Chinese people cherish the relationship between humans and nature. We always seek to strike a balance between nature and human society. Raising pets has helped us find that point at which we can live peacefully and happily together with animals.

3. Are there any safari parks in China?

I think so. In order to protect animal rights, China has set up a number of nature reserves in which animals can move freely and enjoy 100 percent freedom in whatever aspect. By doing so, wild animals can get back to the world under the rule of the jungle, restore their nature and become true animals rather than slaves or clowns in their owners' lives.

4. In your opinion, what improvements should be made to zoos?

To my thinking, zoos need to be larger so that animals kept in zoos can be given greater space to live. Zoos need to improve the living conditions of the animals. A better and more balanced diet is needed to ensure the healthy growth of animals. Besides, a cleaner living place is also necessary.

33. *Describe a popular game that children play.*

You should say:

what it is

where you played it

how many people are needed

how to play it

and explain why you think it is interesting.

The game that comes to my mind is an old Chinese game called "The Eagle and the Chicks". It is great fun, and easy to play.

When I was a child I played this game very often. The game needs at least five kids to start, and the more kids participating, the more fun it is. One child will play the "eagle" and another child as the "mother hen". The rest of the kids will be the "chicks", lining up behind the hen, with both hands holding on to the clothes of the chick in front. In the game, the eagle tries to catch one of the chicks, who then takes his/her role as the eagle. The mother hen tries to protect her children with her arms stretched.

"The Eagle and the Chicks" enjoys great popularity among children in China. They definitely get great satisfaction in the excitement. In addition, they learn how to

笔 记 区

work as a team, which is an essential skill later in life.

Further questions

1. What is the difference between boys and girls in terms of playing games?
   I think that boys like to play games that require more physical strength whereas girls like to play games that require social skills. In general, the games they play more or less reflect the roles they are going to play when they grow up.
2. What is the difference between adults and kids in terms of playing games?
   Sometimes there is no difference! Some adults play games like crazy, while overall kids play games in order to learn. But we play games mostly for fun.
3. What is the difference between games played in the past and those played nowadays?
   Actually I don't see many differences. Football, basketball, pingpong have been with us for decades and remain the most popular sports games.
4. Can you give me more examples of different games?
   Oh sure. Hide-and-seek is a popular game among children. And playing-house, too, where children pretend to be adults and play the roles of father and mother. That's great fun!
5. What age do you think is the best time to play? Why?
   There's no "best" time. One is never too old to play.

34. *Describe a subject you have taken in school.*
You should say:
what it is
who taught it
what you learned from the subject
and explain why you like it.

I'd like to talk about my favourite subject, English. I have always been excellent in English since middle school. This is due to my first English teacher—my mother. By the time I studied in her class, she had taught English for 15 years. She was the course coordinator, responsible for syllabus design and young teacher training.

My mother used a very special kind of teaching method in the class. The whole class was divided into four groups, competing with each other. The group who answered the most questions correctly in the class would be given some prize at the end of the term. Most of the students prepared for the lessons very well in order to answer the questions correctly. We found it very exciting and tried to earn more points for the group.

I have learnt not only the English knowledge such as vocabulary, grammar, and pronunciation, but also communication skills and team spirit. You know I was one of

笔记区

the group leaders. So I needed to communicate with my group members so that we could cooperate well with each other and win the prize.

Further questions

1. What subject do you want to learn in school?

   My favourite subjects in middle school are English and history. I'm always curious about other cultures and what happened, and are happening on the other side of the world.

2. What subject can't you learn in school?

   I think in China children get a very strong education in academic subjects like maths, physics, English and so on. But they are not offered lessons that develop their social skills and life skills. I wish I could learn how to drive or how to cook in school.

3. What do you think of the teachers in the middle school?

   I like most of them because they are nice, patient, and conscientious about their job. But sometimes they are very rigid and strict with us.

4. Could you give some suggestions on child education?

   Well, the most important thing I think is to arouse the children's interests in learning rather than to force them to learn more than they can manage. In China, since school education is still quite exam-oriented, many students have concentrated too much on textbooks and rote learning, neglecting the physical and spiritual dimensions of personal development.

5. What are the benefits of self-teaching and being taught by teachers?

   I think both ways have their advantages and disadvantages. Self-teaching allows the students freedom to choose what they learn and the pace to learn at. You know how you can learn better, after all. But education isn't only about learning. It also provides the students with social experiences and develops their social skills. Teachers play a very important role in the process. They can help the students, guide them a little bit, and organize discussions... So maybe the best way is to combine them both.

四、事件题

35. *Describe an exciting trip / long-distance trip you made.*

You should say:

when you made the trip

where you went

how the trip was

and explain why it was exciting.

笔 记 区

Last summer I had a very nice holiday with my parents in Sanya, Hainan Province. It is a very famous coastal city in the southern part of China. The place is very beautiful!, and each year thousands of tourists spend their holidays there.

We spent four whole days in Sanya. We spent our time visiting tourist sites along the coastal area. The blue sky, navy sea, white beaches, my eyes are filled with beautiful landscapes. My parents and I also took the golden chance to swim and enjoyed the sunbathing on the comfortable beach. One more thing worth mentioning is that I also tried scuba diving there. It was so fascinating. I swam very close to the coral beds and beautiful fishes swam beside me elegantly. Never shall I forget such a unique experience. Well, of course, that did cost me a lot. Apart from seeing the sceneries, we also had many delicious sea foods like lobster, crab, oyster and so on. Even today, I can still clearly remember the feast I enjoyed in Sanya.

For four years, because my parents and I had always been busy about our own business, our family hasn't had a chance to spend such a nice holiday together. That's why this trip to Sanya has been a very exciting one for me. I'll always treasure this long-distance trip as my best memory.

Further questions

1. What is the vehicle that Chinese people often use when they travel?

   I think people usually choose the vehicle in accordance with the distance of their destinations. Coach, train, airplane, ships can all be possible choices for travellers. But mostly speaking, I think in China, people prefer to use the railway system when they travel. Particularly during the Spring Festival, there are always crowds at train stations. I guess this is because trains can offer a way to travel fast at a relatively low cost.

2. What do you think is the difference between individual and group travel?

   I think if people choose to travel alone, they can have a more flexible travel plan than group travellers. There is no holding to a strict time schedule and people can stay at a particular sight as long as they want. But for group travelling, I think it's advantageous in terms of cost. For group travellers, tickets, rooms and board are booked by the travel agent. In this way, people can save money for their trip and they'll have less concern about things besides travel.

3. What do you think are the pros and cons of travelling?

   I like travelling and I've been to many places both in China and in foreign countries. I think travel is a very good way to relax myself from the heavy pressure of working and studying. Moreover, it gives me chances to broaden my scope and to meet interesting people in different places. However, travel is usually time and strength consuming and sometimes it can be very expensive, so I think, definitely, it's not a good choice for everyone.

4. There are a lot of foreign visitors coming to China nowadays. What's your

笔 记 区

comment on that?

I think it's great that more and more foreign visitors are coming to China. I find two advantages of this phenomenon. One is that visiting China is a very good way for foreign friends to learn about the new China and our traditional values, because it is widely recognized that the best way to learn about a country and its culture is to actually visit the place. Further, when these tourists return to their home countries, they will be able to describe what they've seen in China to their friends, and I believe it is a good chance to publicize China on the world stage.

5. Why do many people travel abroad? What do you think are the advantages and disadvantages?

I travelled abroad once to the U.S.A and that was several years ago. I cherish this fantastic experience not only because I've got chances to see some of the world-famous tourist sites, but more importantly, the cross culture experience is interesting and it has actually helped me gain a better understanding about our own culture in reflection to foreign culture. I guess this is the major advantage of foreign travel as well as the reason why people are usually fancied by their travelling abroad. Of course, there is one very obvious disadvantage of travelling abroad. Most often, the expenses are too high for a majority of people to shoulder.

6. What's your comment on the prospect of China's tourism industry?

I expect there will be a prosperous future for China's tourism industry. So far, the tourism is not a major GDP contributor. However, during the last decade, resulting from an improved living standard and a switch of consuming pattern, more and more people begin to choose travel as a way of recreation, and the tourism industry in China has witnessed a significant growth. Now the industry still grows steadily under the current prosperous economic climate. I think if you take a look at the tourism market during the long vacation period you'll agree with me without any hesitation.

7. What kind of foreign people do you think choose to travel in China? Why they do so?

I suppose the foreign friends who choose to travel in China are those who fancy the Chinese culture. The culture I mean here is a broad term. There may be people who are interested in natural sceneries like the Three Gorges and Mt. Huang, while at the same time, there may also be people who are attracted by Chinese civilization, which is amongst the four origins of civilization. Different people have different expectations on their trips to China. Whatever the expectations are, I believe for those travellers, China is the place where their eastern dreams are.

8. Can you predict what kind of vehicle we'll have in the future?

Well, this question reminds me about a film I've recently seen—*Star Wars*

笔记区

Episode III. Besides the exciting plot of the film, one thing that strikes me most is the gorgeous predictions on the lifestyle in the future. It's great that in the film I've actually visualized the kind of vehicle I used to imagine that people will have in the future. As road congestions are becoming more and more severe than before, I do believe it's just a matter of time for us to have private air shuttles that can fly freely in the sky as convenient transport vehicles at our disposal.

9. How would your grandparents travel to other cities? By car or by some other means?

My grandparents live in a small town about 200 km away from my home. I should say, since they're growing older, they hardly ever go to other cities. My grandparents usually visit us during the summer and late winter. There's a highway link between the two cities, and it only takes about 4 hours to travel round trip, so it's fairly convenient. It's economical too, because the one-way fare only costs 50 Yuan. For these reasons, my grandparents often choose express shuttles as their travelling vehicle.

36. *Describe an enjoyable visit.*

You should say:

who visited you

what for

what you did

and explain how your friend felt, why.

On my 25th birthday I invited a lot of friends over to my home. The party was scheduled for 6 o'clock. On the morning of that day, I ordered a birthday cake from the baker's in my neighbourhood. Then I went shopping in a supermarket and bought many balloons, 25 lotus-shaped candles, vegetables such as cabbage, tomatoes, cheese, shrimp, bacon and salad dressing. You know, all the stuff needed to make a salad. On the afternoon of that day I decorated my sitting room with balloons and candles and then at around 5 o'clock I started to prepare dinner. When my friends entered my home at 6, their faces lit up immediately because of what they called "a romantic ambience". During that party I received many gifts. We sat around the table and talked of many beautiful memories from the past. We had a great time that night.

Further questions

1. Do you like people to visit you?

It depends. A visit to you when you are busy with your own business may be a headache. It makes matters even worse if you don't like the visitor. But it's a whole other story if a best friend of yours comes to see you and it happens that

笔记区

you are free.

2. Is there a difference between a visit from a family member and that from a friend?

   Yes, sure. Usually a visit from a family member lasts a bit longer than a friend's visit. But other than that, I cannot think of any other differences.

3. If a foreigner visits you, what will you do to make the guest feel at home?

   First of all, a friendly and warm welcome may make a guest feel at home. Food is also important. Maybe I'll try to prepare some food from his/her home country.

4. If a foreigner visits your country, what advice will you give him or her?

   That's easy. I can give them millions of pieces of advice. But the most important one is to be open-minded. I know some of the things you see, eat, or experience may look absolutely weird and exotic, but try them. You will be proud of yourself.

37. *Describe a project you finished with others.*

You should say:

with whom you finished this project

when it was

how you did it

and whether you received any benefits.

Even until this day I can still remember a project I was involved in when I was at college. I took part in a translation group because I wanted to improve both my English and Chinese. Once, we got a job from a government agency to translate a water supply manual from Chinese to English. It was a document of more than 100 pages. Then our group decided to do it together. We decided the number of steps we must go through and the person in charge. Then we distributed the task, translated our respective parts, exchanged our translations with each other, corrected the mistakes, unified the translation of the same English terms and connected our translations and gave them to the person in charge for final editing. During the whole process we spent a lot of time together translating and discussing. Sometimes we even had quarrels because of our different understandings of a word. Anyway we ironed out all the difficulties and finished the job as scheduled. To our surprise, we got a bonus later for the translation as the agency was really satisfied with our work.

Further questions

1. Is cooperation important?

   The importance of teamwork lies in the significant effect that it produces, especially when being properly applied and managed. It creates flexibility and coordination among members and enables them to use their talents and participate

笔记区

in making decisions.

It also provides a great deal of acceptance, understanding and physical interaction, which cannot be gained individually. That's why members rely on teamwork to get the feedback, attention and moral support which they constantly need. As a result, this leads to a great improvement in the quality of work produced, making the process more fun and less frustrating.

2. Do you like to work alone or with others?

I like to work with people, because I can share my ideas with others and get feedback. I don't think I'm independent enough to work alone. I get more motivated when working with my classmates.

3. What are the advantages and disadvantages of working in a team?

Working in a team brings both benefits and problems. The benefit is obvious—the more people there are, the more ideas. But the biggest problem is that sometimes it takes ages to reach an agreement, especially when there isn't a strong leadership.

4. Should teamwork be encouraged in school? How?

Well, I think so. Schools in the first place are places where students learn the essential skills they need later in their lives. As to how to encourage teamwork, I think the teachers could include projects as part of student assessment. Homework could be assigned in the form of mini-projects that involves groups of students rather than an individual student.

38. *Describe one thing you find interesting about cultural difference.*

You should say:

what it is

how you learned about this cultural difference

and explain why you think it's interesting.

I've been abroad in my secondary school for a period of time, and in my current college, which is affiliated to the China Foreign Ministry, I also have plenty of chances to get in touch with foreign people. They are either worldly renowned scholars or diplomats from around the world; the Arabian world, the European countries, North and Latin America, and Africa... Foreign culture is then becoming a very vague term. The more people I meet, the harder it is to generalize. It's like asking a foreigner who's spent years in China what Chinese culture is. But I can still talk about a most recent case that happened around me though it's not interesting. One of my classmates failed a course because he's got a technical problem identified as plagiarism. The professor is from Yale. I mention this because I discovered that though Chinese teachers don't allow plagiarism, they don't put emphasis on not doing it. None of my Chinese teachers has ever brought our attention to this issue but we are

笔记区

always warned in the first classes given by my 12 foreign teachers since I've entered the college, that plagiarism is seriously banned and we are given detailed training on how to make quotations and bibliography. Though the situation in China is improving, it is still far from enough. I regard this a difference in the degree of respect to people's intellectual property. Plagiarizers are called intellectual thieves among my foreign professors but we don't have that serious of wording in Chinese. That's now what I see about cultural difference, and it's also an issue we should pay special attention to.

Further questions

1. Do you think it is necessary to learn the foreign culture when learning English?

   It depends on the expectations of the learner. For most people, English is just considered a tool necessary for their work. They learn English because they need to read the foreign information on their business for reference. For example, an engineer learns English to understand the latest information in his area. Therefore, background knowledge about English culture isn't strongly desired. However, for people who have higher expectations on their English proficiency, foreign culture is a vital element in knowledge storage. After all, language and culture are not two solely independent concepts. Anyway, learning foreign culture is highly appreciated and can very positively broaden one's scope, not merely within the area of language learning.

2. Do you think that foreign languages are easier to learn if you have interest in their culture?

   Yes, I think so, but I think they are easier to learn if the learners have a talent in language learning. I weigh this factor more than interest. The question is how people develop interest in an area. People are not born with interests in certain fields, but people are born with special talents. This has been proved scientific. Many language learners don't work hard but can still command beautiful language. That is because they are linguistically talented. I think that people have interest in the fields they are good at, not that they perform better because they have the interest. My thought is that I'm interested in English because I'm capable of doing it. Therefore, I think talent, particularly in language studies is more important than interest.

3. Is it necessary for people to go abroad to study English?

   It depends. People learn English for various kinds of reasons. For many of them, English is not that useful considering the nature of their work, but under the current inappropriate system, it is a necessary skill in many posts in order to get a promotion. I think for them, there's no need to spend time and money to learn a foreign language overseas, because what they need is to pass a required exam.

笔 记 区

Further, many people simply cannot afford the expensive price. However, for people who need to have further analysis in English literature and linguistic studies, an oversea studying experience is undoubtedly very necessary.

4. How do you think living in a foreign country can help you understand more about your own culture?

   It helps a lot. We have a term called "culture clash". It is like when you lose something you begin to appreciate its existence. Only when placing oneself in a different culture can one feel the existence of traditional values in his/her home country. Culture is intangible, and during most of the time, it can't be seen but can only be experienced. I've been to the States once, and it wasn't until then when I began to have realistic ideas about what cultural difference is. I guess that's why cultural exchanges are highly encouraged.

39. *Describe an important change in your life.*
You should say:
what it is
what the effect on you is
how you feel about it
and explain why it is important.

Actually, that sounds kind of unusual but one of the turning points in my life was when I got my first bicycle.

I remember it was a present my father gave me on my seventh birthday. It was a brand new bicycle. You know, back in the 1980s, having a bicycle was really something, especially for a boy of only seven.

That was a very important day for me. For the first time, I could go out on my own and go as far as I wanted to. I used to polish the bicycle everyday and take really good care of it. Of course, that only lasted a few months, and then I lost interest in it.

I think the reason that it was an important change for me is that for the first time in my life, I realized what a fantastic thing it was to be free, and to go anywhere with your free will. That was the beginning of a lifelong craving for travelling. By the time I graduated from university, I had almost been to most of the major cities in China. And now I'm thinking of the world outside China. Of course, as a return for his kindness, I will buy my father a brand new car on his 60th birthday.

Further questions

1. What changes are you going to make in the future?

   I don't know. But the immediate one is that I will go and study in the U.K. I believe it is going to be another important change in my life.

笔记区

2. What do you think are the main changes over the past 20 years in China?

   Well, that's a tough question. I think there are drastic changes in China in the last 20 years, in economic terms and in social terms. But the one I feel the strongest about is that the living standard is rising dramatically.

3. Are there any new changes that are taking place right now?

   China is a dynamic and ever-changing country. There are always new things and new ideas coming out. But the one that comes to my mind first is a heightened awareness in environmental protection. Both the government and the citizens are becoming increasingly concerned with the world we live in.

40. *Describe a wedding that you attended.*

You should say:

when it was

who got married

what happened at the wedding

and explain how you felt about it.

OK, I'm going to talk about my own wedding. My wife and I got married in late September, in Xi'an, my hometown. I remember it was very cold. We held the reception 2 months later in Beijing, my wife's hometown.

We had quite a large reception, about 200 guests, I believe. My wife wore a traditional Chinese Qi Pao, but I wore a modern business suit.

We had a lavish dinner, consisting of different dishes from various provinces. Of course, there were the formal speeches, the exchanging of wedding rings, and so on. Afterwards most of the guests indulged themselves in the wedding feast. Quite a number of my friends and I got drunk. My wife was so angry but she was OK the next day though.

Also we took a lot of photos and we even video-taped the whole thing. My wife and I watched the video-tape again and again. We believe that was the happiest moment in our lives.

Further questions

1. What's the difference between Chinese weddings and western weddings?

   I've never been to a western wedding reception so I'm not sure of the differences. But there are some differences which you can tell from common sense. In China the wedding is held either at home or in a grand hotel, while a western wedding is most likely to be held in a church. There's one more difference, which I'm not very sure about. My friends told me that in English-speaking countries, the brides often dress in white, which stands for purity. But in China, red is the colour for such happy occasions.

笔记区

2. What's the difference between weddings in the past and now?

I think the weddings have changed a lot over time. When I was a child, the weddings were mostly held at home and the bride was carried in a sedan chair. But now the receptions are usually held in a big hotel and the bride is picked up at her home by a limo.

3. What kind of people will be invited to the wedding?

The friends and relatives of the bride and the groom will be invited.

4. What wedding gifts do they bring?

Well, the wedding gift is almost the same —a red envelope with money in it.

笔 记 区

III. Part 3 按题型汇总的题目

一、Opinions on Social Issues 社会问题及观点

1. *What is your opinion of the one-child policy?*
   I think the one-child policy is reasonable. I think that China needs to control its population right now. How else can we make China strong and provide enough food and education for all the people? Perhaps in the future when our country is more developed, we can allow people to have more children. But for now, the government's policy on family planning is necessary.

2. *Do you think smoking is a problem that needs special attention?*
   That's an interesting question. I think it does. A lot of people in China aren't aware of the health consequences of smoking. They just smoke because it's socially acceptable to do so. If more people knew they could get cancer from smoking, they'd probably stop, or at least smoke less. I know that the tobacco industry is a big business, and if we tried to get rid of smoking, we'd also be getting rid of jobs, but at the very least, people should be told about the potential dangers of smoking. That way they can make an informed choice about whether to smoke or not.

3. *Do you think China's membership in the WTO will benefit China?*
   Well, it's a big topic and many people are thinking about it. I'm quite sure it'll benefit China and other WTO members as well. The common Chinese consumers, will benefit most from it because prices of imported products will go down. Also, the quality and after-sales services of national products will be improved. I guess the main danger we have to face is the new competition to our national industries but I think they're up to the challenge.

4. *What do you think of the unemployment problem in China?*
   I believe the problem is getting more and more serious now. China's a country with a large population and there has always been more labour than required. It was not a big problem in the past under the planned economic system, but now enterprises can not afford the burden of a surplus labour force and many workers

笔记区

in state owned enterprises are being laid off. Something must be done about it before more serious problems arise.

5. *What do you think is the most serious social problem in China?*
That's hard to say, but I'd guess it's overpopulation, even though we've made a lot of progress. Although China has a strict family-planning policy with one family having only one child, the population is already over 1.3 billion and it's still growing. It not only causes a shortage of food and shelter but also it causes a lot of other problems like unemployment and crime. We can be flexible with this policy, but I think, in general, we need to enforce this policy quite strictly.

6. *What do you think about the environmental problems in China?*
The environment is becoming a more and more serious problem. Well, as far as I'm concerned, I think these problems are solvable if we work together. I also think that people should be more vocal to press for change and I think that people should try to set good examples. The process is beginning to occur but the problem is that we have only scratched the surface of the problem. If we don't pay more attention to it then we will have an unbearable quality of life.

7. *What do you think of using science in food production?*
I guess it's dangerous. We need natural crops to regenerate the soil and when we start playing around with nature we may run into trouble. I think we are getting to a state where we will be dependent totally on our unnatural food processes, and when we have no ability to even use artificial ways to produce food then we will face starvation.

8. *What do you think of advertising in sports and entertainment events?*
I think there are two sides to this issue. On one hand, people say that to have sports you must allow them to find ways to make money. After all, we can't have every athlete only sponsored by the government. On the other hand, when we let advertisements into sports we are allowing big companies to control events.

9. *What do you think of violence on TV and in films?*
I'm very concerned about the violence on TV and in films. It's very bad now and I think it affects the way people think. Children get more aggressive and they use these characters as models. I think the worst thing it teaches people is that justice can only come by force. In that case, how can we trust the processes of negotiation and diplomacy?

10. *What do you think of the problem of piracy?*
I think it's a serious problem that we'd better start addressing because a lot of companies are hurt by it and it affects our foreign investment. I still see a lot of it going on in the streets and sometimes they can get quite pushy. I mean if I were involved in the clothing industry or music or film industry I wouldn't want to sell

笔记区

my things in a place where the risk of having my stuff copied is too high. So we'd better tackle this problem before we get countries complaining about us to the WTO.

11. *What do you think of media in your home country?*

I suppose it needs more improvements. It needs to have more services and start getting more specialized because I know many people are bored with what they currently offer. Also, people would like to see more in-depth coverage of issues and more feedback from a wide section of society. Also, I know many people who think there should be more coverage of events that occur outside of China in the newspapers. Also, I think there should be more channels. For example, I've heard that in some cities in North America there are over a hundred channels with many specialized channels. I think we should have that kind of situation.

12. *What do you think of the transport system in your hometown?*

Personally I think the transport in my hometown is terrible. The buses are just too old and need to be upgraded. For example, it's not that unusual to see a lot of buses broken down on the roads. As for the road system, it's obvious that the roads are not well planned. The roads are wide enough but don't give enough room to let cars exit. The side lanes are always congested and sometimes you can get struck in a traffic jam for over 40 minutes.

13. *What do you think of the education system in your hometown?*

Going to university can help people get a good job in China. But, many courses are too old and not very useful. The professors often have just recently graduated or are very new in their field, or they are older and not very up to date with new developments. Also, we have to take all sorts of courses that are not directly related to our field. This, I feel, is a complete waste of time. We could be learning much more in our own field instead of spending time learning courses that have no use for our future.

14. *What do you think of key schools in China?*

I think it's an old system that needs changing. Not every intelligent student is accepted into a key school, even if they are academically able. Also, intelligent students shouldn't be segregated. They need to learn to deal with all kinds of students. Segregating bright students doesn't provide them with the skills they need to communicate and interact with others, which is what they'll need to do once they start working.

15. *What do you think of fast food restaurants in your country?*

Personally I can't stand them and think there are now too many in our country. I mean take Beijing now. There are currently over a hundred of them and I think we don't need that many. The food is not very nutritious and to be frank it's expensive

笔 记 区

as well.

16. *What do you think of the 3 Gorges project?*

Personally I think there are two sides to this issue. On one hand, it will probably provide a lot of needed electrical energy. I mean take the area of Chongqing. It's a growing city but it's hampered by a lack of energy and it needs to be able to feed more electrical energy to some of the poorer provinces to the west of it, particularly Tibet. Also I think it will make navigation easier along the Changjiang river and that will be good for our industries.

On the other hand, I think it creates some hardships for those people living in that region, since they must be relocated and they are giving up the area that they have lived in for so long. Also, we must be very careful to make sure there is no environmental damage since there are a lot of precious lives that depend on the river.

17. *What do you think of the Olympic Games? Are they necessary for the world?*

I don't think I like the Olympics. As far as I'm concerned they are a waste of time and money. There is just too much nationalism and pressure on the athletes. For example in the last Winter Olympics you had countries threatening to boycott them or pull out for all kinds of reasons, and you had some unethical judging going on. I also think that they have become too commercialized and that they've been taken over by big companies.

18. *What do you think of the popularity of English in China?*

Well, it's quite natural. I mean the world is getting closer and closer and I think it's natural that the world begins to use a common language. Well, that means if you want to do well in business you should at least know a little English. Take the Internet for example. I mean, there are lots of Chinese websites, but as far as I'm concerned, you can get a much better range of knowledge if you can understand English. Some of the best industries in the future will involve international trade so if you are reasonably good at English you will be in demand. So the popularity of English is really for practical reasons. You can get a better job and you can probably have more opportunities.

19. *What do you think of school uniforms?*

Personally I think it is a good thing. I mean it's fine for some countries to let their children have a lot of freedom with their clothing but I think that it only creates problems in many other places. I mean I read somewhere that there is a lot of bullying that takes place in North American schools and that some kids are laughed at because too often their clothes are shabby. Another thing I think you have to understand is that we stress more harmony and unity among our students. It's important for students to have this sense of unity or our nation will fall apart.

20. *Should children be punished in school?*

My opinion is that children should be punished but not too often. I think the best way to deal with children is to guide them through their mistakes and to try to help them see their own errors. I mean, punishment should be used, but only when the children believe that they can get away with something that they shouldn't do. Punishment also cannot be the only way a child learns not to do something, otherwise he or she will only act out of fear of consequences without knowing whether it's truly right or wrong. For example, if a boy passes notes in class and is only punished, he may stop it only as long as the teacher is around. But when he comes to another class with a teacher who's not as strict, he might start doing it again. He hasn't realized why it's not the right thing to do.

二、Opinions on the Meaning of Various Aspects 概念及意义

21. *What does friendship mean to you?*

Well, that's a tough question. Let me see. I think it means almost everything to me except perhaps my family. Friendship, in my mind, means having people who you know will help you if you are ever in trouble. I think it's also people who you feel you can actually tell things to and they will listen. Friends are people who you don't need to be so polite to when you ask them to go somewhere—you can just phone them up and tell them "let's go somewhere" and you know they'll probably go. They are also people who have the same kind of sense of humor when you speak with them so that you will just laugh and laugh together.

22. *What does happiness mean to you?*

Well, it's a big topic. To me happiness means a carefree life, though I think it's impossible to be always carefree. That's why many people think of their childhood as being their time of true happiness because it was a time when they had little to worry about. Also, I think having a lot of very good friends is part of being very happy. It makes me happy to have some close friends who have a lot in common with me. I think happiness will double when it's shared with friends. Finally, I think happiness is knowing that you are useful, and knowing that you can help people when they need it. I feel happy to be able to help other people. I think it's pleasant to feel needed.

23. *What do clothes mean to you?*

In my opinion they are a way of showing respect to the people that you have to meet everyday. If you dress too sloppily or cheaply I think you are essentially saying that you really don't care about others and that is a bad thing. To me, clothes are a kind of presentation to the world and the clothes you wear are a kind of way that you present you character. If you present it with clothes that really

笔 记 区

don't match or have nothing unique to offer, you are not letting yourself have the best image that you can possibly have.

24. *What do you think education really means?*

Well, it's a difficult question to answer but I think that essentially it means anything that may bring positive changes to you. It may be a skill or it may be some information to learn. I think it's also important to include any wisdom or moral lesson that can be learned. I think it's dangerous to concentrate too much on just skills because education to me also means something that gives you a way to shape your behaviour. For example if a student is very good at mathematics but has poor social skills he may use his skills to create some terrible weapons, rather than use them for peaceful purposes.

25. *What do you think "real love" means?*

It's a difficult question. I mean I don't know that much about this topic, but I suppose that it means that you would do everything you could for a person—even give up your life. I think real love is more than just passion. It must be a feeling that this person is so important to you that you would sacrifice everything you could for this person's well being.

三、Stating Your Standards 阐明标准

26. *What do you think the goal of an education should be and tell me why you feel that way?*

Education should really be a time when you learn new ways of thinking and are challenged to go beyond what you know. But if I were to choose between learning useful things versus learning for enjoyment, I would definitely choose learning for enjoyment. I don't mean just learning when I feel like it. Rather, I mean studying things that interest me. If I am truly interested in a subject, I will really try hard to learn it. I think the goals of education should also be to produce a well-rounded person, I mean a person who is not just good in one or two areas but a person who can show knowledge in quite few areas.

27. *What do you think is important in a friend ship?*

I think honesty is an essential part of any relatioship. When I am doing something wrong, a real friend should be able to tell me that I am wrong, though it may casue some hard feelings. Probably I will be angry in the beginning, but when I think about it, I will certainly thank him for that. Only a real friend could be honest enough to do that.

28. *What qualities do you think a good teacher needs?*

I suppose the basic qualities involve two things. First the teacher must understand the process of learning and the ways to make learning more efficient and

笔 记 区

effective. I also think that a teacher must have a good personality that motivates students to learn. I don't think it's necessary for a teacher to have a perfect personality but at least they must show a passion for what they are teaching. The moment the students sense that the teacher just doesn't care about the subject, they also lose their enthusiasm for it. Patience is a key quality too because if there is no patience then students will be ignored.

29. *What do you think the goal of travelling should be?*

Well, I've never thought about that before. I guess the goal of travelling should be to enjoy yourself. For me, I think the goal I usually have is to have an experience that sticks in my mind for a long time and to give me a wider understanding of the world. I like to feel good about visiting a place and I like to think that the place made me a better person. I think often too many people travel just so that they feel they are adventurous and so they can boast to all their friends about all the places they have seen. But I think it is more important to truly relax and take your time exploring things without having to follow some rushed plan of things to see.

30. *How should people be promoted at work, through experience or performance?*

That's a big issue in many companies. I'm not sure how I feel about this issue because I think both experience and performance are important. I mean if you've been working for a long time I think it's natural that you would expect better treatment. On the other hand, I don't think that it's right that experienced people should put little care into their job just because they think that their jobs are well protected because of seniority. In my opinion, people should be promoted based on a combination of experience and performance. If they do not perform well, they may be demoted or even laid off, but if they do perform well, they will be promoted. Those people who perform well but have little experience should be promoted but not too high because this will only discourage those people who have worked in a company for a long time.

31. *What qualities do you think are important for a successful or good film?*

That's hard to say. A good film doesn't have to follow a certain formula. I think there are all kinds of good films and they don't have to be a certain style. I think the basic qualities are commitment and professional acting. I can't stand those actors who star in movies with little concern about how to make their characters seem like real people. I think that the cinematography is quite important because without it you are just resenting images without concern for the meaning they convey. If there is no concern for the way it is shot then you might as well read a book, because the main features of films that make it pleasing are its setting and artistic filming. These days, I think one criterion for a successful film seems to be just good special effects, but I don't care much about that.

笔 记 区

32. *How do you define a good quality life?*

I think a good quality life involves no fear or thought that you are in danger, or being unfairly treated. I think it's a life where there are no serious health risks and there are opportunities to enjoy yourself without feeling worried about the consequences. I mean, if you're worried about the pollution in the water or you are worried about the crime in an area then it doesn't matter how rich you are because you have no opportunity to enjoy your surroundings. A good quality life can probably be found anywhere in the world but I think the conditions in some places make it easier than other places.

33. *What is your standard of a good place to visit?*

I guess the place should first have opportunities for you to see something that you don't see very often. Also I think there should be some reasonable facilities for you to enjoy. For example, there should be, at least, some decent roads to get in and out and some decent place to see. I think that the place should be relatively safe and clean. I also think it should offer some opportunities to see things without getting charged for everything. I mean there are just too many places that charge you for every step you take and I think this is wrong because good places shouldn't be another kind of tourist traps.

34. *What is your standard of success?*

In my opinion, success means reaching the goals that you have for yourself, and it means you have achieved something that is not only good for yourself, but also good for others. I mean, if you have lots of money that doesn't necessarily mean you are a success. It could mean that you were lucky or you just happened to have the right talents. True success means meeting your goals, and if your goals just happen to be raising a happy family, well I think that also makes you a success.

四、Making Predictions 预测未来

35. *What do you think of the future of China if China keeps an open policy?*

Personally I think China's future is very promising. The open policy has brought many benefits to the Chinese. For example, our standard of living has increased, China has become a stronger nation economically, and we've learned a lot about the rest of the world. China needs to continue with an open policy in order for us to gain strength and respect as a world-class nation.

36. *Do you foresee there being more advertisements in the future?*

Well, I think so. We are getting more and more foreign advertisements, and as more investments are coming in, I think this is something unavoidable. The concept of advertising on TV, for example, is just beginning to catch on among the bigger companies and as more and more private businesses grow and increase

笔记区

their advertising budgets they may give TV a chance. Also, I think you'll see more and more advertising agencies that specialize in making good advertisements start up in China and they will be in hot demand in the next few years.

37. *How do you think the Internet will change people's buying habits in the future?*

I guess the change will be incredible in the future. People rely so much on the Internet nowadays that they spend a lot of their time in front of the computer. More and more people are buying things over the Internet, and I think this trend will continue in the future. People will not get out of their houses, they'll just shop at home. The key challenge before this happens is that the stores must find a good way of delivering things at a low cost. This has been the biggest problem for a lot of e-commerce type companies in the past but I have a feeling they'll become more skilled at it in the future.

38. *Do you think that the Internet is going to change the way we get news?*

Well, we have seen that change already. I get my latest news from the Internet. And I believe this will be the trend for the future if more and more people get wired up with the Internet. I'm not sure in the future whether newspapers will survive if more people get the news from the Internet. I think the main way it'll change the way we get news is that we will get the events immediately. We can now get a variety of sources. Also people will become more sophisticated about the things that are happening around the world and they will be able to make up their own minds about issues.

39. *Can you imagine what transport will be like in the future?*

I suppose it will be fueled with different energy sources because there is just no way that we can continue with petroleum for much longer. So I think that when new energy sources come out, you'll see different designed transport. I also predict that some transport will begin to use the air more often just for short distances because I think that the road systems cannot be maintained and repaired forever. We need to find other ways, so I imagine our cars will probably be flying and maybe there will be flying bicycles too.

40. *What would life be like without music?*

That's difficult to say. I mean we just take it for granted that we'll always have music but I guess if there wasn't any music we'd suffer in a very big way because we need music to create some higher form of pleasure. We need music to get in touch with some of our deeper emotions. If I had no music, I'm sure I'd go crazy because music relaxes me and it's a great way to hear some form of communication, which I might not have time for if I didn't put on a song or two.

笔 记 区

41. *Do you think the traffic problem will get better or worse in the future?*

Well, I'm not sure, but I have a feeling it will get better. It may be that the problem will get worse before it gets any better, but I think that there will be a time when something is actually done to tackle the problem. My feeling is that part of the problem will be solved when we actually start to regulate the number of cars on the roads. I also think that once the subway system is improved and can carry people to places they weren't able to go, then the situation will get a bit better.

42. *Do you feel optimistic that environmental problems will be solved in the future?*

I guess you could say I'm optimistic, but only in the long term. I think it will, but only when people begin to realize that there's an actual crisis out there. I remember when it seemed that everyone was talking about the issue. Now a lot of people are just saying, "Well, nothing can really be done about the problem." I think that people could do something about it if they really wanted to but the problem is that they keep delaying the solutions so I think when they realize they cannot delay the process any more then they will actually start doing something concrete about it.

43. *How do you imagine people's lifestyles will change in the future?*

I guess there will be some big changes in lifestyles. We'll be mixing our work and free time more and probably make more of our own choices about when to work and when not to work. I also think that children will become more and more independent and also sophisticated and they will be shouldering more and more housework, as a growing number of households have two income earners. I think we'll also be experiencing more stress and more competition and I think we'll probably be making more and more friends from distant places.

44. *How do you think housing will change in the future?*

In my mind, the housing situation will see a growing number of private developers and more and more housing that is built up high. I think apartment buildings will get much higher and I think the basic facilities of most Chinese housing will be improved. Public housing will probably be upgraded and more responsibility will be placed on the owners to keep the housing clean and well maintained. But I think there will also be a big challenge in the future for public housing to keep pace with the growing demands of the middle-class in China.

五、Making Suggestions or Offering Solutions 解决方案

45. *What do you think we should do to protect the environment?*

I think the main challenge is to create a good staff to enforce the standards we have already set. The key thing about a good, clean environment is that the standards be enforced so that the laws have some teeth to them. I also think that it's necessary to have good technical innovations so that the methods to do such

笔记区

things as water treatment can be developed. I also think it really takes a strong commitment by everyone to make sure that the environment is always the top priority in every new plan that is created.

46. *How do you think global warming can be prevented?*

As far as I know, global warming is caused by the Greenhouse Effect, which results from too much carbon dioxide in the air. I think the government should take measures to limit the number of private cars and make efforts to develop the public transport system. Besides, we should try to replace fossil fuels with new, cleaner energy resources. Once we can reduce the amount of carbon dioxide in the air, the temperatures will very likely stabilize and we can then feel safer that the situation is under control.

47. *How can we preserve our history best?*

I believe the best way to preserve our history is to make sure that we protect all the symbols of our history, and that means that we try to set aside enough room for our old buildings and old sections of town to flourish. I think it's important to make sure that we also try to provide some reenactments of history in our films, books and TV shows and also, if possible, through our tourist areas. I think another very important way is by keeping good records of the events that take place and by getting a variety of interpretations of history.

48. *What should one do to prepare for a good trip to China?*

I think you should get a good phrase book that you can use if you need to get things done. You need a basic level of expressions that will help you make your trip easier. There are some other things that you have to be aware of. For example, you need to beware of possible dangers and people who are trying to cheat you. You also should try to understand the history of China because that will make some of the places that you're going to more interesting. For example, if you watch a film or read a good book on the Forbidden City it will be much more interesting to you when you wander around in it.

49. *What measures should be taken to reduce crime?*

Well, to start with I think we should try to find the root of the crime problem. I mean you can't just scare crime away very easily. Sometimes it's because the gangsters have managed to scare everyone from doing anything about the problem. Other times it's just simply a fact that there are too many people who live in hopeless poverty and they feel they have no other ways to make a living. Then I think it's important to increase our enforcement skills and that means getting more policemen and policewomen and trying to give them the best resources to do their job. I think finally, that there must be a justice system that's fair and won't treat anyone. Once all of these things are done I think crime will decrease significantly.

笔记区

50. *How can traffic problems be best solved?*

In my opinion the best way to solve this problem is by trying to widen our roads and build more flyovers at the exits. Shanghai has successfully done this and now experiences fewer problems as a result. I also think that we may have to encourage people to take public transport lines more often or simply ride their bicycles more. One more thing that should be done is to build better smaller roads that connect the bigger roads. One big problem in bigger cities is that a lot of the connecting roads are often blocked and so everyone has to squeeze into some exit roads to get from one area to another.

51. *How can the tourism industry be improved?*

I believe the first thing to do is to make it illegal for tour operators to collect commissions from various shops or stores and to simply increase the salaries of the tour operators. The second thing that needs to be done is there needs to be more control over the vendors in the famous sites to make sure they don't harass visitors. It can be very unpleasant when people follow you everywhere to sell their things. Finally, I think that there should be more opportunities to do independent travelling by setting up more campsites and clean hostels, to accept the backpacking crowds.

52. *How can education be reformed to meet future challenges?*

I guess the best reforms should be in the area of post secondary education and I think it would be good to pour a lot of money into upgrading the facilities and attracting better university professors to work in them. I also think there should be more community colleges and smaller universities that accept people from all walks of life. One more thing is that I think there should be more opportunities for distance learning programmes from various universities around the world so that many Chinese can get benefit from overseas education without travelling so far to other countries..

六、Explaining Reasons 解释原因

53. *What do you think are the main reasons for the gap between the rich and poor?*

The main reason is that there are some fields that are in demand and there are short supplies of labour, while other fields have too many people in it and the demand may not be that great. Well, if you ask me, I don't think you can expect everyone to become rich at the same time. Some people say that under the market economy system it's natural for the most capable people to make a fortune first. Life is competition after all. Well, I can accept this partly but I think we should still do more to raise the standards of people who are struggling in life.

笔记区

54. *Why do people in China traditionally want to have a son?*

Well in the past, sons were preferred because they carried the family name. Also, when they married, their wife would join the family. This means that the parents would gain a daughter-in-law. But when the daughter married, she would join her husband's family. I think the bigger reason is that in the countryside, sons can help out more on the family's farm, just because they're stronger and have more endurance. There's still a sense that the son can earn more money and then take care of the parents better. I think this is changing because a lot of people are realizing that a daughter tends to take better care of her parents when they get older.

55. *Why does advertising have such a powerful influence on what people buy?*

I think advertising is a very powerful tool and it's getting more and more popular these days. I think many people don't have any real knowledge about a product, so most of the time they rely on advertising for information, which they think is trustworthy. If there is no advertising, consumers will not realize certain products exist so they will not buy them. If you advertise, your customers are introduced to your products and may be encouraged to make purchases.

56. *Why do people like sports so much?*

I'm not very sure because I don't really like sports that much. I suppose it's because sports represent a safe, fun, and fair way to compete. Sometimes in work or in our studies we may feel things are not quite fair and even. Sports are fair and objective. There's also a social function of sports, getting together gives many Chinese a chance to establish and make contact with each other. Sports are fun and they keep both the body and the mind in shape.

57. *Explain people's attitudes toward old buildings.*

Well, I think generally speaking people are fond of them. I mean they are part of our history and culture. But I think a lot of people are also impatient to see China develop and modernize quickly so our attitude towards the old buildings is often... well...preserve them if we can, but if a more modern building needs to be built, why not build it?

58. *Why are so many people buying cars these days in China?*

Well that's an interesting question. I think it's mainly a face thing. It's as if riding a bicycle is a loss of face. I mean as soon as you buy a car people assume that you're doing well in life. We don't really need the car, and it doesn't really improve our actual quality of life, but it's nice to show others you have a car. There's also this sense of freedom you get when you drive a car. I don't know how to exactly explain it but it's the kind of feeling that you are the master of your motion instead of some drivers.

笔 记 区

59. *Why do people like travelling so much in your home country?*

That's a good question. Sometimes I wonder why people just don't try to explore the places around them instead of trying to find paradise so far away. I think that people are just looking for an escape from their lives for a while and I think it's another status thing to say that you've been to all these exciting places. That's why I think you find a lot of people taking so many pictures but not really stopping to feel the places they are going to. I think there are some people who like it because they honestly enjoy learning and experiencing life in a different way but I think these people are a minority.

60. *Do children know the difference between right and wrong?*

Well, I don't know much about this issue because I'm too young to be a parent and I'm no longer a child. But my guess is that they don't really. I mean, I love children a lot but I think it takes a number of years before you can really learn to know the real reason why something is right or wrong and it takes a long time for people to really sympathize with others in a sincere way. One example of this is the kid that teases others. He doesn't really know it's wrong but he hears that his parents and teachers say it's wrong so he doesn't do it. Another reason he stops doing it is because he's afraid he might get teased. But does he really know it's wrong? I doubt it because he doesn't have the ability to know how to think and realize the hurt another person feels.

61. *Why are some arts popular and others not?*

Well, it's hard for me to say because I'm not an expert on art, but I think that the popularity of art depends on the deeper feeling a painting or work of art seems to generate. I mean if you look at art and feel nothing from it then it can't get very far. I also think, to be frank, that a lot of art is just fashion and based on the fame or name of the artist. I mean most people don't really know the difference between one art and another so they rely on the name. It's like name-brand clothing, I guess you could say.

62. *Why do so many people like fast food in China?*

You know I can't figure that out myself. I mean it's not that convenient. Sometimes at lunch you could be waiting to get to the front of the line for quite some time. It's not peaceful, it's noisy. The food is overpriced and not very nutritious. I think the real reason is that the advertising and promotion is good and it has this kind of happy atmosphere that draws people in. People also like the idea of just getting some place to chat freely and not being interrupted by some waiter or waitress. I also think a lot of people like to use their fingers to eat just for a change.

笔记区

七、Explaining Importance, Impact and Role 重要性及角色

63. *What role does tourism play in your country's economy?*

I think tourism is playing a more and more important role in our country's economy. Since the opening up of our economy, the number of tourists has increased dramatically, and this is a useful source of foreign currency for the country. I think for some places it has become almost a lifeline. For example places like Dali and Sanya depend so much on tourism that I think they would literally disappear without it.

64. *What is the impact of technology on human beings?*

That's a big topic. Well, I guess we can say that technology is something that changes the pace of life without us really realizing it. Suddenly, things are faster; travelling, communicating and computing are all faster, and then we get used to that increased pace and we don't think of it as being special any more. I happen to think the impact can be quite a positive one, if we direct this new efficiency in the right direction. My concern is when this technology starts to make us less and less sociable with one another and makes us more impersonal.

65. *What role does natural beauty in nature play for the Chinese?*

I guess that places of natural beauty play a big role in our lives. We take pride in our country's natural beauty and it is a source of strength to us. When we think of our country we don't just think of our institutions and people but also our places. These places help us to relax, to connect us with history, and inspire us to do great things.

66. *What role does music play in our lives? What is its function?*

That's difficult to say. I think that, by and large, music does play a big role in our lives. We kind of take it for granted, but I think we don't realize just how important it is. I think the biggest role it plays is that it communicates a kind of emotion to us and that emotion helps us to get in touch with what we have inside of us as people.

67. *What is the impact of Western music on Chinese music?*

I'm not an expert at this since I basically only listen to Chinese music, but I think that the main impact is that it has taught us to simplify our lyrics and just concentrate on the repetition of the melody. Also, the impact has been that music has become simpler and more directed at the young. Also, Western music has taught us to be a bit bolder with some of our feelings.

68. *What is the importance of playing sports?*

Well it's an interesting question. I mean, we play them and have fun, but we don't really think about their importance. Perhaps the real importance of sports is just to have a good time. They release our energy and keep us in shape and I guess that's

笔 记 区

all I think of for actual importance.

69. *Explain the impact of the Internet on our lives.*

I think the Internet is changing our lives because we can connect to the rest of the world without leaving the house. We can also work at home without going to the office, we can get the latest news without buying a newspaper, and we can also make purchases at home. All these changes have already taken place in some people's lives. Also, we can now contact each other easily and this tends to make communication more frequent but it also makes it shallower, since we don't really write very long messages anymore.

70. *What role do you think old and modern buildings play in our society?*

I think they both play an important role but for different reasons. Old buildings are important for preserving our culture. Modern buildings are important for showing that we are now a modern country and that we will provide the best facilities. I don't think that our country would be as strong if we didn't have both of them to enjoy.

71. *What is the importance of learning a second language?*

Leaning English is getting more and more popular in China. I think the main importance of learning a second language is that you can use it for many career-enhancing purposes. For example, if you know English you can work at any publishing company or language school. You can also get a job much more easily at a foreign company and you can communicate with potential clients. So you see, we consider English to be a very important subject for our careers.

72. *What benefits do hobbies have on a person's life?*

Well, in my opinion, hobbies are the difference between a boring and an exciting life. I mean your work could be exciting but if all you do when you get home is watching TV or surfing the Internet then I don't think your life can be very fulfilling. I think that a hobby is also a very good way to expand your social life. And if you are good at your hobby...Well, who knows? Perhaps you can make your hobby your career, like Bill Gates did when he started making computer programmes in his spare time.

八、Listing the Ways 举例说明

73. *What kinds of possessions create high status in your country?*

Well, that's hard to say, there are so many. You know, everyone is different and some people regard some things as being more important than others. I would say the biggest status possession is probably the car. You know if you drive one of those Santanas or Audis, it's a sign that you've made it. Also, of course, the flat itself is important too. If you live in a 3 bedroomed or even a 4 bedroomed flat

笔记区

that's private and up high, well... that's another sign you've made it.

74. *Can you give me some examples of some negative effects of advertising?*

Well I think these ridiculous advertisements that promise that you can improve your memory by taking a pill are a big scam. I mean they're really misleading and I think that these kinds of ads really need regulation. Another negative effect of advertisements is they try to associate happiness with the objects you buy. Can buying things make you happy? The problem with this way of thinking is, well, what happens when you get tired of the object? Then you have to buy more things.

75. *In what ways do people usually make friends in your country?*

Well, all kinds of ways. I guess the most common way is by acquaintances' introduction. Maybe in your country you like to introduce yourself, but I guess we are a little more reserved and always wait for an introduction. There are also some other ways, for example, classmates. I think classmates are the most common source of friends. You will find that these friends are more lasting than say colleagues from work.

76. *What are some ways people like to travel in your country?*

Well, even though I see a lot more people doing independent travelling, I would still say that tours are the most popular way of travelling. I guess we like to be with groups of people when we travel. Also, we are still a bit nervous to risk doing things by ourselves. Another popular way of travelling is by renting a car and driving to some place in a group. This gives you a bit more freedom but you have to be careful of the regulations.

77. *What factors influence the ways people dress?*

Well, that's an interesting question. It's hard to say. I know weather would be one of the ways. I mean if it's snowing outside you're obviously not going out without a coat. But besides weather I think that clothes are basically chosen by what self-image the person wants and what he or she feels is comfortable. You know women often choose clothing that people tell them suits them and also which seems to give off the best image for them.

78. *What effects or benefits does learning an instrument have on people, especially children?*

Well, I'm no expert on the subject and to tell you the truth I'm not really sure. I don't play an instrument so I have no personal experience to draw from. I suppose if I had to guess I'd say that learning an instrument sharpens your mind because I'm sure it's not that easy. I mean I know some people who'd practise for hours and so I think it must not be easy. I guess it must also make you more creative because now you know a way to put notes together.

笔 记 区

79. *What are the typical characteristics of a modern family?*

Well, I've never thought about what makes a modern family. I suppose it's a family that gives each other a large degree of personal freedom. I mean when I think of a modern family I think of the father and mother both doing the work they want and both sharing the housework. Kids can also make choices about their careers and relationships. I also think that a modern family should be smaller and probably a little better off.

80. *What are the main features of traditional architecture in your country?*

Well, I'm no expert on this topic. I've never really studied the architecture of my country. I guess the main features are the steep roofs and the curvy eaves, which are often decorated at the corners. Also a lot of traditional architecture is held up by pillars. We used to use a lot more wood in our architecture but now it's a lot more cost effective to make things with brick or concrete. Also, windows are much smaller in traditional architecture, but many modern buildings are made completely with glass.

81. *What are the various ways computers can be useful for our learning?*

Well, it would be difficult to come up with a complete list since the number of ways might be unlimited! Well, I can think of one way where computers are helpful, my English. The other day I came across a pronunciation learning website which gave very good explanations about where I should place my tongue and teeth and where a sound should originate. I think, also, that computers are good for allowing us to do drills and practise exercises because I find it embarrassing to do them in front of a teacher.

九、Changes 描述变化

82. *How has technology changed in China over the last few years?*

I think technology has really taken quite a big leap since the open door policy. More and more people are realizing the importance of technology and the good things it brings and the way it increases productivity and efficiency. People are now being trained to use technology in the work place. People are realizing that without technology, it'll be difficult to compete in the new global economy. The Internet is one example. More and more people are connected to the Internet at home or at work. It becomes part of many people's lives to get news, get in contact with people around the world and even receive our entertainment on the net. The amount of information it provides is incredible.

83. *How have Chinese eating habits changed in the last 20 to 30 years?*

I guess that eating habits have undergone some changes. We eat a lot more variety than before. We are more prosperous now and so we can order a lot of different dishes at restaurants. I also find that many people are learning to make dishes

笔记区

from different places. My mother for example, learned to cook Sichuan food, even though we are from the northeast of China. Another way it has changed is that young people are eating a lot more fast food, not just from the West but also Chinese style fast food. We just like the casual style of eating.

84. *How has the environment changed?*

I think the environment has changed a lot. The air has become worse and worse and the water has become more and more contaminated. Because of over-development the sandstorms have gotten worse, as well. However, I think some aspects have also improved. More and more parks are being created and there have been a number of successful tree planting projects.

85. *How has tourism changed in China?*

Well, tourism has become very popular in China and is now a big business. More and more people are taking an interest in travelling to China and so the revenue collected from tourism is becoming significant. This means that many cities have changed a lot to accommodate more tourists. Take Xi'an as an example. Tourism has become one of the major industries there and so a lot of shops now carry souvenirs as well as other things.

86. *What are the differences between entertainment media, such as TV and movies in the past and now?*

There are big differences. I mean in the past everything we heard was directed from just a few sources and now there is a lot more diversity. Our movies now come from all over the world and directors now have a lot more freedom to choose the themes that interest them. Also, there's a lot more English in the films and on TV these days. In fact there are now even a lot of English-only programmes.

87. *How have families changed? What's the difference between families now and in the past?*

I think families have changed in some very significant ways over the last 10 or 20 years. For one thing they are a lot smaller than they used to be with the implementation of the one-child policy. Also, the roles of fathers, mothers and children have changed. It used to be that the father was the all-powerful figure and now I think it's the child. Since there is only one child now, you can say that the child is the new emperor in many families. Also, a lot more mothers are now working full time and many of them are earning more than their husbands.

88. *How have buildings and construction changed in the last 20 years in China?*

In my opinion architecture is, of course, no longer relying so much on brick and a lot of the new buildings are using different materials. Basically you can say that buildings are getting higher and they look cleaner and shiner than even before. But in my view, I think the construction standards are getting worse and worse. I

笔记区

think too many developers are trying to rush projects and are cutting corners along the way. If this problem continues you're going to see more and more cases being brought to court.

89. *What are the differences between hobbies today and hobbies in the past?*

Well I guess that hobbies in the past were simpler and usually didn't involve much more than a person's own skills at things. Since many of us weren't as well off as we are now, I guess you could say that we had to be careful about not spending too much on our hobby. These days I see people spend a fortune on their various hobbies, so I think that is the biggest difference.

90. *How has transport changed in the last 20 years?*

Transport hasn't changed that much, except that there is just so much more of it. I mean, look at the number of cars on the roads—it's almost quadrupled since the eighties. There is a lot more public transport and some of the buses are much cleaner and more modern than they used to be. Also, the subway system covers more places. But in my opinion, the changes in public transport haven't kept pace with the growth of cars and that's a serious challenge for our cities.

91. *How has clothing changed in the last 20 years?*

I think clothing has changed quite a bit these years. I mean 20 years ago we just started the open door policy and so many people were beginning to test out new styles of clothing. In those days perhaps you could say that fashionable clothing like that seen in Europe was a bit adventurous. Now it's very common. It seems everyone is wearing namebrand clothing these days. Another thing that's quite interesting is that a lot of traditional clothing that many people thought was so old-fashioned and useless a few years ago is now becoming fashionable again. It seems we are beginning to take a new interest in our traditional dressing styles and combine them with the styles of today.

十、Comparisons 比较

92. *What's the difference between Western and Chinese culture?*

Well, in fact I know very little about it, but my guess is that Chinese culture is based on Confucianism while Western culture is more based on individual liberalism. This means that we have more acceptance of authority and are more likely to accept conditions and try to find more subtle ways to change things. I think Western culture emphasizes the benefits of conflict to create change. I also think that Chinese culture places a lot of importance on the family and respect for the elders. Well, Western culture does too but it seems that this importance is a preoccupation with Chinese.

93. *What's the difference between the way children and adults make friends?*

笔记区

Well I think the main difference is that children start their friendships very accidentally and they don't really have to make so many gestures in words. Adults try to use the power of their words and their conversation to secure friendship. Children, on the other hand, just start sharing things or playing together, and instantly, if they enjoy being together, they continue the friendship. Also, children more quickly forgive their friends for the things they do wrong to each other but I think adults take matters more seriously.

94. *Can you compare different types of transport in your hometown?*

In my hometown it's a bit hard to get around on a bicycle. I mean, it's certainly cheaper but it's also a bit tiring going up all these hills. A taxi is convenient and there's no problem in my hometown finding one, but they can get a bit expensive if you take them everyday. A bus is probably the best option if it's not rush hour, but if it's a busy time you'd better expect to squeeze in. I think subways are the best but the problem is that they don't go everywhere. I guess a car is the most convenient, except when you get stuck in some traffic jam. Also, cars just add to our pollution problems.

95. *Compare the difference between middle school and university life.*

I think middle school life is quite structured, and so all you really need to worry about are your grades and your friends. Your classmates are people you see everyday and your teachers are always on you about your behaviour. There's a lot of stress about your exams and I'd say that learning is rather forced. With a university life you have to structure your life more on your own and you are responsible for your own behaviour. The big challenge in university is not so much on getting good grades but getting along with all your roommates in the dormitory.

96. *Compare traditional food and fast food.*

I think traditional food just means that the dishes are served on separate plates and people share the same plate. Fast food means you generally go up to the counter to order it and you bring it back to your table. The food is usually something simple and informal. You can also eat with your fingers and you can be as casual as you want to be.

97. *What are the main differences between flats and traditional houses in China?*

I think the main differences are in the facilities. In a flat you have all of your facilities in working order and you don't really need to share much with other residents except maybe the playground if you have kids. With a traditional home, a lot of the facilities like telephones and water are shared. Flats are also centrally heated, while traditional homes may not be heated at all. Traditional homes are usually made of brick and often they are no more than one floor high, whole flats

笔 记 区

can go up to 12 floors. Traditional homes are quite neighbourly, since you share so much with each other, and many people complain that flats encourage people to just keep to themselves and ignore their neighbours.

98. *Compare hobbies of Chinese with hobbies of Western people.*

Well, that's an interesting question. It's a bit hard for me to say, since I've never been to a Western country, but I guess that the hobbies there probably involve more collecting things, especially collecting older things. I know a lot of Westerners like to collect stamps or antiques. I think Chinese are more interested in mastering certain skills like calligraphy or the right way to pour tea. Chinese probably like keeping their hobbies to themselves while Westerners like joining clubs and stuff.

99. *How do the younger and older generation in China differ?*

You see many of the older generation came from more difficult circumstances, and they had a harder life. So they often think that we just do things without thinking about it. I often hear my father complain that there are too many rude youngsters around who show no regard for money and don't treat the elderly with any respect. The elderly are usually more cautious and slower to accept new ideas. The younger generation is quick to adopt new things like the Internet and we tend to accept fads. We dress, take guided tours and even eat differently and we think that the older generation should respect our points of view more.

100. *Compare Western and Chinese art.*

This is a difficult question for me. I'm not really that keen on art. I suppose it's nice to look at, but I won't waste much time or money on it. But I guess the difference is just that Western art usually seems to disguise some hidden meaning and it focuses more on the texture of its art and the details. Chinese art is meant to have more rhythm and perfect strokes and simplicity is more important than the symbolism it contains if there is any.

101. *What are the differences between objects you make by yourself and objects you buy?*

I think objects you make are of course cheaper! Seriously though, I think that objects you make are more meaningful because they've come out of your labour and your care. On the other hand, objects you buy are probably done more professionally and they certainly save you a lot of hard work. Personally, I prefer things I make unless I have no talent at it.

十一、Advantages and Disadvantages 评价优缺点

102. *What are the advantages and disadvantages of space research?*

I think one of the advantages is certainly that it's interesting, and it feeds our

笔 记 区

knowledge about the universe. I mean, we need to know things. Also, it can be turned into a commercial enterprise. For example many countries now sell satellites for commercial purposes and that couldn't have been achieved without some space research. The disadvantage is, of course, money. It's expensive, and you get a lot of people complaining that the money could be used for better purposes. I agree with this argument somewhat but I think the problem is that we need to research things in space or we may face a disaster like an incoming asteroid that we can do nothing about one day.

103. *What are the advantages and disadvantages of watching a sports game on TV compared to watching it live (in a stadium)?*

I think watching a game on TV has several strengths. For example, you can hear the commentary and you can see the action repeated again. You are given more knowledge about the game and things are not so noisy for you. You also have the freedom to eat what you want for free and get up and do something else. The seats are more comfortable, and the volume is yours to control. But there is one main disadvantage that is hard to deny. You cannot capture the feeling and excitement of watching something live. Also you cannot share your joy with other fans at the time that it's happening.

104. *What are the advantages and disadvantages of having a part time job while at school overseas?*

I think the main advantage of having a part time job is that it eases the financial burden on your parents. You are able to have a little pocket money without going to your parents all the time. Another advantage is that you can generally improve your English a lot if you can work part time overseas. You're working with your colleagues and they can communicate with you daily. The main disadvantage is that it's tiring and the time you spend working could be spent getting good grades. Also, overseas part time work is usually not very well paid so the added pocket money may not really be worth it.

105. *What are the advantages and disadvantages of public transport?*

I think the main advantage of using public transport is that it's cheap and generally much better for the environment, because you are only using one vehicle instead of many. Especially if your buses run on clean air, you can reduce a lot of emissions. Another advantage of public transport is that it reduces traffic jams. I think public transport is less stressful because you don't have to worry about parking and all that kind of things. The big disadvantage of public transport is the wait. It's much more convenient to just jump in your car and take off. Also, you have to follow a route and you have no flexibility with public transport. Sometimes it can be very uncomfortable, especially during rush hours.

笔记区

106. *What are the advantages of getting your news from the newspaper?*

Well, I like knowing what's going on, so newspapers are a good way for me to know what's happening. I won't say that I completely believe everything that I read in the newspapers, but I do find them very interesting and entertaining. I'm sort of an information junkie, so I just like to know current things. Because before a newspaper is printed, the editor will check through the articles and the sources where the news was derived from, it's often more reliable. In TV news, the news broadcaster may say something he or she thinks is right. So I feel newspapers are more reliable.

107. *What are the good things and bad things about Western food?*

I'm afraid I rarely eat Western food, I'll just make a few guesses then. Let me see...well, perhaps the good thing about it is that there might not be as much oil since a lot of the food is baked and boiled. I think another good thing is that the hamburgers are quite delicious sometimes. Well, the bad things I think are many. I think the food is tasteless, at least a lot of the food I've tried. Also, I think with hamburgers, they are quite bad for you and the fat content is very high. That's about all I really know about Western food.

108. *What are the advantages and disadvantages of giving projects in school instead of exams?*

You know, probably every teacher has weighed the advantages and disadvantages of them. I think the main advantage is that they encourage students to do their own thinking and in the process they take pride in what they create. They also gain more practical knowledge. The problems are mainly related to time. It takes a lot of time, not only for a student to do such a project but also to grade it. Also, how do you grade something like that? To grade something it's hard to be objective.

109. *What are the advantages and disadvantages of a traditional family?*

Well, my family is quite traditional so I guess I can tell you a bit about this. It's difficult to say what the advantages of a traditional family are. I guess the main thing is that things are probably more stable and everyone knows their role. In my family, for example, we don't really question my father's authority. It's also cheaper for us because you do everything together as a family. The disadvantage is that you have less freedom to do the things you really want. I mean, it seems that my parents are always questioning my decisions.

110. *What are the advantages and disadvantages of reading books for entertainment compared with watching TV or films?*

Well, I think the main advantage of reading books is that they do a lot for your imagination. It is more challenging and you have to work harder to gain your knowledge. TV is less challenging and doesn't make you think as much. But the

笔记区

main disadvantage is that books just take too much time to get through. TV is more convenient and time efficient and that's why I think so many people like it.

111. *What are the advantages and disadvantages of living in a small city?*
Well, I guess the main advantage of living in a small city is that you feel closer to the people around you and so you get a good social life. You have more chances to enjoy nature and the air is much fresher. The disadvantages are the lack of career opportunities and the facilities are generally not as good. Life in a small city may have fresher air and vegetables but it's hard to think about all that when you're worried about sending your kids to a good school.

笔 记 区

第四章
雅思口语考试常用词语和句型

I. 词 语

1. Hometown

1. architecture: There's some nice, German-style architecture in my hometown.
2. city centre: I live just within the city centre.
3. coast/coastal city: My hometown is a coastal city.
4. countryside: The surrounding countryside is very beautiful.
5. crowded: One drawback of my hometown is that it's quite crowded.
6. fresh air: I really miss the fresh air there.
7. grassland: Nearby my hometown you can visit many grasslands.
8. high-rise building: There are a lot of new high-rise buildings in my hometown.
9. historical site: There are a lot of famous historical sites in my hometown.
10. hospitable: The people in my hometown are always very hospitable.
11. industrial: My hometown is an industrial city with lots of pollution.
12. lively: My hometown becomes very lively in the evening.
13. located: My house is located alongside a small river.
14. main industry: The main industries in my hometown are steel and manufacturing.
15. make a living: It is a little difficult to make a living in my hometown.
16. market: The markets are all very colourful.
17. medium-sized: My hometown is a medium-sized city.
18. modern: There are a lot of modern buildings in my hometown.
19. open-minded: Usually the people in my hometown are very open-minded.
20. opportunity: There are not many good job opportunities in my hometown.
21. pace of life: The pace of life is fast in the city.
22. population: The population of my hometown is rather small.
23. prosperous: My hometown has been getting more prosperous recently.
24. shore: We do have a very nice sea shore with many coconut trees.
25. traditional: The people are still very traditional compared with city people.
26. valley: My hometown is situated in a big valley.

笔 记 区

2. Weather

1. breeze: I just love the cool sea breeze.
2. clear sky: Unlike this city, my hometown has a clear sky everyday.
3. climate: The climate of Dalian is quite pleasant, I think.
4. degree: It never goes below 10 degrees for more than three days.
5. drought: In Northern China there is always the danger of a serious drought.
6. dry: Beijing's weather can be very dry in winter.
7. dust-storm: We usually get dust-storms in spring.
8. flooding: If there is a lot of rain we may experience flooding in the spring.
9. fluctuate: The day and night temperatures fluctuate a lot in spring and autumn.
10. fog: Heavy fog can cause accidents on the road.
11. humid: Beijing is quite humid in July.
12. mild: The weather in my hometown is quite mild.
13. minus: The temperatures can go as low as minus 5 degrees.
14. misty: This afternoon was quite misty due to the heavy rain in the morning.
15. season: The four seasons are not very distinct in Southern China.
16. snow: There is a lot of snow in Harbin, especially in November.
17. storm: There are hardly any storms as far as I know.
18. sunny: Autumn is sunny most of the time.
19. temperature: The temperature can reach up to 40 degrees in summer.
20. wind: The wind is so strong that it picks up all the dust from the road.
21. winter: Beijing's winter has been getting milder in the last couple of years.

3. Studies

1. analytical thinking: Schools should also emphasize analytical thinking.
2. assignment: I spend my weekends doing the assignment.
3. bachelor/master degree: First I'll get my bachelor's degree and then I will study for a master's degree.
4. cafeteria: I often eat in the cafeteria.
5. class monitor: I was a class monitor for three years in my primary school.
6. classmate: My classmates are all very friendly.
7. competitive: Education is getting more and more competitive.
8. creativity: Creativity is important in a student's development.
9. critical thinking: We need to sharpen student's critical thinking skills.
10. develop: I hope my child will develop an interest in playing the piano.
11. discipline: Strict discipline is important for our teachers.
12. dormitory: We have eight people in the dormitory.
13. drill: Our education system tends to teach by drilling and practice.
14. emphasize: Education should also emphasize personal development.

笔 记 区

15. encourage: Children should be encouraged to be independent.
16. entrance: I passed my entrance examinations last year and now I am a freshman at Peking University.
17. exam based: The Chinese school system is exam based.
18. examination: The examination system is quite different.
19. extracurricular: I often spend my time doing extracurricular activities such as playing ping-pong and I am a member of the English club at school.
20. facility: Many schools lack facilities because of lack of money.
21. first year: My first year university life is quite fun and I'm enjoying it.
22. focus: This scholarship focuses more on leadership instead of grades.
23. foundation: Chinese education provides a good foundation for learning.
24. grade: Good grades do not mean a student is creative.
25. graduate from: I graduated from Fudan University in Shanghai.
26. headmaster: The headmaster in my school is relatively young compared to others.
27. homework: I do a lot of homework in the evening.
28. independent work: Many teachers prefer students that come out with independent work.
29. interaction: There isn't enough interaction in Chinese classrooms during class.
30. key school: Many parents hope their kids will get into key schools.
31. lecture: Biology lectures are always boring.
32. major in: I major in economics.
33. memorize: I used to memorize vocabulary but I realize that is not a good way to learn.
34. obedience: Obedience is still used to judge whether a student is good or not.
35. obey: We were taught to obey the teachers.
36. post-graduate study: I am thinking of doing my post-graduate studies in England and then come back to China to work.
37. private school: A private school's tuition is more expensive than a public school's.
38. problem solving: We should try to encourage more active problem solving.
39. professor: My professor encouraged me to go on studying.
40. project: Sometimes students can learn more from projects.
41. roommate: I have 5 roommates in my dormitory.
42. scholarship: I hope to get a scholarship to go abroad.
43. semester: Last semester was the most difficult.
44. special need: Some students require special needs in school.
45. stressful: Large amounts of homework can be quite stressful for some kids.
46. subject: How many subjects are you studying this semester?
47. teaching style: My English teacher's teaching style is very relaxed.
48. textbook: Most of the textbooks are printed locally.
49. training: We need to give students special training in certain areas.

笔 记 区

50. under stress: Sometimes I feel under stress from all the pressure.
51. well-rounded: Schools should aim to turn out well-rounded graduates.

4. Work

1. ambitious: There is nothing wrong with being ambitious when it comes to a career.
2. announce: The union announced a ban on overtime.
3. assist: I hope one day I can assist in the family business.
4. balance between: People should try to balance between work and family life.
5. be preoccupied with: People are too preoccupied with work.
6. be replaced: Many fear being replaced, they tend to work harder.
7. benefit: There are fewer benefits for employees in the private sector.
8. boss: My boss is very generous.
9. career: People are concentrating on their careers.
10. challenging: The most challenging part of the job is the research.
11. colleague: Colleagues may not cooperate as much as they used to.
12. condition: My company provides very comfortable working conditions.
13. contribute to: We cannot deny the fact that workers from other provinces have indeed contributed to the city.
14. coordinate: It is important to coordinate the activities of different departments.
15. day off: My day off is always on Monday.
16. day to day: My day to day work is very routine.
17. deadline: My supervisor always gives me a tight deadline.
18. duty: My duties involve supervising the production.
19. employ: Most of the people we employed have a degree.
20. foreign owned: Most foreign owned companies require people with a good command of English.
21. handle: I believe I can handle jobs under high pressure.
22. headhunter: We see more and more headhunter firms operating in China.
23. hire: I was first hired as an assistant manager.
24. in charge of: I'm in charge of hiring new staff for the company.
26. individual success: I am not sure how a person can judge individual success.
27. intense competition: Intense competition has forced companies to put more pressure on their workers to perform more quickly.
28. job hopping: Nowadays, job hopping is popular in China.
29. job title: My job title is managing director.
30. joint venture: My company is a joint venture with a German company.
31. laid off: I'm sure it wouldn't feel good to be laid off from work.
32. overtime: Many employees are made to work overtime without pay.
33. position: This position needs to be filled soon.

笔 记 区

34. promote: I was promoted to chief engineer after six months.
35. promotion: Promotions are being made based on merit rather than experience.
36. quit: Very few people quit because the company takes good care of its people.
37. represent: I represent my company at overseas conferences.
38. resign: I resigned from my last job after four months because it wasn't going anywhere.
39. responsibility: My responsibility is to ensure sales targets are achieved.
40. rewarding: I guess you could say that my job is very rewarding.
41. routine: My work is quite routine and not very challenging.
42. salary: The salaries have gone up for many people in the last two years.
43. state owned: My company is a state owned company.
44. under pressure: I am always under pressure to meet deadlines.
45. under stress: Many people are under stress to complete their work on time.

5. Traffic and Transport

1. bridge: There are many bridges in old Suzhou city.
2. bus/subway line: Beijing will get 6 more subway lines before the 2008 Olympics.
3. construction: Most of the construction is carried out in summer.
4. convenient: Getting around town is getting more convenient with more bus lines in service.
5. cyclist: Cyclists are still very common in China.
6. exhaust: The exhaust of so many cars in the city creates a lot of pollution.
7. exit: There should be another exit since this one is always jammed.
8. flyover: Shanghai has more flyovers than Beijing.
9. highway: We need highways to improve the infrastructure of our country.
10. intersection: Accidents always happen at the intersections because people are careless.
11. lorry/truck: Many trucks come into the city at night because they are not allowed in during the day.
12. obey traffic rules: If more people would obey traffic rules, there would have been fewer accidents.
13. overhead crossing: Overhead crossings can help to reduce the number of accidents.
14. parking lot: Most business areas have assigned parking lots.
15. pedestrian walkway: Most cities have pedestrian walkways.
16. restriction: It would be nice to have more restrictions on where cars can park.
17. rush hour: The traffic is very congested in rush hours.
18. slippery: Roads are very slippery in winter.
19. traffic accident: Most of the traffic jams are caused by traffic accidents.
20. traffic jam: To avoid the traffic jams, I suggest you leave after peak hour.

笔 记 区

21. traffic light: We need traffic lights at the intersections to regulate the traffic.
22. well-maintained: Most of the buses are well-maintained and can be quite comfortable to travel in.
23. wide/narrow road: The old roads in my hometown are very narrow but the new ones are wide enough for three lanes of traffic.

6. Hobbies, Spare Time

1. a fan of: I am a fan of Gong Li, a famous Chinese actress.
2. calligraphy: It takes lots of patience to learn to master Chinese calligraphy.
3. collecting: One of my hobbies is collecting stamps.
4. crazy about: I am quite crazy about watching old films.
5. enjoy chatting: Many young people enjoy chatting on the net.
6. get some exercise: I enjoy just getting some exercise whenever I can.
7. get together with: I enjoy getting together with old classmates once in a while.
8. go on the Internet: I often go on the Internet.
9. go out with: I often go out with my friends and have a good time with them.
10. have a good time: I often have a good time just chatting with my friends.
11. hike: I like hiking in the wilderness whenever I can.
12. It takes a lot of practice... : It takes a lot of practice to get good at it.
13. It takes persistence... : It takes persistence to do a good job in sculpting.
14. keep fit: You have to exercise daily to keep fit.
15. keep in touch: I wish I had more time to keep in touch with old friends.
16. opera: If I have time I like to watch Chinese opera.
17. play cards: I play cards with my friends in the evening.
18. require a lot of skill: Such an activity requires a lot of skill.
19. shopping: Most of the time I just do window shopping.
20. sleep in: I usually sleep in on Sunday mornings.
21. spend time with: On the weekend, I always spend time with my family.
22. take a trip: I enjoy taking a trip to the countryside.
23. take classes in: On the weekends I take classes in English.
24. take pictures: I like going to beautiful places to take pictures. Photography is my hobby.
25. take up: I have decided to take up a speaking course to improve my oral English.
26. teahouse: Suzhou has some nice teahouses that are more than a hundred years old.

7. Future

1. adapt to: I must try to adapt to the new environment.
2. ambition: My ambition is to become a doctor.
3. apply: I hope I can apply my medical knowledge to help the poor.
4. balance my time: If I want to achieve my goal, I would need to balance my time

笔记区

between work and study.

5. career: Everybody wants a stable and good career.
6. concentrate on: I think I should concentrate on pronunciation rather than grammar.
7. concern: I have many concerns about living overseas.
8. contribute: I hope I can contribute to my country's development.
9. culture shock: It is very common for many overseas students to experience culture shock.
10. custom: I'll have to get used to the different customs in Canada.
11. get accustomed to: I need some time to get accustomed to my new environment.
12. get established: It is very important to get your career established before you get married.
13. get used to: My father couldn't get used to the weather when he was in London.
14. goal/aim: My goal is to get a doctorate degree.
15. home stay: I prefer a home stay situation to staying in a dormitory.
16. homesick: I'll probably get homesick from time to time.
17. independent: I want to be independent when I grow up.
18. lonely: There is no doubt I will feel lonely sometimes.
19. manage my time: There should not be any problem to manage my time if I plan it properly.
20. mannerism: I must get used to his mannerisms.
21. mindset: To be able to adapt to the changing environment, we need to have an open mindset.
22. prove myself: I hope I can prove myself in the more difficult assignments.
23. settle in: It will take some time before I can settle in the new environment.
24. try out: I'd like to try out many different things overseas.
25. upgrade: I need to upgrade my computer knowledge.

8. Families

1. argue: Sometimes we argue but I think it is a waste of time.
2. be brought up: I was brought up in a very loving home.
3. birth control: Birth control is important to curb population growth.
4. broken family: Broken families can sometimes affect the children.
5. close-knit: My family is a very close-knit one.
6. collect a pension: In the West, it is common for the elderly to collect a pension.
7. cousin: I have a cousin that is one day older than me.
8. discipline: My mother was very strict with her discipline.
9. divorce: Divorce used to be taboo but not anymore.
10. elder: The elders always have lots of experience to pass down.
11. extended family: An extended family has its advantages and disadvantages.

笔记区

12. family size: Family size is small in China nowadays.
13. fight: Although we sometimes fight we do love each other a lot.
14. filial duty: Filial duty is important in Chinese society.
15. financially independent: Sometimes, the younger people want to be financially independent before they're ready to get married.
16. get along: I do get along with people quite easily.
17. get together: Chinese new year is an important time for families to get together.
18. grow up: I grew up in a small town.
19. keep in touch: I keep in touch with my family by e-mail.
20. life expectancy: Life expectancy has lengthened in some areas because of improved healthcare.
21. live apart: Many people would love to live apart and be independent.
22. look after: It is the job of children to look after their parents when they age.
23. make ends meet: In rural places, children started working at a young age to make ends meet in the family.
24. model: Parents always try to be good models for their children.
25. move out: We moved out from the area last year.
26. nag: People always say old people nag a lot but I have never noticed that.
27. nuclear family: Nowadays there are many nuclear families.
28. one child policy: China is adopting the one child policy to control the population.
29. only child: I am the only child in my family.
30. opposite: My best friend lives in the block opposite me.
31. pass away: My grandfather passed away three years ago.
32. raise...(e.g. children): It's a bit easier to raise a child than it used to be.
33. resemble: I resemble my father the most.
34. retired: Both my parents are retired.
35. scold: My mother sometimes scolds me for being too noisy.
36. single parent family: I don't think single parent families provide any less quality care than families with both parents.
37. spoil: Some kids are spoiled because all the attention was given to them.
38. strict: My father is quite strict.
39. support: My father is the one that supports the whole family.
40. the generation gap: The generation gap is getting wider and wider.

9. Shopping

1. store: There are more and more computer stores in town.
2. retail goods: There are wider selections in all kinds of retail goods nowadays.
3. gift shop: You won't miss the gift shops at the tourist site.
4. necessity: This store sells all kinds of necessities.
5. department store: There are three department stores in my hometown.

笔 记 区

6. cheat: The shopkeeper is quite honest and he will not cheat you.
7. imported goods: The shops in my hometown have a lot of imported goods.
8. luxury item: Nowadays more shops are selling luxury items.
9. price: The prices are very high here.
10. good deal: You can find some good deals if you look hard.
11. quality: The quality of goods in my hometown is quite high.
12. window shopping: I enjoy going only window shopping.
13. pirated goods: There are many pirated goods, especially DVDs.
14. modern: Many young people like to wear modern clothing.
15. service: The stores here emphasize their excellent after-sales service because of competition.
16. parking: Parking is always a problem especially in the CBD areas.
17. sales staff: The sales staff have been through training to provide good service.
18. on sale: You can find many goods on sale in my hometown.
19. bargain: You must bargain hard because the asking price is very high.
20. fashion: People are more fashion conscious nowadays.
21. in style: There are lots of things you can buy which are in style these days.
22. cost of living: The cost of living is relatively low in Gansu province.

10. Language Studies

1. accurate: I find it difficult to be accurate when we speak.
2. brave: One key strategy is to be brave with foreigners.
3. confident: When you speak, it is important to be confident.
4. familiar: There are many words I am still not familiar with.
5. fluent: My best friend can speak fluent Spanish.
6. grammar: Grammar can be complex sometimes.
7. hesitate: I often hesitate when I speak.
8. idiom: There are many idioms in English.
9. learn by heart: The teacher learned all the students' names by heart.
10. memorize: I spend a lot of time memorizing words.
11. native speaker: Forget about the accent, you will not speak like a native speaker.
12. persist: I think it's important just to persist with a language.
13. phrase: There are still many phrases which I can't understand.
14. practise: If you often practise speaking, you will be fluent.
15. pronunciation: I would say pronunciation is more important than mimicking the accent.
16. recite: Sometimes I'll recite a paragraph.
17. rhythm: Developing rhythm in your speech isn't easy.
18. smoothly: I hope one day I can speak English smoothly.
19. strike up: Yesterday I struck up an interesting conversation with an African

笔记区

woman.

20. stutter: It is common to stutter when you first speak the language.
21. tone: Chinese language has four tones.
22. tongue tied: I get a bit tongue tied when I speak.
23. translate: I can get my classmate to translate the essay into Japanese.
24. vocabulary: He has a large vocabulary but he couldn't speak a full sentence.
25. word block: I often get word blocks when I try to say something.

11. Sports

1. compete: If I cannot make it this time, I can always compete again next year.
2. exciting: I find sports exciting.
3. field: The field is often too wet to play football.
4. graceful: I like to watch female figure skating because it is so graceful.
5. keep active: It is important to keep active in life.
6. keep fit: I go swimming just to keep fit.
7. keep in shape: I hope I can always keep in shape if I control my diet.
8. live broadcast: Live broadcast is just as good as being there.
9. live game: Watching a live game can be very exciting.
10. match: This football match won't be exciting since both teams are not that great.
11. out of shape: I'm a bit out of shape now so I have to practise.
12. participate: Every student has to participate in extracurricular activities.
13. play for fun: I'm not a serious player. I just play for fun.
14. practise: To be competitive, we must practise everyday.
15. release stress： Exercise can help us release stress.
16. score: I think the yellow team will score more than the red one.
17. skill: Developing skills requires practice.
18. stadium: The stadium can accommodate 50,000 people.
19. strength: I don't have the strength to pick up the weights.
20. team: Our team won the first gold in ten years.

12. Food

1. baked: I like baked potatoes.
2. bitter: Some Chinese herbs are very bitter.
3. boiled: Westerners like to eat boiled potatoes.
4. chopsticks: I learned how to use chopsticks when I was four years old.
5. delicious: I like my mother's cooking because it is always so delicious.
6. dumpling: People in the north like to eat dumplings.
7. fresh: The fish is fresh.
8. helping: The helpings are large in that restaurant.
9. herb: More and more people are talking about herbs as an alternative to western

笔 记 区

medicin.
10. high in fat: McDonald's foods are high in fat.
11. hot pot: In the winter time, people like to eat hot pot.
12. hygienic: I prefer home-cooked meals because they are more hygienic than those of the restaurant.
13. lamb: Most of the lambs come from Inner Mongolia.
14. mixed: I like to eat mixed vegetables.
15. nutritious: It is important to eat nutritious food.
16. oily: Sichuan food can be quite oily.
17. salty: I can't take salty food at all.
18. smell: I like dishes that have a nice smell.
19. snack: I'm not used to having snacks between meals.
20. spicy: The food is so spicy that it numbs my tongue.
21. steam: Since the fish is so fresh, it is better that we steam it.
22. stir fried: Stir fried dishes are common in Chinese restaurants.
23. sweet: Shanghai food is quite sweet.
24. unique taste: I love Indian food because it has a unique taste.
25. variety: I prefer to have a variety of dishes when I go to a restaurant.

13. Clothing

1. baggy: I like to wear baggy pants.
2. brand named: Many people are wearing brandnamed clothing.
3. casual wear: Sometimes people think casual wear makes a person look cool.
4. colourful: Colourful clothing seems popular these days.
5. conscious: I am not that conscious of my appearance but many people are these days.
6. conservative: Very seldom I wear sleeveless shirts because I am conservative.
7. designer clothes: Designer clothes are very expensive.
8. dull: People used to wear very dull clothing in the 60s and 70s.
9. fashionable: More and more people are buying fashionable clothing.
10. in style: I'm not the best person to ask what is in style this summer.
11. jeans: Many people are wearing jeans nowadays.
12. keep up with: It is hard to keep up with the changes.
13. loose fitting: Loose fitting clothes are more comfortable.
14. spend a fortune: Older people complain that many youngsters spend a fortune on clothes.
15. tight fitting: Young girls like to wear tight fitting skirts that older people hate.
16. trendy: Many trendy clothes are appearing in stores now.
17. up-to-date: Fashion magazines can provide up-to-date designs.

笔 记 区

14. Music

1. band: These people formed a band and played in the pub.
2. classical: I enjoy classical music the most.
3. concert: I have never been to a concert.
4. dance to the beat: When the music starts, my daughter will dance to the beat.
5. folk: I always enjoy watching folk dance by minority people.
6. heavy metal: Heavy metal music is quite popular.
7. hum along: I am not good at singing but I like to hum along when I listen to a song.
8. instrument: Pi Pa is a Chinese instrument.
9. jazz: This pub plays only jazz music.
10. love song: There are just too many love songs nowadays.
11. lyrics: I like to study the lyrics of the song. They are usually very meaningful.
12. meaningful: The lyrics of this song are very meaningful.
13. melody: I like singing along to the melody.
14. piano: I used to attend piano lessons but I stopped.
15. pop: I like pop music because it makes me feel free and easy.
16. relax: When I am free, I like to listen to music to help me relax.
17. rock: I prefer rock to other kinds of music.
18. sad song: Sad songs make me feel moody.
19. stimulate: I guess I like this kind of music because it stimulates me.
20. voice: I like listening to the voices of these singers.
21. well-known: I mainly listen to well-known songs.

15. Places

1. altitude: Many tourists feel dizzy in Tibet because of its high altitude.
2. deep gorge: The Three Gorges between Chongqing and Yichang are very deep gorges.
3. deep impression: The sunrise at Taishan mountain made a deep impression on me.
4. deep valley: The place is in a very deep valley, which seems so mysterious.
5. flight: There are many flights from Beijing airport.
6. glacier: My dream is to visit the north pole and see the glaciers.
7. grassland: Inner Mongolia is famous for its vast grasslands.
8. Great Wall: Chinese people say that you are not a real man until you climb the Great Wall.
9. Imperial Palace: If you go to Beijing, you must visit the Imperial Palace.
10. on tour: I prefer to go on tour because everything is arranged.
11. pagoda: You will see a nice pagoda on top of the highest hill there.
12. plant life: The park has a rich variety of plant life.

笔记区

13. reach the summit: For climbers, the biggest satisfaction is to reach the summit.
14. rich culture: China has a very old and rich culture.
15. shore: I love to go to the shore and feel the sea breeze.
16. shrine: There are many shrines, a couple of which are famous.
17. souvenir: Many tourists like to buy souvenirs while on tour.
18. spectacular view: You can get a spectacular view on the top of Huangshan mountain.
19. statue: There are many important statues in the square.
20. steep canyon: The steep canyons will take your breath away.
21. steep cliff: Along the famous Three Gorges, there are many steep cliffs on both sides.
22. sunbathing: Sunbathing can be quite fun provided you don't burn your skin.
23. sunrise: Have you every tried to get up early and see the sunrise?
24. sunset: Standing on the Great Wall and watching the sunset is very captivating.
25. temple: There are many temples in China especially in the South.
26. tourist: More and more tourists are coming to China every year.
27. twisted rock: Those twisted rocks inside the Imperial Palace are beautiful.
28. waterfall: If you hike into the park you will see a very pretty waterfall.
29. wave: The waves can be quite strong during the monsoon season.
30. wildlife: You can observe a lot of different wildlife in that region.

16. People

1. admire: Michael Jordan is the person I admire the most.
2. behaviour: Some people consider his behaviour a bit odd, but I like him very much.
3. depend on: I feel I can always depend on her.
4. diligent: Few of my classmates are as diligent as her when they study.
5. easygoing: My friend is a very easygoing person.
6. extrovert: My best friend is sometimes too extroverted.
7. hang around: We like to hang around together at Internet cafes.
8. high cheek bones: My sister has high cheek bones.
9. in common: My friend and I always have a lot in common.
10. introvert: I am much more introverted than my brother.
11. lost contact/touch: I have lost contact/touch with my old classmates.
12. loyal: My sister is very loyal to me.
13. mutual respect: We seem to have mutual respect for each other.
14. reliable: I feel my best friend is very reliable and will not break promises.
15. rely on: We can always rely on each other for help.
16. same interest: My father and I share the same interest in sports.
17. secret: I share my secrets with my best friend.

笔 记 区

18. sense of humour: My best friend has a good sense of humour.
19. stand by me: My parents will always stand by me.
20. trustworthy: Many people say I am trustworthy.

17. Experiences

1. be scared to death: I was scared to death giving that speech in front of everyone.
2. celebrate: More people celebrate Christmas in China nowadays.
3. couldn't believe my eyes: I couldn't believe my eyes when I saw such a beautiful site.
4. deep impression: If you visit the exhibition, you will get a deep impression of it too.
5. effect on me: The effect this trip had on me was something I can hardly describe.
6. encourage: It was my piano teacher who encouraged me to take part in the competition.
7. enjoy myself: I enjoyed myself very much when I was in Malaysia.
8. finally: Finally, she arrived and we met for the first time.
9. impress: I was impressed by the artist's work.
10. in a daze: After I heard the news I was in a daze.
11. jump for joy: My parents jumped for joy when I was admitted into university.
12. learning experience: I treat this trip as a learning experience, and will try to do things differently next time.
13. never forget the time: I'll never forget the time when I represented the school in a Chinese chess competition which was held by the city.
14. once I... : Once I was picnicking on the beach, it suddenly started raining.
15. overjoyed: Many Chinese were overjoyed when Beijing got to host the 2008 Olympics.
16. put all my effort into: I put all my effort into learning Chinese painting.
17. realize: The bus had already moved when I realized I was on the wrong bus.
18. recall: Whenever I recall that trip I get such a warm feeling.
19. shock: Everyone was shocked by the news.
20. stay in my mind: The little girl that died of cancer will always stay in my mind.
21. think it over: After I thought it over, I felt so stupid lending him money.
22. took...seriously: I took my first job very seriously and always worked overtime.
23. unforgettable: The most unforgettable moment was when I broke my leg in school.
24. with all my might: I tried with all my might to complete it on time.

18. Buildings and Homes

1. architecture: I prefer traditional architecture.
2. brick: Brick houses are very common here.

笔记区

3. concrete: The walls are made of concrete.
4. corridor: The longest painted corridor is in the Summer Palace.
5. design: The design was done by a European.
6. dining room: The dining room can accommodate 1,000 people.
7. empty/vacant: The apartment has been vacant for 3 months.
8. entrance: I can't find the entrance to the park.
9. furniture: All the furniture here is from Spain.
10. high quality material: It is made of high-quality materials, so it looks very classy and solid.
11. kitchen: I like a kitchen that is bright and clean.
12. living room: The living room is at least 20 square metres.
13. old fashioned: Even though it is designed that way, it is not necessarily old fashioned.
14. roof: The roof is red.
15. skyscraper: There are many skyscrapers in Shanghai.
16. tile: Tiles come in different colours to choose from.
17. traditional-style: It is made from traditional-style architecture.

19. Gifts and Meaningful Objects

1. aluminum: It is made out of a light type of aluminum.
2. antique: I guess you could call it an antique, even though I don't know the age of it.
3. be used to: It is used to store words and definitions.
4. breakable: This bottle is breakable, so handle it with care.
5. decorate: It is decorated with many different pictures.
6. function: It has many functions and features.
7. hollow: It is actually hollow inside so that you can keep coins.
8. metal: It is a metal object with many designs on it.
9. plastic: The edge of it is made of very hard plastic.
10. plug: You can just plug it in and cook what you want.
11. precious: The crown was set with precious jewels.
12. priceless: My dad gave me this watch, and I considered it to be priceless.
13. rare: This is a rare piece of artwork.
14. rectangular: It has a rectangular shape which is quite interesting.
15. replace: The sentimental value of this gift cannot be replaced.
16. reward: I was given it as a reward for getting good grades in school.
17. round: The top of it is round.
18. shiny: The surface is very shiny and smooth.
19. surface: The surface is very smooth and shiny.
20. texture: The texture is quite rough.

笔 记 区

21. well made: I can see that is a well-made piece of work.
22. wooden: It is a wooden object with a plastic cover.

20. Favourite Animal

1. adorable: Pandas are adorable animals.
2. avoid: This animal tends to avoid humans so they are hard to see.
3. bamboo: Bamboo can be used to make different objects.
4. be found in: Polar bears are to be found only in the North Pole.
5. claw: The tiger has sharp claws.
6. conservation area: Many of them live in conservation areas, which protect them from hunters.
7. crawl: The crocodile crawls on land.
8. cunning: I think the wolf is a cunning animal.
9. cute: The koala is a very cute animal in Australia.
10. elegant: The rooster looks very elegant with the crown on its head.
11. endangered: The white tiger is an endangered species.
12. extinct: This kind of species has become extinct.
13. fierce: The lion is a fierce animal.
14. graceful: Most people agree that this animal is very graceful when it moves.
15. habitat: Its habitat is in Northeast China.
16. hunting: These animals have been disappearing due to hunting.
17. instinct: Sharks have a very good instinct of where the food is.
18. paw: They have sharp claws on their paws.
19. population: The population of the panda has decreased drastically over the last 20 years.
20. protected area: These animals mostly live in protected areas around China.
21. shy: The panda is also a shy animal.
22. spot: The leopard has spots on its body.
23. stripe: Zebras have stripes on their bodies.
24. tail: I love the long tail of a tiger, and the way it moves.

21. Festivals and Holidays

1. carnival: There are different carnivals held during summer in my hometown.
2. celebrate: Chinese New Year is celebrated all over China.
3. customary: It is customary for people to exchange gifts on Christmas Day.
4. decorate: It is customary for people to decorate their houses during the festival season.
5. family reunion: Most people look forward to a family reunion during festival seasons.
6. feast: My mother always cooks up a big feast on this day.

笔记区

7. fireworks display: We end the event with a huge fireworks display.
8. honour: Qing Ming is the day when the living honour the deceased.
9. Labour Day: Labour Day falls on May the first.
10. legend: There is a legend which explains why we set off firecrackers.
11. Mid Autumn Festival: Mid Autumn Festival is a time when people can get together briefly, have a nice feast together and perhaps watch the moon.
12. National Day: National Day falls on the first of October.
13. parade: During the 50th Anniversary, there was a big parade at Tian'anmen Square.
14. pay respect to: Kids should always pay respect to their elders.
15. red packet: The younger children receive red packets from the elders during Chinese New Year.
16. reestablish link: It's a good time for us to reestablish our links with each other.
17. reminisce: Sometimes we just sit around and reminisce about the old times.
18. round table dinner: Round table diners are common for Chinese people during this festival.
19. set off fireworks: Many people in rural areas set off fireworks during Spring Festival.
20. significance: The significance of such an event is mainly symbolic.
21. Spring Festival: We get seven days of holiday for Spring Festival.
22. superstition: We do it out of superstition but we really don't take it seriously.

节日用语

Customs:

1. bid farewell to the old year 辞旧岁
2. dragon dance 舞龙
3. exhibition of lanterns 灯会
4. firecrackers 爆竹
5. fireworks 烟花
6. get rid of the ill-fortune 去晦气
7. gift money 压岁钱
8. Guo-nian 过年
9. lantern 灯笼
10. lion dance 舞狮
11. New Year paintings 年画
12. offer sacrifices to one's ancestors 祭祖宗
13. paper-cuttings 剪纸
14. pay New Year's call; give New Year's greetings; New Year's visit 拜年
15. poetic couplets 对联
16. propose a toast 敬酒
17. red packets 红包

笔记区

18. riddles written on lanterns 灯谜
19. special purchases for the Spring Festival ; do Spring Festival shopping 买年货
20. spring cleaning 扫房
21. Spring Festival couplets 春联
22. staying-up 守岁
23. taboo 禁忌
24. traditional opera 戏曲
25. variety show 杂耍

Food names:

1. assorted candies 什锦糖
2. candied lotus root 糖藕
3. candied lotus seed 糖莲子
4. candied winter melon 蜜冬瓜
5. candy tray 糖果盘
6. cumquat 金橘
7. eight treasures rice pudding 八宝饭
8. family reunion dinner 团圆饭
9. Jiao-zi: Chinese meat ravioli 饺子
10. Nian-gao; New Year cake 年糕
11. peanut candy 花生糖
12. red dates 红枣
13. red melon seed 西瓜子
14. Tang-yuan 汤圆
15. the dinner on New Year's Eve 年夜饭

22. The Environment

1. air/water/soil quality: The air quality is getting worse and worse in some cities.
2. carbon dioxide: Excessive carbon dioxide can cause weather change.
3. chemical: There are a lot of chemicals being dumped in the water.
4. coal: Our country relies too much on coal.
5. contaminate: The river is contaminated by the nearby factories.
6. dumping: Waste dumping at improper areas can cause pollution.
7. endangered: The panda is an endangered species.
8. exhaust fume: Exhaust fumes can cause respiratory problems.
9. extinction: Some animals are close to extinction.
10. garbage: You can see garbage on many streets.
11. give fines to: The government should give fines to those who break the rules.
12. Greenhouse Effect: I think everyone is worried about the Greenhouse Effect.
13. litter: We shouldn't litter and we must keep our city clean.

笔记区

14. logging: Illegal logging is a big problem in this town.
15. over-(e.g. over-logging, over-fishing): The fish population has decreased dramatically because of over-fishing.
16. plant trees: Many students learn how to plant trees in school.
17. poach: Bear poaching is still going on in the northeastern part of China.
18. pollution: Pollution is a big problem for many cities in China.
19. recycle: We should do more to recycle bottles and papers.
20. regulation: The government is passing new regulations to deal with the problem.
21. resource: We need to protect our resources better.
22. restriction: Strict restrictions should be imposed to protect the environment.
23. reuse: As they become wealthier, many people no longer reuse things.
24. soil erosion: Soil erosion is a big problem in Inner Mongolia.
25. waste: We need to adopt better waste treatment of the water.

23. Technology

1. accurate: People expect programmes to be accurate and reliable.
2. advance: Technology is getting more and more advanced.
3. automatically: Many new facilities work automatically.
4. automation: Full automation is what many factories are hoping to achieve at year's end.
5. brand new: We need brand new technology for our industries to prosper.
6. connect: The Internet connects people around the world.
7. electronic: Electronic goods such as hand phones are getting smaller.
8. globalization: Globalization will help to improve living standards.
9. hardware: We can produce good computer hardware.
10. high-tech industry: There are many high-tech industries in Zhong Guan Cun.
11. information age: We are living in the information age because things move fast.
12. latest development: It's important for a company to be on top of the latest developments or it will fall behind its competitors.
13. modernization: Modernization opens up many opportunities for people.
14. outdated: Many computers are outdated.
15. restructure: Many companies have to restructure.
16. retraining: Many laid-off workers go for retraining to improve their skills.
17. revolution: Computers have gone through quite a revolution in the last twenty years.
18. stay on top: People have to stay on top of all the latest developments.
19. technical: If there are any technical problems, it's difficult to get them fixed.
20. top notch: Many companies like top notch people to work for them.
21. transfer: Many banks will do money transfers from one account to another.
22. upgrade: These days it's necessary to constantly upgrade our skills.

笔记区

23. wireless: We can expect much of our technology to be wireless in the future.

24. Societal Changes

1. acknowledge: Most people acknowledge that this is a serious problem.
2. article: I have read an article about the bank robbery in today's newspaper.
3. at a...rate: Things are changing at an alarming rate.
4. awareness: Consumer awareness is growing.
5. bias: A good newspaper will try to be free of any bias.
6. can't take: I can't take the blame because I wasn't there when it happened.
7. censorship: Censorship is sometimes necessary for a number of reasons.
8. century: I hope the world will be at peace in this century.
9. come together to solve: I hope people will come together to solve the problem.
10. corruption: Corruption is rampant in some companies.
11. day by day: Our lives are getting better day by day.
12. dependent: People are more dependent on computers than ever before.
13. discriminate on/against: I would say some foreign workers are discriminated against in big cities.
14. equality/inequality: There still exits some inequality although it's a bit better now.
15. experiment: Countless experiments were done to make sure it works.
16. expose: Many cases of this have been exposed.
17. feel the strain: I can feel the strain with the increased competition.
18. gap: The gap between rich and poor is enormous.
19. global village: We truly live in a global village.
20. growing demand: There is a growing demand for new solutions.
21. ignore: Society cannot ignore the disadvantaged people.
22. impact: There are many ways that this problem has impacted society.
23. impersonal: Unlike letters, I find e-mail more impersonal.
24. innovation: Innovation is important for any company that wants to survive.
25. keep pace: We have to keep pace with the changes.
26. (can't) keep pace with: The world is changing so fast that I almost can't keep pace with the changes.
27. keep up with: It is hard to keep up with the changing technology.
28. libel: Sometimes restrictions are necessary to protect people from libel.
29. look into: If you look into the problem, you might find it is more complicated than you think.
30. neglect: The poor are the ones that are often neglected in the society.
31. opening up: China is slowly opening up to the world.
32. over dependence: I think we should not create any over dependence on one source.
33. pass legislation: We need to pass legislation that stems the problem.

笔记区

34. pressure: The pressure can sometimes be too great to handle.
35. print: The magazine print is getting more and more attractive.
36. publish: This magazine is published once a month.
37. rapid development: Beijing has seen some rapid development in the last three years.
38. reliable/credible/accurate source: It's important for a good reporter to have reliable sources or the story may turn out to be false.
39. repress/suppress: Some women feel they are still suppressed in society.
40. rise in...: There's been a sharp rise in crime.
41. rising/on the rise: Crime has been on the rise for the last couple years.
42. root/underlying cause (of the problem): The root cause of the problem is the low pay they receive at work.
43. self-sufficient: The main challenge is to make them more self-sufficient.
44. special effect: American films are good at special effects.
45. steadily: The revenue has changed steadily over the years.
46. stem from: Such abuse stems from a lack of awareness.
47. substantial: You can see substantial changes were made over the years.
48. surface: Although it seems to work on the surface, the reality is different.
49. take over: Tall buildings are taking over those low flats.
50. transform: In ten years, I'm sure China will be transformed into one of the superpowers.
51. verify: It is not difficult to verify whether it is true or false.
52. violence: There is just too much violence on TV.
53. voice concern: Many people are voicing their concerns about this issue.
54. way of thinking: People now are more receptive to new ideas, and the way of thinking has changed.
55. way of thinking: The younger generation has a different way of thinking.

25. Media

1. broadcast: These days television can be broadcasted around the world.
2. check source: A reporter must check his sources very carefully.
3. download: You can download games from the Internet.
4. gossip: Gossip news keeps readers entertained.
5. irresponsible: Some reporters are irresponsible when it comes to reporting.
6. journalist: It is not easy for journalists to do reports in war zones.
7. objective: A reporter has to be objective for his/her reporting.
8. professional: It is important to act professionally as a journalist.
9. report: Sometimes we have to be sharp if the report is not true.
10. sensationalism: The entertainment news often likes to engage in sensationalism.
11. standard: I would say our newspaper adheres to high industry standards.

笔 记 区

12. tabloid: Some people like to read tabloid news.

26. Lifestyles

1. cool: Young people like to look cool and think it is attractive.
2. disposable income: In the cities, you can see that disposable income has increased.
3. fashion: Many people are getting more fashion conscious.
4. image: Image is only a disguise to what a real person is.
5. keep fit: One needs to keep fit to be healthy.
6. more open towards...: Many people are more open towards inter-racial marriages.
7. pace of life: I prefer the relaxed pace of life in the country.
8. rebel: Teenagers like to rebel rather than conform to the norm.
9. recreation: Recreation areas are lacking in many cities in China.
10. social life: I try to keep my social life minimal during the weekend.
11. standard of living: Many people are enjoying a higher standard of living.
12. status: High status does not mean happiness is achieved.
13. take life easy: We live only for so long, so I feel we should take life easy.
14. take up: I hope to take up diving courses when I visit Thailand.
15. trend: The trend towards healthy eating is to go organic.
16. way of life: The way of life is very different in different provinces.

II. 句 型

1. Describing Objects, Clothing, Buildings and Housing

1. It's round with a long handle and lots of different functions.
2. It's made of silk.
3. It has many features.
4. It can be used to make phone calls or you can use it for playing games.
5. It has a lot of patterns.
6. It is red coloured with a steep roof.
7. The whole building is covered with designs.
8. It's a 3-room apartment, and it's about 80 square metres.

2. Recalling Events

1. I can still remember the time when I passed my entrance examinations.
2. I'll never forget the time when I first went to primary school.
3. It all started when I landed at the airport.
4. Once, when I was a college student, I went on a trip which I will never forget.

笔记区

3. Describing Moods

1. I felt so happy that I could jump for joy.
2. I was in a great mood.
3. I felt like I was in heaven.
4. I was scared to death.
5. I was overcome with joy.
6. It impressed me deeply.
7. I felt so depressed.
8. I felt like a millionaire.
9. I was worried to death.
10. I was filled with joy.

4. Giving Instructions

1. The first thing you should do/need to do/is to plug it in.
2. To start with, you should/need to turn on the power.
3. First, you need to take off the lid.
4. The first step is to get the ingredients prepared.
5. After that, you need to find the right switch.
6. Next, you should select the function you want to use.
7. After that, you should press the button.
8. Then, bring it close to your ear.
9. Finally, switch it off by pressing the red button.
10. The last thing you need to do is to turn off the stove.
11. Don't forget to check to see if the batteries are inside.
12. Make sure you recharge it at night.
13. Make sure you won't forget to turn it off when you are finished.

5. How to Hesitate

1. Well, ...
2. Actually, ...
3. In fact, ...
4. You see, ...
5. You know, ...
6. How shall I put it, ...
7. Let me think for a second, ...
8. Give me a few seconds, ...

6. Commenting on the Issue Itself

1. That's difficult to answer, but (maybe)...

笔记区

2. I'm sorry, but I don't know much about...but perhaps...
3. Maybe I can answer your question by telling you about a personal experience I had.
4. That's an interesting question...let me see. Well, I suppose that...
5. Yes, that's a big issue.

7. Talking about the Changes

1. More and more people in China are learning English.
2. The environmental problem is getting more serious.
3. Cities in China have been going through some big changes.
4. These days, computers have become very popular.
5. Prices of computers are falling rapidly.
6. There has been a rapid increase of farmers moving to the cities.
7. The number of engineers has risen rapidly over the last few years.
8. China's population has remained about the same over the last few years.

8. Talking about the Role or Importance of an Issue

1. Yes, computers play a big role in our lives.
2. Yes, I think it's an important issue for us in China these days.
3. You're right, sports are playing an increasingly big role in our lives.
4. Entertainment has always been important to our lives.
5. Friendship is something we all take seriously.
6. In China we consider the family to be key to our society.

9. Giving an Anecdote Related to the Issue

1. I can remember seeing the Olympics and thinking how wonderful it must be for people from Sydney.
2. Yes, I personally have experienced some of these changes growing up here in Beijing.
3. In fact, I had a personal experience with this issue of crime last year.

10. How to Make Generalizations

1. In the vast majority of cases, the accidents are caused by neglect.
2. In most cases, divorce is something that both parties realize is necessary.
3. Generally (speaking), Chinese people love sports.
4. By and large, Chinese people are very respectful of the elderly.
5. On the whole, Chinese students receive a good education in the basics.

11. Speculating the Reasons for a Trend

笔记区

1. Probably the main reason that technology has increased is that we are now more

open to outside ideas.

2. The best reason I can think of for the increase in crime is our changing social conditions.
3. I would guess that fast food restaurants are becoming more important because of their convenience.
4. I'm not sure, but from my own observation, I would say that most people are buying cars because they're symbols of prosperity.

12. Speculating the Reasons for a Situation

1. Although I'm no expert, I'd guess that children learn instruments more easily because they are not so dependent on human language and therefore more susceptible to alternative ways of expression.
2. It's hard to say, but if I were to guess I'd say that many people are doing their MBAs because they think it is much easier to get a job with one.
3. If I had to guess I would say that children make friends easier than adults because they are more carefree.
4. I'm not that familiar with art but I'd say that some art is more popular because it connects better with its audience.

13. Speculating the Importance or Effect of Something

1. I'd probably have to say that the real importance of sports is that they allow us to release our energy.
2. I'm not sure, but I think the biggest role that a teacher plays in education is that he/she guides you to success.
3. I had to say that the biggest impact of machinery is on human beings. I'd guess it has made us more demanding in producing things.

14. Speculating the Important Factors that Cause or Contribute to Something

1. I imagine that the most important factor to a long lasting friendship is trust.
2. There are many ways, but I suppose that the most important way a foreign language affects us is that it opens up a whole new world to us.
3. I'd say the biggest way that music contributes to our world is that it helps make us feel calmer.

15. Speculating about an Issue in the Future

1. It probably won't change much in a short period of time.
2. Perhaps not in the short term but it will get better in the long run.
3. I'd say it will probably get better because more people are concerned.

笔 记 区

16. Giving Opinions

1. I think it's a matter of a person's choice whether they want to learn it.
2. I think it's hard to judge now but we'll be able to tell later.
3. I'd like to point out that pollution is not a new problem.
4. As far as I'm concerned, the Internet is a waste of time.
5. In my opinion, we should stick together as a group.
6. From my point of view, I think you should look for other ways out.
7. Personally, I think the time could be better spent doing other things.
8. Frankly, I think it's a waste of time.
9. I reckon we should consider other options.
10. If you ask me, that's not a good solution.
11. I'd say that we should think about a range of solutions.

17. Expressing Your Argument Immediately by Giving a Counterargument

1. Well, I know many people like it but I think it's wrong.
2. Yes, these days it is quite popular to go on these chat lines, but I think it's not very good.
3. A lot of people think the environment is getting better but frankly I think it's getting worse.

18. Giving Reasons for Arguments

1. Well, I think there are 2 (or 3 or more) reasons: First, I think it is part of our culture. Second, I think it is good for our economy. Finally, it gives us time to recharge and be rested for the next working year.
2. Well, the main reasons I think this would be dangerous are...
3. The best reason I think the examination system should change is because it prevents too many people from pursuing their dreams.
4. I can come up with about 3 reasons for the change in people's diets.

19. Supporting Arguments by Giving Examples

1. Take the problem of traffic jams at the intersection for example.
2. The ping-pong champion is a good example.
3. Well, just to illustrate my point, 30 years ago we had few cars.
4. One example of this is the carnival at Longtan Park.
5. I think I can give you one particular example of a policy that has really helped to protect the environment.

20. Supporting Arguments by Giving Hypothetical Logic

笔记区

1. If you allow your traditional customs to disappear, this will have a very bad effect

on your culture.

2. If everyone were to eat fast food, we would have a lot of health problems to deal with.
3. If animals were to disappear, we would indeed be showing our irresponsibility to the animal kingdom.

21. Supporting Opinions by Offering Solutions

1. I think what should be done is to give students more opportunities to demonstrate their creativity.
2. If I had the power to change things, I would start by relocating factories to places outside the city.
3. What ought to be done is a complete ban on such practices.
4. I think this problem could be solved by creating more job opportunities.
5. To solve this problem, I think we should try and set up more facilities for elderly people to meet each other and socialize.

22. Stating Differences

1. The main difference between the way younger people think of clothing and the way older people think of clothes is in the styles.
2. The biggest difference between construction about 20 years ago and today is that 20 years ago much construction was done manually.
3. There are some key differences between Western and Chinese food.
4. One large way that big cities differ from small cities is the air.
5. Yes, there are quite a few differences between the way children and adults make friends. A good example is the way they just start using each other's toys happily without needing permission.
6. The difference between Western movies and Chinese movies is that Western movies tend to be more action-based while Chinese movies focus on the relationships between people.

23. Making Comparisons

1. Big cities have more opportunities than small cities.
2. University life is more interesting than middle school life.
3. Key schools are cleaner than regular schools.
4. There is more oil in Chinese food than in Western food.
5. Families in the past were more dependent on each other, but now they are more independent.
6. An apartment is not as big as a house but in many ways it is more convenient. For one thing, you can use the facilities in the apartment block, like the gym,

笔记区

swimming pool and playground.

7. There were fewer cars on the roads 20 years ago, compared to now.

24. Pros and Cons

1. There are two sides to this issue. On one hand, we need tourism to develop our economy. On the other hand, we shouldn't let it destroy our natural beauty.
2. This issue is complex. On one hand, people say it's healthy to play sports but on the other hand playing them too competitively may lead to some harmful things.

25. Advantages and Disadvantages

1. There are many advantages and disadvantages of watching sports versus playing them.
2. The main advantage of getting your news on the Internet is that it is fast and you can choose what news you want to learn. The disadvantage is it may not be as reliable.
3. The strengths of a traditional family are in its close family support, but the weakness is that often the husband and wife feel trapped in the relationship.
4. The positive side of technology is its contribution to our convenience, but the darker side of it is that it may make us lazier.
5. While many point out that uniforms save students form buying clothes, I think it also teaches students conformity.

26. 其他用语

1. 当你没有听懂时，可用：
   1）Could you please rephrase that question/topic?
   2）I'm not exactly sure what you mean...
2. 当你对考官所提问的内容不熟悉或完全没有听说过时，可用：
   1）I'm not exactly sure how to answer that question, but（perhaps）...
   2）That's a rather difficult question, but（maybe）...
   3）I'm sorry, but I don't know much about...
3. 当你联想到其他相关答案进行回答时，可用：
   1）However, it might be possible that...
   2）Maybe I can answer your question by telling you about a personal experience I had.
   3）That's an interesting question...
   4）Let me see. Well, I suppose that...
4. 当你进行逻辑型论证时，可用：
   1）Well, I think there are 2（or 3 or more）reasons: First, ... Second, ... Finally, ...

笔记区

2）In my opinion there are three ways of looking at it: First of all, ... Next, ... Then, ...

5. 当你论证完毕，询问考官是否还需补充其他信息时，可用：

1）Have I given you enough information?

2）Would you like me to tell you more about...?

3）Is that all you'd like to know?

6. 当你认为自己已将所知道的都表达清楚，再无补充时，可用：

1）I'm afraid that's about as much as I know.

2）I think that's all.

3）I can't think of anything else right now...

4）Is there anything else you wish to know?

7. 当谈到现在和将来打算时可用：

1）Well, ... as you know, at the moment I'm studying at...

2）Well, ... as I told you before, at the moment I'm working at...

3）I'm preparing right now to go to...so my short-term plan is to...

4）I've already found out a lot about my intended course, for instance, ...

5）If I'm successful, I'll probably...so, in the long-term, I hope to...

6）If I'm not successful, that is, if something goes wrong, I think I'll probably...

7）I'm certain I'll (do something).

8）I'm going to (do something).

9）I'm intending to (do something).

10）I'm thinking of (doing something).

11）I'm hopeful to (do something).

12）I'm certain I'll be (doing something).

13）I'm going to work.

14）I intend to be (doing something).

15）I think I'll be (doing something).

16）I hope to be (doing something).

17）I'll probably (be able to) (do something).

18）I possibly won't (be able to) (do something).

19）I probably won't (be able to) (do something).

20）I most probably won't (be able to) (do something).

21）I might even...

22）Of course, I could always...if...

23）It's always possible that...

24）Perhaps I'll even...

25）I've thought about (doing something).

26）I've got a good chance of (doing something).

27）I've got a 50-50 chance of (doing something).

笔 记 区

28) I've got a reasonable chance of (doing something).

29) I've got little chance of (doing something).

30) I've got no chance of (doing something).

笔记区

附录 1

模拟口试

Exam One

Part One

Hometown

Where are you from?

Where do you live now?

Which part of the city do you like best?

Is there any part of the city that you don't like?

Are you going to stay there for a long time?

Films

Do you like films?

What kind of films do you like?

How often do you watch films?

Do you like to watch alone or with your friends?

Do you prefer to watch films in the cinema or at home?

Birthdays

How important are birthdays in your country?

What do children get on birthdays in your country?

What is the most important birthday celebrated in China?

Part Two

What kind of books would you like to write? (e.g. textbook, history book, story book)

You should say:

what kind of books you would like to write

what you would write in your book

and what kind of people would read your book in your opinion.

Follow up

When would you plan to write it? Do you like writing?

Part Three

Writer

What is the most important quality about a writer?

笔 记 区

Why do people choose to write for a living?

What kind of difficulties would a writer come up with?

Library

What do you think of libraries in your society?

How can libraries encourage people to read or learn more?

What do you think of the amount of money the government spends on libraries?

Exam Two

Part One

Work and study

Do you work or do you study?

Do you like your job?

Would you change jobs?

Memories

Do you keep photos? Why?

How do you feel when other people talk about their past experiences?

What can you learn from other people's experiences?

Public transport

What kind of public transport do people around you use?

Do you use public transport often?

What can the government do to improve public transport?

When is public transport most crammed?

Part Two

Describe the happiest person you've ever known.

You should say:

who the person is

why the person is happy

how the person shows happiness

and explain how you feel about this person.

Part Three

Happiness

What can be done to help other people to be happy?

What are the sources of happiness?

Government and happiness

Is there anything the government can do to increase people's happiness?

Do you think that the standard of living affects people's happiness?

笔记区

Exam Three

Part One

Hometown

Where are you from?

Where do you live now?

Which part of the city do you like best?

Is there any part of the city that you don't like?

Are you going to stay there for a long time?

Restaurants

How often do you go to restaurants?

Do you like to eat out?

On what occasions do you eat out?

What kind of restaurants do you like best?

Seasons

Talk about the seasons in your hometown.

Which season do you like most? Why?

What do people do during this season?

Part Two

Describe the clothes you wear on special occasions.

You should say:

what type of clothes you would choose for such occasion

what you will look like when you wear them

how you feel when you wear them

and explain why you wear it.

Part Three

Are there any traditional costumes or national costumes in China?

Why do people like to wear traditional clothes?

What is the meaning of fashion?

What is the difference between the clothes people wear now and those in the past?

Do you think clothing is more important than before? Why?

What's the main difference between men's fashion and women's fashion?

What can you tell from the way people dress themselves?

What are the advantages and disadvantages of people wearing uniforms?

What will make a person change his/her clothing?

笔 记 区

Exam Four

Part One

Do you work or do you study?

How do you like your job? / How do you like your studies?

Are you interested in other jobs?

Is your university a good place to study in?

Do you have any plans for the future?

Have you ever been to the seaside?

Why do some people take their holidays at the seaside?

Do you want to live near the sea?

Do you like writing?

What do you like to write in your free time?

What is the biggest problem with English writing for you?

Part Two

Describe a project you finished with others.

You should say:

with whom you finished the project

when you finished it

how you did it

and whether it brings any benefits.

Part Three

Is cooperation important?

How to cultivate students to cooperate?

What do you think about teamwork?

What may be the problems of working in a group?

What are the benefits of teamwork?

Exam Five

Part One

Accommodation

What kind of place do you live in?

Describe your neighbourhood.

笔记区

Photos

Do you keep photos? Why?

Do Chinese people like to take photographs?

How do you feel when other people talk about their past experiences?

What can you learn from other people's experiences?

Music

What kind of music do you like? Why?

When do you listen to music?

Can you play a musical instrument?

Should children learn to play instruments?

Part Two

Describe a film you like.

You should say:

what the name of the film is

when and where you saw it

if it is a happy story or a sad one

and explain why you like it.

Part Three

What kind of films do you like best?

What kind of films are most popular in China?

What is the main difference between modern films and those in the past?

Do you prefer to see a film at home or in a cinema?

What is the difference between young people's taste in films and that of adults?

What do you think of Zhang Yimou's films?

What do you think of using the same actor/actress for different films?

Who is the most famous film star in China?

What do you think of violence in films? Why is there so much of it?

Is there censorship in China? Why?

What is the most important quality of a successful film?

Exam Six

Part One

Work and study

Do you work or are you a student?

What is your major?

笔记区

How do you like your studies?

Hometown

Where are you from?

Where do you live now?

Which part of the city do you like best?

Is there any part of the city that you don't like?

Are you going to stay there for a long time?

Films

Do you like films?

What kind of films do you like?

How often do you watch films?

Do you like to watch alone or with your friends?

Do you prefer to watch films in the cinema or at home?

Part Two

Describe your favourite (wild) animal.

You should say:

what it is

how you know it

what it is like

and explain why you like it.

Part Three

Wildlife conservation

Can you think of some reasons why some species become endangered?

What are the advantages and disadvantages of having a pet?

What are some other purposes for which animals are used?

Do you find using animals for medical research acceptable?

Safari parks and zoos

What do you think are the benefits of keeping animals in a zoo?

Any improvement?

笔记区

附录 2

口试实例

下面的口试实例包括在MP3中。为了达到真实的效果，考生的回答中包括一些错误，不要模仿。所有错误都用彩色印刷并在随后的括号中附有正确答案。

Sample Interview

（Stage 1）

I: Good afternoon. My name is Clive. May I have your full name please?

C: My name is Zhouqi.

I: What shall I call you?

C: You can call me Sandy.

I: And can you tell me where you are from?

C: I'm from Wuhan in Hubei province, China.

I: Can I see your identification please?

C: OK. Here you are.

I: That's fine. Now, in this first part, I'd like to ask you some questions about yourself. Let's talk about your hometown. What kind of place is it?

C: I was born and grow（grew）up in Wuhan, the capital of Hubei province. It is a（an）industrial big（big industrial）city in the middle of China. The city is actually divided into three towns by two big rivers. Have you ever gone to（been）there before?

I: No. I haven't. What is the most interesting part of your hometown?

C: I think it's the climate. It's very hot and humid in summer. The temperature sometimes reaches 40 degrees and it is often rains（it often rains）.

I: Are you a student or do you have a job?

C: I'm a college student. I study in Wuhan University.

I: And what's your major? What do you study?

C: My major is Accounting.

I: Why did you choose to study this as your major?

C: Well, the reason is very simple. I think it's easy to me（for me）to find a job after my graduation because every business needs accountants.

I: Now let's move on to what you do in your spare time. Do you like reading?

C: Yes, I like reading very much. I used to reading（read）a lot, but I'm too（so）busy now with my study that I have fewer（less）time to read.

笔记区

I: What kind of books do you like to read?

C: I like to read novels, all kinds of novels, especially those written by famous writers.

I: And do you have a favourite writer?

C: Yes, my favourite writer is Mark Twain. His works are full of humour and deep thoughts.

I: When do you like to read?

C: I like to read in the evening because it's very quiet then. I can concentrate to (on) the books I read.

I: How about your holidays? How do you usually spend them?

C: I like to travel very much. I usually go to a different place every year.

I: Is there anywhere in particular that you would like to visit?

C: I like to go to places with beautiful scenery but not too many people. So I don't usually travel in(on) national holidays to avoid the crowded (crowds of people).

I: Let's talk a little bit about travelling and transport. What is the most common way that you like to move around?

C: I beg your pardon?

I: Well, How do you prefer to travel for long trips?

C: Oh, I prefer to travel by train. It's cheaper than travelling by air and you can also enjoy to look(looking) at the scenery.

I: Do you see any changes in transportation over the past 20 years in China?

C: Yes, there are more and more people buying their own cars. The traffic is much more heavier(heavier) than before.

(Stage 2)

I: Now in the next part of the interview I'm going to give you a topic and I'd like you to talk about it for one or two minutes. Before you start talking you've got one minute to think about what you are going to say. And you can make some notes if you wish. Do you understand? OK. Here is your topic and here is some paper and a pencil for making notes. I'd like you to describe a film you have seen and have enjoyed very much.

(The candidate begins to read the card and write notes while the interviewer looks at his watch.)

...

Verbal Prompt Card

Describe a film you enjoyed a lot.
You should say:
- when and where you saw it
- what the story was about (briefly)
- why you like it

笔记区

and explain the effect the film had on you.
INSTRUCTIONS
Please read the topic carefully. You will be asked to talk about it for 1 to 2 minutes. You have one minute to think about what you are going to say. You can make some notes to help you if you wish.

Candidate's Notes on Paper

2ys ago
home
辛 list
War2
辛 save Jews labour list
historic truth
斯皮导 style other Jaws, Save 大兵Ryan, 朱park
Chinese same suffer

（One minute later）

I: All right, remember you have 1~2 minutes for this and don't worry if I stop you. I'll tell you when your time is up. Can you start speaking now please?

C: The film that gave me a deep impression is called "Schindler's list". I saw it two years ago on DVD with a group of my friends. At that time the film was not showed（shown）in the cinema so we just saw the English DVD at home. I saw the film because my friend recommended me（recommended it to me）and borrowed（lent）me the DVD.

The story happened in the Second World War. It was about a German factory owner tried （who tried）to save Jews from dead （being killed）. The factory owner is （was）called Schindler. He tried to put as many Jewish workers as possible on his list of employee names so that they could be saved. He didn't really need so many people to work in his factory, but he decided to try his best to save the poor Jewish people. The film also showed how the German soldiers killed Jewish people with uh ... poison gas. It was really terrible. After the war many Jewish survivors came to Schindler's tomb in memory of him. Without his help they wouldn't have been alive.

The reason I like this film is because it tells us the truth in history, in spite of（although）it was horrible. I remember the famous director Mr. Spielberg directed this film, and it wins （won）an Oscar award. I like Spielberg's films because he is good at showing the truth with details, and he knows how to touch the uh viewers.

笔记区

I also like some other Spielberg's films such as Jaws, "Saving Private Ryan" and "Jurassic Park". Another reason why I like this film is that we Chinese people has (have) suffered the similar experience in the past.

I: Did your friends like this film as well?

C: Some of them like (liked) it. Others don't (didn't) feel good after seeing the film because it is (was) full of uh, how to say, violent (violence).

(Stage 3)

I: OK, so far you've told me about a film you've seen and enjoyed very much. Now I'd like to discuss with you one or two more general topics. What are some differences between films nowadays and those in the past?

C: I think the most (biggest) difference is the development in technology ([tek'nɔlədʒi]). With modern science and technology ([tek'nɔlədʒi]), especially computer skills, we can produce more excited (exciting) films. I think it costs much more money to make a film today than in the past.

I: What kind of films is more popular in China?

C: I think Hollywood films are more popular in China now. Nowadays people are very busy with their work or study. They go to the cinema just to relaxing(relax). Hollywood films can make people excited and relaxed.

I: And what is your favourite type of films?

C: Well, I like to see the big-show films too, especially when I'm tired. But I more like (like...more) uh uh tragedy films. I think they can really make you think about and remember something. But many Hollywood films just make you feel happy for a short time and you usually forget them soon.

I: How different is teenagers' taste in films from that of adults?

C: I think most teenagers like to see uh uh comedy films. They also like to see films because they can see their favourite film stars. Adults usually do not run after film stars. They just like to see a film because they like it for what it is.

I: What's the difference between Chinese film stars and international stars? Which are more popular in China?

C: There are not so many Chinese film stars are (who are) world-famous. They are not so good at acting skills than (as) international stars. And they don't make so much money, too (either).

I: What do you think of the violence in films? Why do you think there is so much violence in films?

C: I think it's not good (I don't think it's good)for young people, because young people can not distinguish between good and bad and will be influenced by the bad behaviour in the films. The reason why there is so much violence I think is that the producers of the films want to make more money. They know the violent scenes in the films can attract more people to see the films.

笔 记 区

I: What kind of qualities do you think one should have to be a good actor or actress?

C: Well, a good actor should be intelligent and be good at performing naturally. And may be more emotional than others. He should understand the director's intention quickly. And a good actress should be beautiful usually.

I: Thank you very much. That's the end of the interview. Goodbye.

C: Thanks very much. Goodbye.

附录 3

雅思(IELTS)与新托福(iBT TOEFL)考试的异同

考试形式

新托福： 新托福通过互联网与ETS总部组成局域网，为每个人发出不同的考题，而且考题一次有效，不会再有题库。此外，网考通过电子方式记录答案后，将答案传输到人工评分网络，并予以客观、可靠的评分，从而确保考试的公平合理性。

雅　思： 目前官方并未公布采用"机考"的消息，中国考生所参加的雅思考试仍然是以笔试的方式进行，考试会有一定的题库，部分题目会在考试中重复出现。2006年雅思作文的评分标准将会更加细化。

考试结构——听力

新托福： 原来的短对话被取消。听力部分内容更加学术化，演讲篇幅大大加长。此外，听力部分出现了5种新题型：选择两个正确答案的题目、听部分文章摘要后完成的细节题、根据文章内容点击图片相应位置的题目、通过拖动来选择答案的多选题以及点击表格的题目。

雅　思： 听力部分出现多个经典场景，对细节的考核更贴近国外生活要求。此外，听力部分将出现一些新场景，比如商业场景、超市、纪念品销售点等。考核题型也趋向多样化，不再是单纯考查填空或选择题。

考试结构——口语

新托福： 口语部分采用人机对话，模拟正式的上课讲演来考查学生。考试共有6道题目，一、三、五针对的是校园生活，而二、四、六都是相对学术性的题材。

雅　思： 口语采用"人人对话"形式，客观性相对减弱。2006年的考试不仅会在原有话题的基础上增加部分新问题，而且会将第二部分的话题具体化。

考试结构——阅读

新托福： 阅读部分内容变得更加学术化，其涵盖的题材也更加广泛，包括了历史、科学、教育、商业、社科、艺术文学、工程技术、体育文娱八个方面。此外，阅读部分还出现两种新题型：插入句子题和拖动选择的多选题。

雅　思： 文章内容基本来自传统的题库，比如有关古代文明、移民史的社会科学话题，英国农业和动物特征介绍的自然科学话题等。新题的出现都比较有规律，阅读部分新题约占20%~30%。

考试结构——作文

新托福： 作文部分新增一篇考查综合能力的文章。要求考生用3分钟的时间读一篇学术性文章，然后听2~3分钟的相关演讲的录音，最后要求考生在20分钟内写下一篇字数在150~225的短文。大作文部分基本不变，字数比旧托福要求稍长。

雅　思： 一大一小两篇作文，小作文中的各种常规图表、柱状图、线图、饼图等交替出现。大作文的话题比较全面，包括了政府、环境、科技、媒体、犯罪、文化、动物等各种争议性话题。

托福、雅思认可度异同

美　　国： 两者都承认，3,000多所大学中有接近700所承认雅思成绩（根据雅思官方网站，有380多所学校正式认可）。

澳大利亚： 两者都承认。大学承认托福成绩，但政府签证要求雅思成绩。

日　　本： 两者都承认，但偏向承认托福。

韩　　国： 两者都承认，但偏向承认雅思。

加 拿 大： 两者都承认。

英　　国： 两者都承认。

新 西 兰： 两者都承认。

新 加 坡： 两者都承认。

欧　　洲： 两者都承认。荷兰只承认雅思。

新托福最低分数线为80分

近日，美国教育考试服务中心(ETS)官方网站公布了北美各大学对新托福网考成绩要求及新旧托福分数换算表，部分大学对申请就读美国大学本科和研究生院的学生的托福成绩划出最低分数线。从公布的新托福网考成绩分项要求可以看出，各高校均十分重视考生的口语与写作能力，具有良好的自我表达能力的留学申请者将在考试和申请过程中有较大优势。

笔 记 区

附录4

中国内地雅思考试中心

北京语言大学
考点代码：1
地　　址：100083 北京市海淀区学院路15号
笔试考场：教1楼
口试考场：逸夫楼
电　　话：(010)82303550
交　　通：乘坐331，375，398路

天津外国语大学
考点代码：2
地　　址：300204 天津市河西区马场道117号 天津外国语大学
笔试考场：逸夫教学主楼
口试考场：逸夫教学主楼
电　　话：(022)23286085
交　　通：乘坐4，13，26，871，904，906路

黑龙江大学
考点代码：3
地　　址：150008 哈尔滨南岗区学府路74号
笔试考场：试验楼
口试考场：外事处3号楼
电　　话：(0451)86608579
交　　通：乘坐11，106路

辽宁师范大学
考点代码：4
地　　址：116029 大连市黄河路850号
笔试考场：南院田家炳书院
口试考场：南院外语楼
电　　话：(0411)84258728
交　　通：乘坐101，708，705，715路或522，534路小公共汽车

沈阳师范大学
考点代码：5
地　　址：110032 沈阳市皇姑区黄河北大街253号

笔试考场：信息技术中心四楼
口试考场：信息技术中心四楼
电　　话：(024)86909660，86892233-161
交　　通：乘坐255，236，326，338，4301，4302路

山东大学
考点代码：6
地　　址：250061　济南经十路73号
笔试考场：南校区(原山工大)东配楼
口试考场：南校区(原山工大)东配楼
电　　话：(0531)8903388
交　　通：乘坐K51，K93，K56，2，8，16，18路

中国海洋大学
考点代码：7
地　　址：266071　青岛市香港东路23号
笔试考场：外语学院A区
口试考场：外语学院A区
电　　话：(0532)5901710
交　　通：乘坐501，11，801，321，304路

西安外国语学院
考点代码：8
地　　址：710061　西安市长安南路437号
笔试考场：2号教学楼
口试考场：6号教学楼
电　　话：(029)85309384
交　　通：乘坐603，504，527，215，19路

新疆财经学院
考点代码：9
地　　址：830012　乌鲁木齐市新市区北京北路15号
笔试考场：5号教学楼
口试考场：信息化中心
电　　话：(0991)7843882
交　　通：乘坐2，54，152路或民航班车

郑州轻工业大学
考点代码：10
地　　址：450002　郑州市东风路5号
笔试考场：国际教育学院

笔记区

口试考场：国际教育学院
电　　话：(0371)3836837
交　　通：乘坐2，28，64，86，87路

湖南大众传媒学院
考点代码：11
地　　址：410007　长沙市雨花亭新建西路77号
笔试考场：教学楼
口试考场：教学楼
电　　话：(0731)5602228，5602476
交　　通：乘坐7路到雨花亭

湖北大学
考点代码：12
地　　址：430071　武汉市武昌区学院路11号
笔试考场：3号楼南楼
口试考场：外国语学院
电　　话：(027)87122395
交　　通：乘坐573，215，543，554路

吉林大学
考点代码：13
地　　址：130021　长春市前卫路10号
笔试考场：前卫校区南区第三教学楼
口试考场：前卫校区南区第三教学楼
电　　话：(0431)5651004
交　　通：乘坐13，222，154，239路

华东师范大学
考点代码：14
地　　址：200062　上海中山北路3663号
笔试考场：文史楼
口试考场：文科楼四楼或心理学二楼
电　　话：(021)62233151
交　　通：乘坐69，224，524，567，754，765，829，909路

东南大学
考点代码：15
地　　址：210096　四牌楼2号
笔试考场：礼东楼
口试考场：外语系3楼

电　　话：(025)83793242，83791474
交　　通：乘坐31，2，特1，52，11，15，304路

浙江省高等教育自学考试办公室
考点代码：16
地　　址：310007　文晖路321号浙江教育大厦
笔试考场：省教育厅内一层
口试考场：省教育厅内一层
电　　话：(0571)88008098，13600511882
交　　通：乘坐6，42，45，74，203，316，534路公交车到市交警支队站下车

安徽中澳科技职业学院
考点代码：17
地　　址：230031　合肥市濉溪路312号
笔试考场：学院办公楼
口试考场：学院办公楼
电　　话：(0551)5148001
交　　通：乘坐112，124，131，143，22，300路

仲恺农业技术学院
考点代码：18
地　　址：510225　广州市纺织路东沙街24号
笔试考场：新教学楼
口试考场：新教学楼
电　　话：(020)89003878，89003877
交　　通：乘坐8路公共汽车可到达考点

深圳赛格人才培训中心
考点代码：19
地　　址：518031　深圳市华强北路赛格经济大厦7楼
笔试考场：深圳市华强北路赛格经济大厦7楼
口试考场：深圳市华强北路赛格经济大厦7楼
电　　话：(0755)83780139，83217093
交　　通：乘216，225，212，9，410，446，466，469，470，407，411，413路公共汽车可达

福建师范大学
考点代码：20
地　　址：350001　福州市仓山区上三路
笔试考场：外国语学院

笔记区

口试考场：外国语学院
电　　话：(0591)87676583，87616544
交　　通：乘1，4，20，702，726，813，815，945，963，978路公共汽车可达

厦门大学

考点代码：21
地　　址：361005　厦门市思明南路
笔试考场：基金楼
口试考场：基金楼
电　　话：(0592)2185305
交　　通：乘1，15，17，21，29，43，87路公共汽车可达

海南大学

考点代码：22
地　　址：570228　海口市人民大道
笔试考场：旅游学院2号教学楼
口试考场：旅游学院2号教学楼
电　　话：(0898)66521995，66521985
交　　通：乘5，11，17，18，20，26，30，207，209路公共汽车可达

广西大学

考点代码：23
地　　址：530004　南宁市大学路100号
笔试考场：中加国际学院
口试考场：中加国际学院
电　　话：(0771)3233884
交　　通：乘4，222，218，28路公共汽车可达

四川外国语学院

考点代码：24
地　　址：400031　重庆市沙坪坝区烈士墓
笔试考场：出国留学人员培训部教学B区
口试考场：出国留学人员培训部教学B区
电　　话：(023)65385446
交　　通：乘坐210、801路

四川大学

考点代码：25
地　　址：610065　成都市一环路南一段24号(四川大学北门磨子桥方向)
笔试考场：出国留学人员培训部(四川大学西区)
口试考场：出国留学人员培训部(四川大学西区)

笔记区

电　　话：(028)85407413
交　　通：乘坐27，34路

云南大学
考点代码：26
地　　址：650091 昆明市翠湖北路2号
笔试考场：外国语学院（英华园）
口试考场：外国语学院（英华园）
电　　话：(0871)5032252
交　　通：乘坐22，64，84，96路

贵州大学
考点代码：27
地　　址：贵州省贵阳市花溪区
笔试考场：外国语学院
口试考场：外国语学院
电　　话：(0851)8292035
交　　通：乘公交210，202，203，204路，中巴89，90，97，109路可达

笔记区

附录 5

雅思考试成绩单

INTERNATIONAL ENGLISH LANGUAGE TESTING SYSTEM

Test Report Form ACADEMIC

NOTE *Admission to undergraduate and postgraduate courses should be based on the ACADEMIC Reading and Writing Modules. GENERAL TRAINING Reading and Writing Modules are **not** designed to test the full range of language skills required for academic purposes. It is recommended that the candidate's language ability as indicated in this Test Report Form be re-assessed **after two years** from the date of the test.*

Centre Number CN001 Date 23/OCT/2004 Candidate Number 002853

Candidate Details

Family Name [redacted]

First Name [redacted]

Candidate ID [redacted]

Date of Birth Sex (M/F) M Scheme Code Private Candidate

Country of Origin China (People's Republic of) First Language Chinese

Repeating IELTS (Y/N) Y Previous Test Date 13/SEP/2003 Previous Test Centre BRITISH EMBASSY, BEIJING

Test Results

Listening	Reading	Writing	Speaking	Overall Band Score
9.0	9.0	8	8	8.5

Administrator Comments

Education Australia idp

Centre stamp: BRITISH EMBASSY CULTURAL & EDUCATION SECTION BEIJING

Validation stamp: VALIDATION STAMP IELTS CAMBRIDGE ESOL/BRITISH COUNCIL/IDP:IA

Writing Examiner Number 003246 Administrator's Signature

Speaking Examiner Number 997892 Date 03/11/2004 Test Report Form Number 04CN002853HEG001A

BRITISH COUNCIL IELTS AUSTRALIA idp UNIVERSITY *of* CAMBRIDGE ESOL Examinations

新东方独家引进

《剑桥雅思考试全真试题集 6》
(含光盘 2 张)
剑桥大学考试委员会　编著

定价：110 元　开本：16 开　页码：176 页

《剑桥雅思考试全真试题集 5》
(含光盘 2 张)
剑桥大学考试委员会　编著

定价：110 元　开本：16 开　页码：184 页

◎ 4 套完整的学术类雅思全真试题

◎ 2 套培训类雅思阅读与写作全真试题

《剑桥雅思考试全真试题集 6 精讲》
周成刚　主编

定价：25 元　开本：16 开　页码：168 页

《剑桥雅思考试全真试题集 5 精讲》
周成刚　主编

定价：35 元　开本：16 开　页码：296 页

《剑桥雅思考试全真试题解析 4 精讲》
(含光盘 1 张)
周成刚　主编

定价：28 元　开本：16开　页码：256 页

◎ 洞悉雅思出题规律，精确剖析雅思真题

◎ 针对中国雅思考生的特点和需求，分题型全面破解

《剑桥雅思常见错误透析》
Pauline Cullen，Julie Moore　编著

定价：18 元　开本：32 开　页码：136 页

《剑桥雅思语法》(附赠 mp3 一张)
Diana Hopkins，Pauline Cullen　编著

定价：45 元　开本：16 开　页码：272 页

◎ 雅思备考资料官方出版机构推出的权威雅思语法教程

◎ 剑桥资深语法专家为全球雅思考生量身定做

《雅思口语特训》(含光盘 1 张)
孙涛　编著

◎ 收录最新口语真题和话题卡片，将常考话题进行分类、分级，实现逐级突破

◎ 随书配有 420 分钟录音光盘，内含所有话题题目及经典答案

定价：45 元　开本：16 开　页码：292 页

《雅思听力特训》(含光盘 1 张)
彭新松　编著

◎ 洞悉雅思听力出题规律，提供最新模拟试题

◎ 针对中国雅思考生的特点和需求

定价：30 元　开本：16 开　页码：176 页

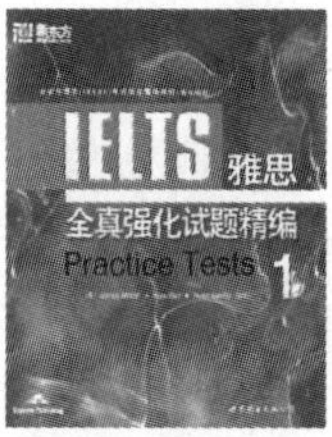

《雅思全真强化试题精编 1》
(含光盘 1 张)
James Milton, Huw Bell, Peter Neville　编著

定价：30 元　开本：16 开　页码：132 页

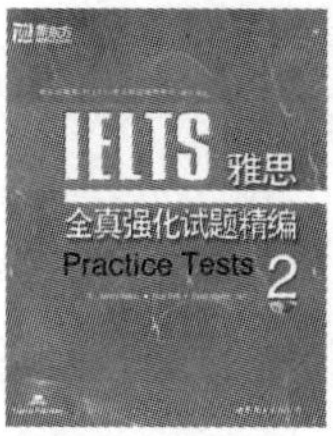

《雅思全真强化试题精编 2》
(含光盘 1 张)
James Milton, Huw Bell, Peter Neville　编著

定价：30 元　开本：16 开　页码：132 页

◎ 4 套完整学术类模拟试题，2 套培训类模拟试题

◎ 随书附赠 120 分钟录音光盘 1 张，模拟真实考场情境

《雅思应试指导及模拟试题》
(含 1 MP3＋1 CD-ROM)
Mark Harrison　编著

◎ 6 套完整学术类模拟试题，2 套培训类模拟试题

◎ 前 2 套模拟试题中配有按题型分类的解题指导

定价：48 元　开本：16开　页码：264 页

《雅思考前突破与冲刺试题》
(含光盘 1 张)　Lin Lougheed　编著

◎ 四套全真模拟练习题，提供真实的考场氛围

◎ 包含详细题解、答案及听力原文，供考生自我检测

定价：48 元　开本：16 开　页码：356 页

《雅思写作套路剖析与范例大全》

顾家北　编著

- ◎ 250 道改错，230 道翻译
- ◎ 114 篇范文，420 个表达

定价：45 元　开本：16开　页码：384 页

《雅思考官口语实战指导》

（含光盘 1 张）　　**Mat Clark**　编著

- ◎ 分析中国考生的成绩现状，阐释评分系统的逐项要求
- ◎ 详尽介绍考试三部分程式，收录最新问题与话题卡片

定价：35 元　开本：16 开　页码：212 页

《雅思口语胜经》（含光盘 1 张）

新东方教育科技集团雅思研发团队　编著

- ◎ 收录口语考试最新问题和卡片话题
- ◎ 精选口语考试常用词汇和句型

定价：35 元　开本：16 开　页码：216 页

《雅思听力胜经》（含光盘 1 张）

新东方教育科技集团雅思研发团队　编著

- ◎ 以雅思听力真题为蓝本，细分常见题型和场景
- ◎ 提供大量听写和分项练习，帮助考生提高听力单项技能

定价：30 元　开本：16 开　页码：216 页

《雅思写作胜经》

新东方教育科技集团雅思研发团队　编著

- ◎ 系统说明写作准备过程及步骤
- ◎ 提供同题各档次作文比较，方便考生自测自学

定价：25 元　开本：16 开　页码：188 页

《雅思阅读胜经》

新东方教育科技集团雅思研发团队　编著

- ◎ 词汇、语法、语篇三大层次剖析雅思阅读
- ◎ 精选 16 篇时文，全真模拟雅思阅读考试情境

定价：30 元　开本：16 开　页码：224 页

《雅思词汇词根+联想记忆法》

（附赠 mp3 1 张）

俞敏洪　编著

- ◎ 原汁原味的真题例句收词全面，涵盖雅思四大题型词汇
- ◎ 标出听力、口语单词，有针对性进行记忆

定价：28 元　开本：32 开　页码：456 页

《词以类记：IELTS 词汇》

（附赠光盘 1 张）

张红岩　编著

- ◎ IELTS 最新词汇：覆盖听说读写
- ◎ 按学科和意群分类：细分至最小同义词区间，符合大脑分类记忆规律

定价：35 元　开本：32 开　页码：400 页

《雅思分级词汇 21 天进阶》

耿耿　编著

- ◎ 电脑统计雅思高频词汇，释义准确并配真题例句
- ◎ 收录雅思最核心 1228 词，方便考生高效把握词汇考点

定价：25 元　开本：32 开　页码：484 页

《雅思词汇精选》（含光盘 1 张）

孙涛　编著

- ◎ 词条精选自雅思权威语料库
- ◎ 中英文双解释义，确保词义注释的准确性

定价：39 元　开本：16 开　页码：482 页

《600 词走遍英联邦——最新英语口语学习词典》（含光盘 1 张）

段立新　编著

- ◎ 全面收录英联邦国家高频率的日常英语口语
- ◎ 词条所配音标突出重音、语调、弱读

定价：32 元　开本：32 开　页码：520 页

读者反馈表

尊敬的读者：

您好！非常感谢您对**新东方大愚图书**的信赖与支持，希望您抽出宝贵的时间填写这份反馈表，以便帮助我们改进工作，今后能为您提供更优秀的图书。谢谢！

为了答谢您对我们的支持，我们将对反馈的信息进行随机抽奖活动，当月将有20位幸运读者可获赠**《新东方英语》**期刊一份。我们将定期在新东方大愚图书网站 www.dogwood.com.cn 公布获奖者名单并及时寄出奖品，敬请关注。

来信请寄： 北京市海淀区海淀中街6号新东方大厦750室 北京新东方大愚文化传播有限公司图书部收

邮编：100080 E-mail：club@dogwood.com.cn

姓名：________ 年龄：________ 职业：________ 教育背景：________ 邮编：________

通讯地址：________________ 联系电话：________

E-mail：____________ 您所购买的书籍的名称是：____________

1. 您是通过何种渠道得知本书的（可多选）：
   □书店 □新东方网站 □大愚网站 □朋友推荐 □老师推荐 □其他________
2. 您是从何处购买到此书的？ □书店 □邮购 □图书销售网站 □其他________
3. 影响您购买此书的原因（可多选）：
   □封面设计 □书评广告 □正文内容 □图书价格 □新东方品牌 □新东方名师 □其他________
4. 您对本书的封面设计满意程度： □很满意 □比较满意 □一般 □不满意 □改进建议________
5. 本书配哪种音像资料更适合您？ □磁带 □光盘 □MP3 □其他________
6. 您认为本书的内文在哪些方面还需改进？ □结构编排 □难易程度 □内容丰富性 □内文版式
7. 本书最令您满意的地方：□内文 □封面 □价格 □纸张
8. 您对本书的推荐率：□没有 □1人 □1—3人 □3—5人 □5人以上
9. 您更希望我们为您提供哪些方面的英语类图书？
   □四六级类 □考研类 □雅思考试类 □GRE、GMAT类 □NEW SAT类 □实用商务类
   □休闲欣赏类 □初高中英语类 □其他________
   您目前最希望我们为您出版的图书名称是：________
10. 您在学习英语过程中最需要哪些方面的帮助？（可多选）
    □词汇 □听力 □口语 □阅读 □写作 □翻译 □其他
11. 您最喜欢的英语图书品牌：____________
    理由如下（可多选）：□版式漂亮 □内容实用 □难度适宜 □价格适中 □对考试有帮助 □其他________
12. 看到"新东方"三个字，您首先想到什么？____________
13. 您的其他意见和建议（可附在本页背面）：____________
14. 填表时间：______年____月____日